BILLY
AI

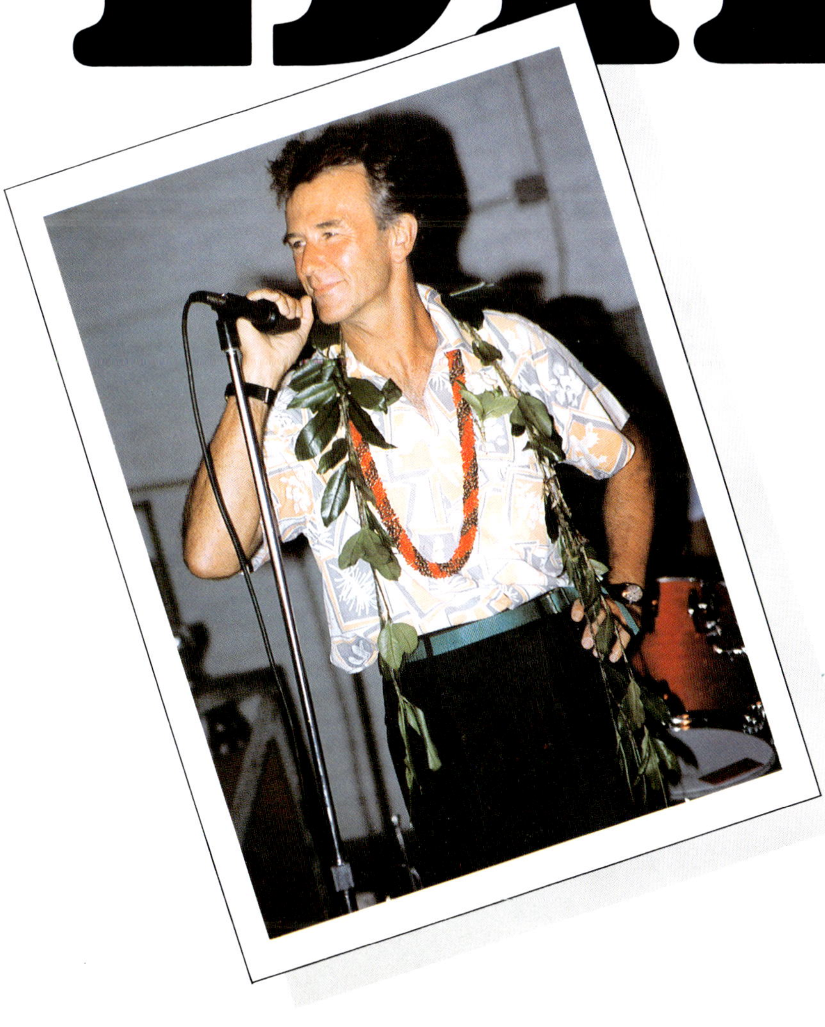

RENG

Paintings of Three Decades

STON

Contemporary Arts Museum, Houston
The Oakland Museum
Chronicle Books · San Francisco

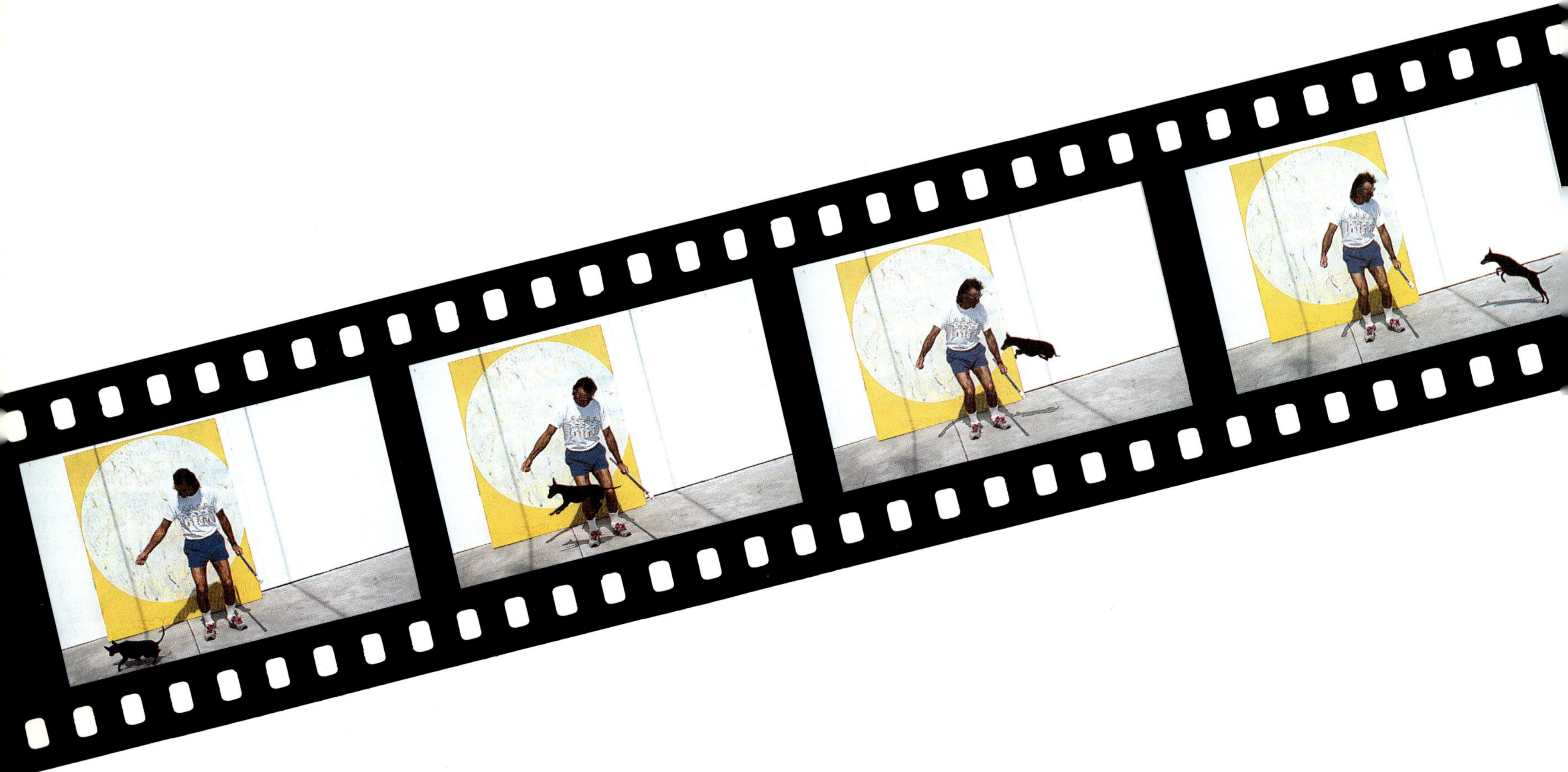

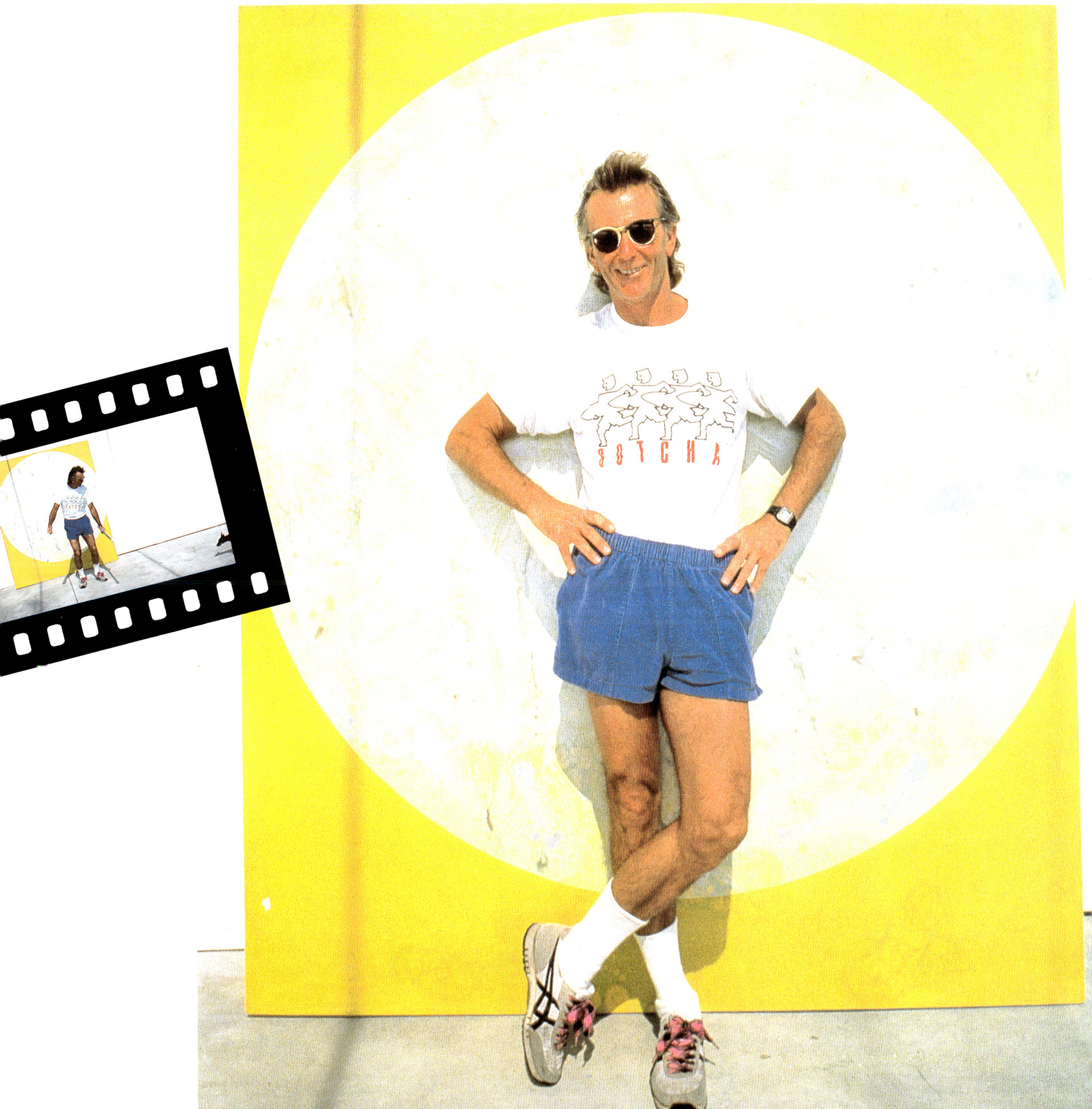

GOTCHA

Exhibition Itinerary

Contemporary Arts Museum, Houston   14 May–26 June 1988

The Oakland Museum   23 July–30 October 1988

Los Angeles County Museum of Art   30 November 1988–29 January 1989

Contemporary Arts Center, Honolulu   6 March–30 April 1989

Library of Congress Catalog Card Number 87-062703
ISBN: 0-87701-473-6

Distributed in Canada by
Raincoast Books
112 East Third Avenue
Vancouver, B.C.
V5T 1C8

10 9 8 7 6 5 4 3 2 1

The exhibition, *Billy Al Bengston: Paintings of Three Decades*, has been coorganized by the
Contemporary Arts Museum, Houston, and The Oakland Museum,
California. The book accompanying the exhibition is
copublished with Chronicle Books, San Francisco.

Contemporary Arts Museum
5216 Montrose Boulevard
Houston, Texas 77006-6598

The Oakland Museum
1000 Oak Street
Oakland, California 94607-4892

Chronicle Books
San Francisco, California

Contents

Preface with Acknowledgments

HE CULTURE OF LOS ANGELES, THE TICK BEHIND A CITY unique in the world, has been the subject of innumerable histories and analytic essays. Whatever happens seems to happen more in Los Angeles, and what strikes us as important about Billy Al Bengston is that his work over the last three decades has been on the cutting edge of the Los Angeles experience.

As Los Angeles has defied the tradition of American cities, Bengston's art has defied the tradition of American painting. Perversely out of the art mainstream, Billy's work has baffled east coast critics. But, as we have come to understand and appreciate Los Angeles for its individuality, we must also come to acknowledge and embrace Bengston's painting as part of the fabric of American art history.

Billy, along with a coterie of artist friends including such luminaries as Ed Ruscha, Ed Kienholz, and Frank Gehry, took the air and space technology that California revered in the sixties and applied it with the spirit of rebellion to their art. They pushed and pulled until they made something beyond the expected. Many have acknowledged Billy Al Bengston as having a significant influence on that experimental generation and most certainly on the generation of Los Angeles artists who followed.

In the sixties Bengston created a series of works of highly symbolic shapes exquisitely painted on distressed aluminum sheets. He intended to break up the surface so that the eye would have to look at these pictures in a new way. Throughout the seventies Billy continued to paint on and with whatever took his fancy.

He found subject matter wherever he went, and he went many places. He discovered Hawaii in 1974 and subsequently returned to compete in the Rough Water Channel Swim with his longtime friend and fellow athlete Penny Little. He found Hawaii was a place he couldn't leave behind. Splitting his time between studios in Oahu and Venice, Bengston continues his romance with the islands.

Bengston, who always denied interpretation of his art, has changed a great deal in recent years. The first large-scale watercolors inspired by Hawaii signaled a major shift in Bengston's work. These paintings had let go. They depicted Billy's life, and they were uproariously funny and outrageously narrative. Billy had taken beautiful and lush watercolors of the foliage, sky, and sea, mixed them with a little boy's joy at being able to identify each airplane that takes off from the nearby Honolulu airport, and had cut them up and made them into stories. There were figures—stick figures—Billy jogging perhaps? There was the proverbial beach threesome, "guy, wahine, guy" to use Billy's words, doing what such threesomes always do. You could see Billy and all his friends and also his new pet dog Dodger; even Billy thought it was funny.

As Billy approached his fiftieth birthday, his subject matter again changed radically, although his inventive use of painting materials continued. Recently he has made a series of paintings of moons seen through window frames at night. Again, although Bengston does not occupy himself with symbolic readings of these works, we can not help but think that these pictures mark the artist's awareness of mortality. The heavens with the moon shining, painted so gracefully and with luminosity, can also be seen as abstract. The surface of the moon is painted to change with each nuance of light. They are not gloomy or unhappy; they do not suggest death. They instead reflect the endless cycles of the universe in which all art and life are made into other art, other life, and the evolution by which each artist makes his own discoveries from the ideas that come to him.

With enthusiasm and pleasure, our two organizations have cooperated on this book and retrospective exhibition, which were suggested in 1982 by Christina Orr-Cahall, chief curator of art at The Oakland Museum, and Marti Mayo, then curator at the Contemporary Arts Museum. Billy was enthusiastic about this proposition, as it marks twenty years since his last survey at the Los Angeles County Museum of Art. Asked to join in the current exhibition tour, the Los Angeles County Museum of Art enthusiastically agreed, and the exhibition will also be seen in the new Contemporary Arts Center in Honolulu. Each of these cities is a place where Bengston's work has been collected and admired. We trust that this exhibition and book will reward those who want to know more about Bengston's art.

We would also like to acknowledge the following individuals for their participation. At the Contemporary Arts Museum: Lou Cinda Holt and Sandra McMain for their careful and diligent coordination of loans; Pamela A. Riddle and Valerie Bell Greiner for their fund-raising efforts; and Cheryl Blissitte for administrative and secretarial assistance. At The Oakland Museum: Barbara Bowman for her exhaustive research; Barbara Levine and Gail Bernstein for their administrative assistance; and Christine Droll for her aid in manuscript preparation.

Our project drew the enthusiasm and participation of three authors who have known not only Bengston's work but also the artist for more than twenty years. Henry T. Hopkins, Jane Livingston, and Maurice Tuchman have supplied us with highly informative and, in some cases, very amusing accounts of the Los Angeles art world and Bengston over the last three decades. Finally, we must give our deepest appreciation to Karen Tsujimoto, who acted as guest curator and essayist for this exhibition and whose devotion to the show and its publication are unparalleled.

This book is funded in part through Houston's Contemporary Arts Publication Fund (established with the generous support of the Charles Engelhard Foundation in May 1982, and with additional support in 1986–88 from Tenneco Inc.), and with funds from The Oakland Museum Women's Board and the Art Guild of the Oakland Museum Association. In addition, we are pleased that Chronicle Books joins us in publishing and distributing this book. We also wish to acknowledge the Board of Trustees of the Contemporary Arts Museum for its continuing support of exhibitions of new work.

The many lenders to *Billy Al Bengston: Paintings of Three Decades* receive our greatest appreciation for their cooperation in making this book and exhibition possible. Billy's assistant Gretchen Corners, friend Penny Little, along with the artist's dealers, James Corcoran and Barbara Whiting of James Corcoran Gallery, Fredericka Hunter and Ian Glennie of Texas Gallery, and Thomas Babeor of Thomas Babeor Gallery, provided invaluable assistance.

Billy Al Bengston has been the essential ingredient in the success of this project. His knowledge, eagerness, and wit have allowed us to enjoy the preparation and presentation of his work.

LINDA L. CATHCART
Director
Contemporary Arts Museum
Houston

CHRISTINA ORR-CAHALL
Chief Curator of Art
The Oakland Museum

Ann Janss, Billy Al Bengston
(center), and Ed Janss, aboard
yacht *The Disappearance*, Baja,
California, ca. 1974. Photo:
Penny Little.

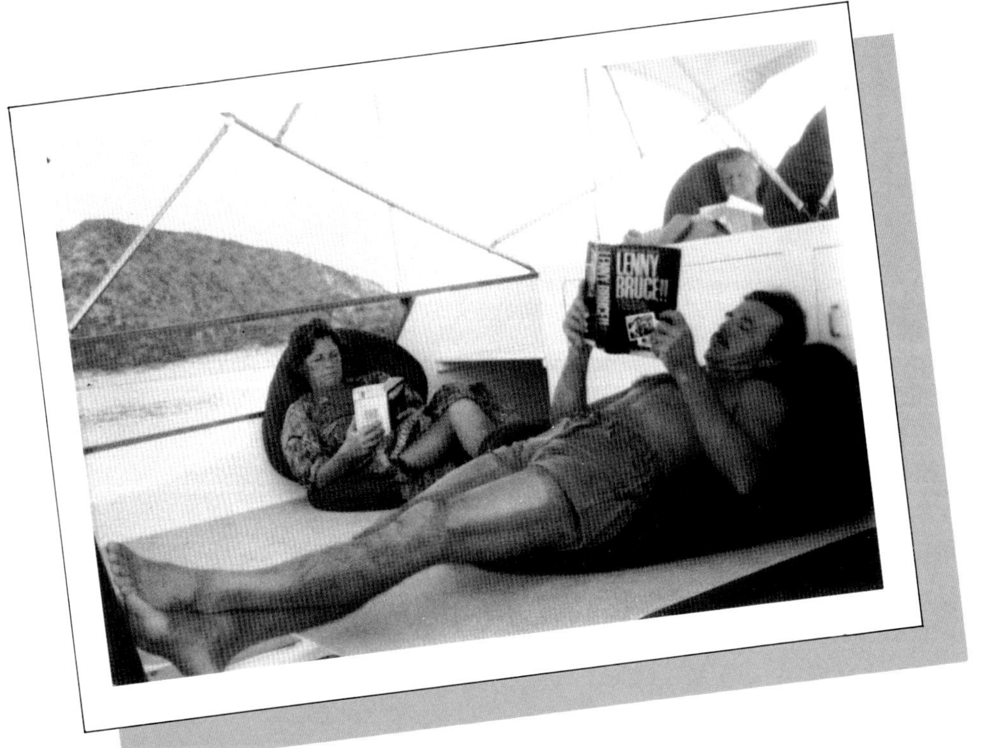

Billy Al Bengston:
Some Retrospective
Thoughts

by Jane Livingston

S THE SIXTIES DAWNED, THE ART WORLD WAITED FOR A sequel to the great New York school in American avant-garde painting. What succeeded the generation of action painting proved neither monolithic nor even readily definable as a mainstream development in American art.

Different agendas were drawn on the two coasts. Critics and artists in New York rallied around the opposing tenets of color field painting and minimalism, espousing, on the one hand, painting that continued to develop toward literalness, and on the other, objects that demanded a condition of theater for its presence *qua* art. In California (and, less vociferously, elsewhere in the country), blithely independent, even sly, strategies were developed by artists who considered the argument raging in New York, gauged its relevance for their work, and placed themselves squarely outside its rules.

California in the sixties embodied many different traditions. It was the locus of a deep-rooted counterculture, whose political and cultural rebellions were centered on the Berkeley campus and in the Haight-Ashbury district of San Francisco. In southern California, the developing aerospace industry began to rival the film and communications business as the symbol of its cultural base. From the fifties through the seventies, the longstanding craft-influenced visual arts tradition hung on in Los Angeles, maintaining a climate against which artists could rebel. The "funk art" of the Beat generation filtered from northern to southern California, introducing such influential artists as Peter Voulkos, Bruce Conner, George Herms, and Wallace Berman.

In the sixties, younger artists migrated to southern California, transforming the aesthetic tradition already established by California-raised artists, such as John Altoon and Craig Kauffman. Robert Graham came from northern California via Korea and Ed Ruscha from Nebraska. Billy Al Bengston had moved with his family from Kansas in 1948, quickly joining a group of artists who had grown up in southern California—Edward Moses, Kenneth Price, Bruce Nauman, Ron Davis, and Larry Bell. The culture that developed depended both on the personalities of these artists and on their presence in the rapidly changing southern California scene of the sixties, expected both to fulfill an idyllic New World dream and realize a technological future. This environment demanded an independent culture.

No artist was more equipped, temperamentally and aesthetically, to respond to challenges to be different than Billy Al Bengston. Bengston's earliest paintings and ceramic sculptures were precocious: informed by an almost eerie awareness of the indigenous art-craft antecedent, they nonetheless pointed ahead to the glittery style that would soon follow. Billy Al, unlike some artists, did not pay lip service to the new artistic vocabulary while surreptitiously cultivating the old. Instead, along with Larry Bell and Robert Irwin, he began to look to technology rather than art-craft, after a relatively brief apprenticeship to that formula. One of the key forces allowing Bengston to bridge this gap was Peter Voulkos, whose influence was decisive, albeit brief.

The peculiar significance of Billy Al Bengston's early art to the *new* Los Angeles movement derived, in part, from its inspiration in the automobile/bike culture. Bengston knew and loved motorcycles; in southern California he was surrounded by a uniquely obsessive and decorative car culture. He naturally adapted its techniques, appropriating the lacquered, layered, metallic surfaces of the car. But, despite publicity to the contrary, he never imitated its look. Instead, he used spray painting to reveal a beautiful, flat-but-deep surface, which characterized his early emblematic paintings.

In the sixties, Bengston seemed not only a member of but perhaps the very exemplar of an iconoclastic aesthetic movement. Associated with both the California bikers' culture and the space technology ethos, his art seemed securely grounded in a high-tech/futuristic mode. But this would prove a transient phase: Bengston eventually revealed himself as essentially a conservative artist, whose deepest allegiance has always been to decorative pictorial values. He remains more allied to Matisse than to Duchamp, closer to Diebenkorn than to Bruce Nauman.

One factor that made Bengston's work in the sixties and early seventies seem so *outré*—uprooted and defiant—was the almost ritualistic repetition of two successive forms—the chevron (or sergeant stripes) and dracula (or iris)—as iconic, centered images. Not quite a pop use of an image or object, nor quite an abstract device, these half-organic, half-geometric signs seemed to define a realm of communication somewhere between pop art and mysticism that was uniquely Bengston's.

During the later seventies, as his work embraced a variety of media ranging from furniture (tables and screens) to watercolors, Bengston became an increasingly romantic and decorative painter. Paradoxically, this development continued his strange disjunction with trends in the art world: at just the moment when his early oddness might be fully appreciated in the increasingly anti-commodity, avant-garde European art market, Bengston had shifted course.

The paradox that is Billy Al is evident in several aspects of his career. First, although his name is identified with the late sixties southern California style, and he truly was one of its inventors, Bengston has not shared in the recent international acclaim accorded (perhaps temporarily) to some of his peers. Second, while he was for a decade widely considered to be in the vanguard of a futuristic use of form and materials, his instincts regarding technique and scale are more attuned to familiar artistic canons, well within the confines of the modernist tradition at its most serene. Besides these seemingly contradictory tendencies, another quality is perhaps most revealing of his elusive singularity, which distinguishes him from all others. Billy Al Bengston is an artist who, throughout his career and its many vacillations and shifts, has simultaneously embraced and scorned inventive technique.

This last characteristic reveals itself in Bengston's work by a peculiar, incessant tug-of-war between an obsessive craftsmanship and a stubborn spontaneity in physical execution. His water-colors—which I consider some of his best work since those extraordinary and inimitable chevron paintings—sometimes break with convention by cutting into and reconstructing the physical object, but they never contrive to be anything but lyrically seductive paintings. The subjects, most often employing images suggested by vegetation and fragmentary architectural elements, suggest an airy landscape, yet they are supremely experimental.

These are simple, seductive paintings on paper, but their apparent accessibility does not negate their sometimes subtle, sometimes aggressive differentness. Neither the watercolors nor any of Bengston's works of the late seventies and eighties can be adequately characterized as "decora-tive." In the apparently conservative yet also eccentric nature of Billy Al's recent work, his uniqueness as an artist throughout his career becomes evident.

An artist who matured at the moment when American art evolved into an open-ended stylistic riddle, Billy Al Bengston chose the safe harbor of physical and stylistic decorum. The earliest works in this exhibition present Bengston at his most radical, most exploratory phase. His subse-quent aesthetic choices have proved, although perhaps not theatrically shrewd, artistically sound. His overriding loyalty to his imperatives as an artist, rather than to a temperamental inclination to the role of showman, has paid off. This exhibition celebrates not the histrionic feats of an unusu-ally stylish magician, but the rigorously achieved oeuvre of a careful, masterful artist.

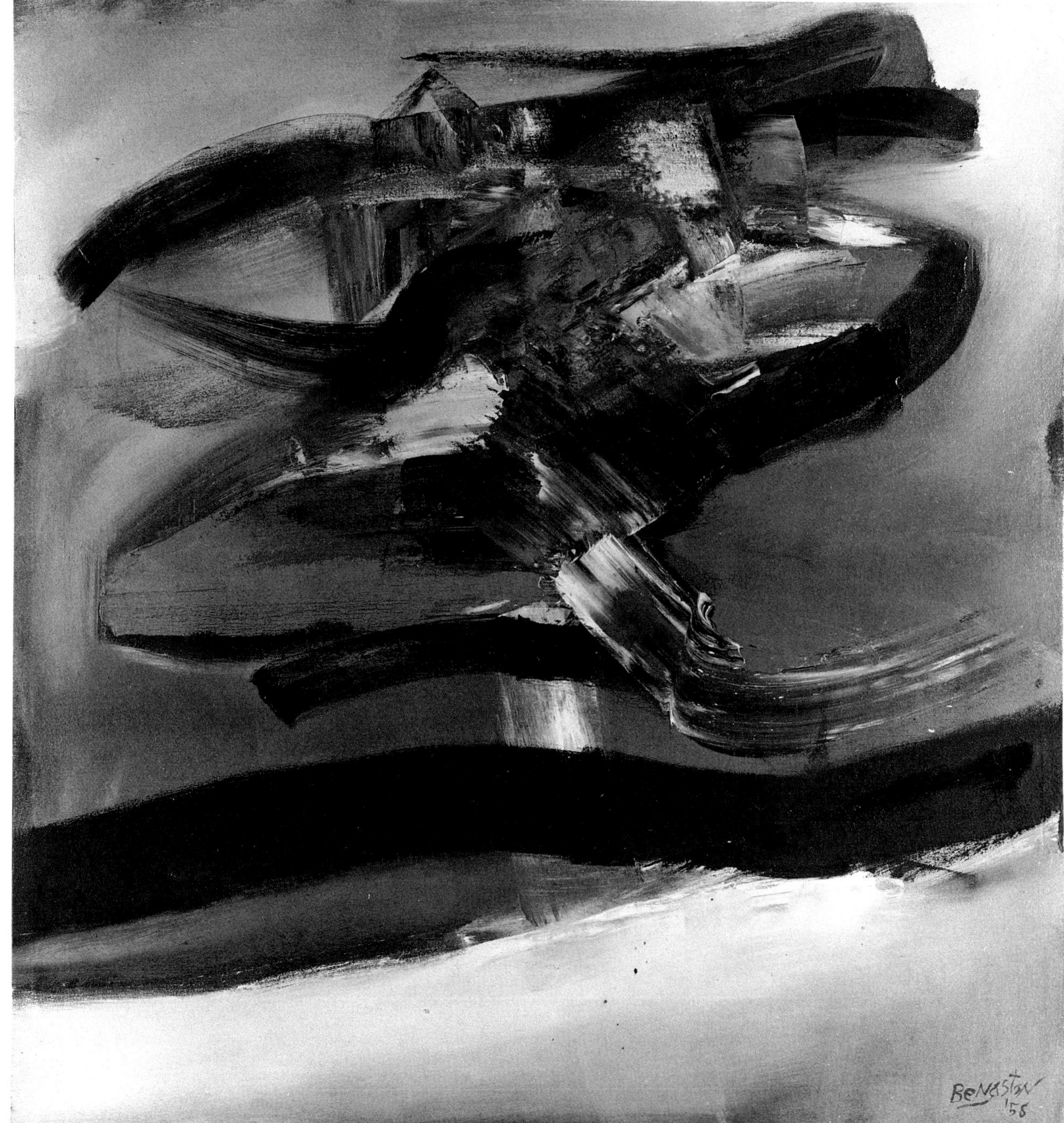

Fig. 1 Billy Al Bengston, Untitled,
1958, oil on canvas, 36 × 36″
(91.4 × 91.4 cm.).
Dr. and Mrs. Merle S. Glick.
Photo: Art Waldinger.

Painting as a
Visual Diary

by Karen Tsujimoto

BILLY AL BENGSTON'S ART OF THE LAST THREE DECADES IS remarkable not only for its importance in the development of contemporary art on the west coast, but in its pure verve and audacity. Collectively seen, his work more frequently challenges taste than confirms it and unequivocally declares the open-ended nature of the creative process. In the sixties Bengston startled the art world with his lustrous, metallic sprayed paintings that summoned images of the Los Angeles car culture. The following decade found him producing elegantly colored screens and bannerlike paintings. In the early eighties, the artist radically changed his tack once again, expressing in caricature symbolic images drawn from his impressions of Hawaii. Now there are new paintings of moons, luminous and tranquil.

But this appearance of flux and change masks the unwavering foundation upon which Bengston's art is grounded: a very personal inquiry merging art and life experiences. The radical shifts that have occurred in his work reflect how Bengston has changed as he has traveled abroad, had new experiences, and matured as both painter and person. His progression has largely been directed by experiential rather than theoretical concerns. The division between art and life—the mystique of the artist, his environment, and what he creates—has been intentionally blurred by the artist. "The process of making a painting is the process of living," Bengston observes. "Every day an artist wakes up with a slightly different idea. He takes that idea to the studio and he modifies the work he has done before. When it's all over, he has made a diary about his life."[1]

Bengston's public persona has contributed to this dichotomy. Outwardly he is gregarious and quick-witted, a dedicated athlete and bon vivant. Inwardly he is a measured and deliberate artist who believes strongly in the ethics of self-discipline and hard work. Painting for Bengston is a very individual and private undertaking; he does not attempt to indoctrinate the viewer or to have his paintings function as a public affirmation of a prescribed dogma.

Although critics have tried to align his art with various schools, from pop art to p & d—pattern and decorative painting—Bengston has eluded specific classification. No movement has convincingly described his work because its core has never been art history or theory. The artists he respects—John Altoon, Robert Graham, Kenneth Price, Edward Ruscha, and H. C. Westermann—are those he sees as having single-mindedly pursued their personal visions. Bengston's regard for other painters like Henri Matisse and Willem de Kooning derives from their persistence in free expression and experimentation. Bengston's art, while seemingly eclectic, is firmly circumscribed by a singular refusal to be categorized.

EARLY YEARS

Born in Dodge City, Kansas, in 1934, Bengston and his family settled in Los Angeles in time for him to enter Manual Arts High School in 1949. There he developed a strong interest in art, especially ceramics, as well as gymnastics, which set the pattern for Bengston's lifelong interest in sports. These classes, however, were not quite enough to sustain his interest, so on school days he could often be found at the beach or wandering through the Los Angeles Museum of History, Science, and Art, studying its Egyptian glass collection or puzzling over paintings by Jackson Pollock and Josef Albers.

Following his graduation from high school in 1952, Bengston began an erratic college career, studying first at Los Angeles Junior College (now Los Angeles City College) from 1953 to 1955. He pursued his interest in ceramics, encountering an inspiring ceramics teacher, Bernard Kester, who encouraged experimentation in cross disciplines, but "with good taste."[2] But Bengston soon left for northern California to continue his studies.

In 1955 Bengston enrolled in the California College of Arts and Crafts in Oakland. Given the school's emphasis on training students in the crafts, as well as fine arts and art education, it appeared to be a logical place for Bengston to pursue his interest in ceramics. But the courses were too predictable and confining for Bengston and within the year he moved back to Los Angeles.

The year he spent at the school proved valuable, however, because two inspiring teachers Bengston encountered in the painting department, Sabro Hasegawa and Richard Diebenkorn, helped the young artist affirm that his artistic instincts were valid. A native of Japan, Hasegawa was influential in spurring interest among Bay Area artists in Japanese calligraphy and Zen Buddhism and its relationship to abstract expressionism. Through Hasegawa, Bengston discovered a model of personal style and learned to value intuition—a lesson reflected in his characteristically uninhibited and spontaneous handling of paint. From Diebenkorn he learned how to approach a painting physically and how to see the difference between what an artist wants to paint versus what it is actually possible to do on canvas. Importantly, Bengston also learned from Diebenkorn that "the mystery of art was real." While painting attracts curiosity and speculation, the visual experience cannot be fully expressed in words; it cannot be understood by human reason alone.

Bengston returned to Los Angeles to enroll at the Los Angeles County Art Institute (now the Otis Art Institute of Parsons School of Design) in 1956. The choice was fortuitous as he finally sought and found—at least temporarily—a dynamic and flexible environment that complemented his own restless energy. By the time he arrived at the school, word had already spread that something extraordinary was happening in the ceramics department, headed by the iconoclast and teacher Peter Voulkos. In his own work Voulkos had broken from the tradition of functional ceramics to create larger, sculptural pieces. He worked with an expansive sense of color that exceeded mere surface decoration and drew his inspiration from myriad sources, ranging from flamenco music to the ceramic work of Picasso and abstract expressionist paintings. Enthusiastic and encouraging, Voulkos, "the master," as Bengston saw him, inspired his students to be similarly freewheeling and experimental.

Bengston readily participated in this lively and exciting period of exploration. He shared, for example, Voulkos's interest in Picasso's idea of painting ceramics in the round. In studying books on Japanese decorative arts, Bengston became especially drawn to teaware of the Momoyama period (1573–1615). What attracted him was the near-perfect synthesis of form, function, and beauty that he felt these simple objects possessed. He was also intrigued by its Zen qualities, the imperfection and irregularity of the shapes and glazes, and the spontaneously painted surfaces.

Cups such as *Phoney Whiteware*, 1956 (fig. 2), reflect the influence of Japanese ceramics. With its rough, crude shape and extemporaneous design, the piece visually expresses the Zen concept that beauty does not necessarily mean perfection in form and craftsmanship.[3] The rich, spontaneous surface incident found here later occurs in Bengston's paintings, where pigment is applied instinctively to create irregularly patterned and energized surfaces. Through such ceramic cups, Bengston reaffirmed his appreciation for art based on risk, expression, and intuition.

In spite of the flexibility of the ceramics program, after a year Bengston left the school. Shortly thereafter he abandoned ceramics—in part due to lingering doubts that it could ever fully divorce itself from its crafts connotations—and turned his attention to painting. "The fault lies not with the art but with the ceramicists," he explains. "They regard it as merely a craft. They fail to set criteria. They play in the mud, unimaginatively making *things*, and that defeats them."[4]

The broad sweeping gestures of an untitled canvas from 1958 (fig. 1) suggest the influence of abstract expressionism in Bengston's first paintings. Having lived in the Bay Area, he was attuned to the work of established northern California painters in this mode such as Diebenkorn, Clyfford Still, and Jay De Feo, and particularly admired De Feo's work at the time. Bengston also followed the east coast development of abstract expressionism through reading *It Is*, a vanguard New York art magazine in which discussions and reproductions of this new painting style were prominent. But while the energized brushwork of Bengston's canvases at that time was similar to that of de Kooning and Franz Kline, his work did not share the emotional subjectivity that distinguishes the work of those painters. Rather, the canvases record his impressions of birds in flight, the ruffled sound of wings visually translated into paint. Even at this early stage, impressions of the natural world were crucial in Bengston's work, a factor that has remained constant.

Bengston premiered a selection of these paintings at his first solo exhibition at the Ferus Gallery in Los Angeles in 1958. Reviewing the show, Jules Langsner, the most prominent art critic in Los

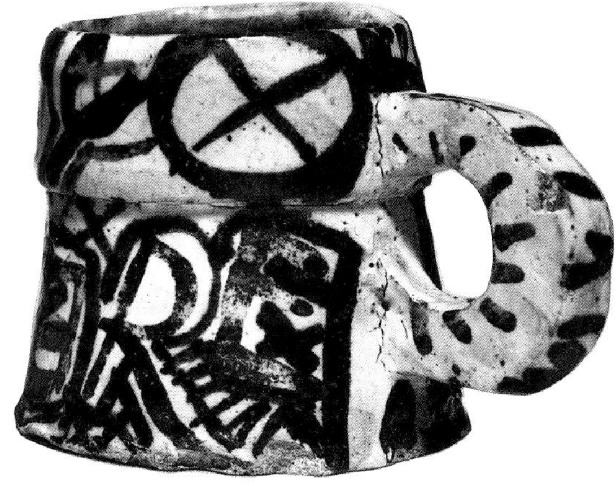

Fig. 2 Billy Al Bengston, *Phoney Whiteware*, 1956, glazed stoneware, 3 × 2¾ × 5″ (7.6 × 7.0 × 12.7 cm.). Kenneth Price.
Photo: Frank J. Thomas

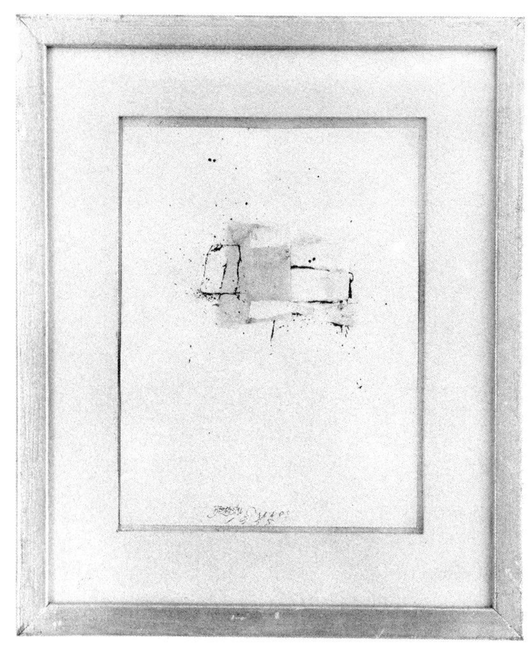

Fig. 3 Billy Al Bengston, Untitled (Cannes), 1958, collage: paper, ink, and gouache on paper, 12½ × 9″ (31.8 × 22.9 cm.). Collection of the artist. Photo: Brian Forrest.

Angeles at the time, wrote in *Artnews* of this "gifted" artist whose paintings displayed "a remarkable degree of authority . . . by the sheer liveliness of brush color and racing passages of pigment."[5] The response was gratifying because Bengston was only twenty-four years old when he had his first solo show, and because he had come to painting after first working in ceramics. But Bengston did not continue long in the abstract expressionist mode despite the positive response, recognizing that he was only belatedly following in the footsteps of other artists.[6]

The period between 1958 and 1959 was a time of crucial reassessment for Bengston, prompted by a six-month trip to Europe. Traveling abroad for the first time, he absorbed a vast range of visual information which suggested a new direction in his work. In Milan he was impressed by two Tintoretto portraits in which the head of each model was centered in its canvas. At the Louvre he was intrigued by what he recalls as a small "minimalist" Vermeer, *The Lacemaker*, in which the content and subject of the image is extremely focused and concise. He also encountered for the first time the work of Jasper Johns, whose paintings of targets and flags were exhibited in the 1958 Venice Biennale. Bengston immediately responded to the subtly articulated surfaces of Johns's canvases and his use of preconceived imagery such as a flag or target isolated in the middle of the canvas.

While abroad, Bengston produced almost a dozen paper collages, such as an untitled piece made in Cannes (fig. 3), in which the focus of the collage is directed to the center of the paper. Of necessity these pieces were intimate in size, as Bengston was constantly on the road and living out of a suitcase. The Cannes collage—like the sun-filled environment in which it was created—is also luminous, the pervasive lightness and openness of the white paper delicately enhanced by the fragile wisps of color and line. Encased in an aluminum painted frame, the cumulative effect is of a hand-sized parcel of light. A world apart from the dark expressionist paintings he had exhibited only months earlier in Los Angeles, these collages hint at the importance environment and light would play in Bengston's later work.

THE FORMATION OF AN AESTHETIC

Upon returning from Europe in early 1959, Bengston undertook a new direction that marks the commencement of his mature work. He began by addressing fundamental issues about painting. First he tackled the question of composition: what elements contribute to a resolved painting? Bengston minimized the problem by focusing on what he considered the most neutral composition possible: a square centered in the middle of a canvas that is almost square. Then, in a move that recalls what he had seen in Europe, he placed dead center in the central square of the painting a cross, star, or most often a heart, or valentine, as the artist prefers to call it. Traditionally these images are highly symbolic, but Bengston was not concerned with their emblematic meaning. The choice of these common shapes was pragmatic; they freed Bengston from having to design imagery that fit within his preferred square format. Each image was meticulously defined, reinforcing the clarity of his composition.

Having established a consistent format and motif, Bengston next addressed questions about paint handling and color. He experimented with a vast palette of hues and often incorporated geometric patterns such as checkerboards or stripes. The canvases were variously thinly painted, heavily impastoed, or softly scumbled so that their surfaces are subtly shimmering in texture. In his black valentine painting *Grace*, 1959 (pl. 1), Bengston pushed his exploration to an extreme, producing a work he viewed as essentially devoid of color and composition. *Grace* is simple, direct, and complete, suggesting the precision that Bengston admired in Vermeer's painting.

The choice of the valentine as his predominant subject was somewhat serendipitous: Bengston's 1960 solo exhibition at the Ferus Gallery was scheduled to open near Valentine's Day, so he selected the heart as an appropriate subject for the event. Titling these paintings after Hollywood starlets—*Grace* (Kelly), *Ingrid* (Bergman), *Kim* (Novak)—was likewise an arbitrary convenience and is a tactic Bengston has consistently employed over the years. Whether naming paintings after John Wayne movies or constellations as he does in later work, Bengston selects his titles after the paintings are completed for the pragmatic reason of identification. Rarely is there a direct corollation between the meaning of a name and the painting itself.

When these canvases were exhibited at the gallery in 1960, the response from critics was positive, although interpretations of the work were surprisingly diverse. Reviewing the exhibition in *Artnews*, Jules Langsner perceived strong ties in the work to surrealism and dada, writing that "Bengston manages very well indeed to convey the Dada aspects of Hollywood without falling into the trap of a hackneyed Surrealist imagery."[7] Gerald Nordland, however, commented on the "machine-like precision" of the paintings and Bengston's imagery, which he saw as harking back to impressionism in the choice of "banal" subject matter raised to a level of significance. "They are ultimately unimportant as subjects," Nordland observed. "Yet they achieve the mysterious monumentality, dignity and intensity of a Motherwell *Elegy* or a Duchamp *objet trouvé*."[8] To his fellow Los Angeles artists, the paintings were refreshingly new and precedent setting. Edward Ruscha recalls that Bengston's break with the prevailing aesthetics of abstract expressionism introduced the concept of symmetrical compositions and "hard-edge" painting to Los Angeles artists.[9]

In 1960 Bengston expanded his repertoire of central-image shapes to include a personal adaptation of sergeant stripes, now sometimes referred to as chevrons. That year, returning from a trip to Europe with Robert Irwin, he decided while on the airplane—instantaneously and capriciously—to use this image. For the next ten years Bengston incorporated the sergeant stripes into his work almost exclusively. He also consciously chose to paint on Masonite, and later aluminum, surfaces he felt were compatible with the rigidness of the image.

It is virtually impossible to suppress the impulse to read military symbolism into the sergeant stripes. This tendency is compounded when one considers that many of the titles Bengston later selected for the paintings are derived from John Wayne movies. Titles such as *The High and the Mighty*, *Two Fisted Law*, and *Hellfighters* reinforce the machismo interpretations of the motif. In choosing to paint sergeant stripes, Bengston perceived a special challenge: to adopt this hard, masculine symbol and transform it into a work of art; to take something mundane and make people stop and notice it. He has also explained that the image functioned as his identifying signature. Because the sergeant stripes became so strongly linked to him, he felt no compulsion to sign his work. But the motif has never held any symbolic meaning for the artist, despite the obvious social and political connotations one may assign to it. Bengston's choice of the sergeant stripes occurred during a relatively calm period of American political activity, and when they first appeared in his work they caused little controversy. The Korean War had ended several years earlier and the turmoil surrounding Vietnam would not occur for almost another decade. Contrary to one's natural inclination, the sergeant stripes are not to be read as an emblem or symbol. Rather, the repeated motif, like his repeated composition, provided Bengston with a consistent context in which to explore his growing interest in color and light and its relationship to environment.

In his first chevron paintings Bengston worked with traditional oil and enamel paints on Masonite, juxtaposing various colors to create luminous effects. In *Stainless Bob Steel*, 1960 (pl. 4), for example, the bright, central yellow square seems to glow like an interior light from the gray, black, and dulled yellow that surround it. But Bengston quickly turned his attention to a radically new painting method: the spray-painting technique and scintillating metallic colors associated with customized-car shops. He became familiar with this method of painting with lacquer when he began to ride motorcycles in 1960, the same year he adopted the sergeant-stripe motif. What started as a hobby soon turned into a vocation, as Bengston raced motorcycles professionally for the next four years, winning enough money to supplement his art income.[10]

Bengston became a master of spray painting, creating dazzling optical and colored effects. In *Buster*, 1962 (pl. 6), for example, meticulously feathered circles of paint seem ethereal, like glowing halos of light; a flawlessly sprayed shadow gives the illusion of deep pictorial space. Collectively seen, these paintings evoke the sumptuously light-filled Los Angeles environment in which they were created. "My earlier work took off from things I saw in the street: cars, signs, etc.—man-made things that we see in harsh California light," Bengston has acknowledged. "And Los Angeles, of course, was and is a car culture. . . . So I used car- and sign-painting materials and colors the way an artist would any other kind of color."[11]

Bengston was intrigued by both the metallic surface quality and depth of color he could achieve by using the spray-painting technique. The process was toxic, and sometimes tedious and time-consuming, requiring as many as ninety coats of sprayed lacquer, but what resulted were paintings that appear simultaneously translucent and dense in color and depth. In *Mr. Britt*, 1960 (pl. 3), the color seems to recede palpably into space as the viewer looks into and beyond the flat picture plane. At the same time, the hard, polished surface acts like a mirror, tossing back reflections. The ubiquitous sergeant stripes act as a visual cue that differentiates these readings. The image variously is immersed within lacquered depths, floats decallike on the painting's surface, or is brushed rather than spray-painted in oil to reinforce contrasts of field perception.

Bengston's preoccupation with the perception of color and light was shared by many of his Los Angeles peers. Robert Irwin, Craig Kauffman, and Larry Bell similarly experimented with new forms and painting techniques, working with industrial materials and methods including Plexiglas, aluminum, cast acrylic resin, vacuum-formed plastic, and spray-painting techniques. Col-

lectively the concerns of these artists paralleled that of their east coast counterparts such as
Donald Judd, Dan Flavin, and Robert Morris, who were also preoccupied during the sixties with
issues of perception and maximizing the viewer's attention to the physical properties of a work: its
color, reflectiveness, transparency, density, or texture. In the course of their explorations, the Los
Angeles artists unwittingly formed a loosely bound art movement, variously referred to as the
"Cool School" or the "L.A. Look," which helped to establish Los Angeles's international art reputation in the sixties.[12]

Bengston premiered a selection of his paintings of sergeant stripes in a solo exhibition in New
York at the Martha Jackson Gallery in 1962. Reviewing the show, the critic Irving Sandler
bypassed any in-depth discussion about the color and luminosity of the paintings. Rather, he
focused his attention on the sergeant stripes, interpreting them as a symbol of "the American
Dream."[13] When the paintings were exhibited later that year in Los Angeles at the Ferus Gallery,
Henry J. Seldis, critic for the *Los Angeles Times*, took another approach. He praised the "coloristic
virtuosity" of *Mr. Britt* (pl. 3), but responded negatively to the rest of the paintings.[14]

John Coplans, then editor and publisher of *Artforum*, was one of the most astute critics to appreciate Bengston's work. A passionate advocate of Los Angeles art, Coplans perceived that Bengston
introduced new visual possibilities through the spray-painting technique and experiments with
surface variability and illusionary depth. He recognized that Bengston's technical procedure
unleashed a new range of coloration totally unlike the use of stain, conventionally applied color, or
the optical type of painting then being explored. "It would not be too much to say," Coplans
observed, "that by the early sixties Bengston had probably extended the notion of a complex synthetic order of color far in advance of anyone else working at the time."[15]

In late 1961 Bengston interrupted his work with spray paint when he was unexpectedly offered an
exhibition at the Ferus Gallery. Because he did not have enough completed paintings of sergeant
stripes to exhibit, he chose to create representational works based on a BSA motorcycle he had
recently purchased. In only a month of preparation for the exhibition, Bengston completed over a
dozen oil paintings, ranging from a complete rendition of the motorcycle (fig. 4) to images of its
various parts—the tachometer, carburetor, license plate, and BSA name plate—isolated in the
middle of the canvas. Some of the works, such as *BSA*, 1961 (pl. 5), were closely related in look to
the sprayed lacquer paintings. The medallionlike BSA logo is centered in the canvas and suspended in a spray-painted ambience of radiant, glowing color. However, in other canvases such as
Gas Tank and Tachometer II, 1961 (fig. 5), Bengston rendered the motorcycle parts in a straightforward, representational manner. Set against sparse white backgrounds, the images were thinly
painted, almost drawn, in oil paint. The motorcycle paintings, produced quickly during a
momentary detour in Bengston's early oeuvre, were ultimately a route he did not further pursue.
Ironically, these images, along with those of the sergeant stripes, helped Bengston to secure
national attention, as they were quickly swept up in the pop art discussion then emerging.

Given the imagery Bengston chose—sergeant stripes and a motorcycle—and his penchant for
titling his paintings with suggestive Hollywood names, such as *Chaney* and *Tyrone*, it is not sur-

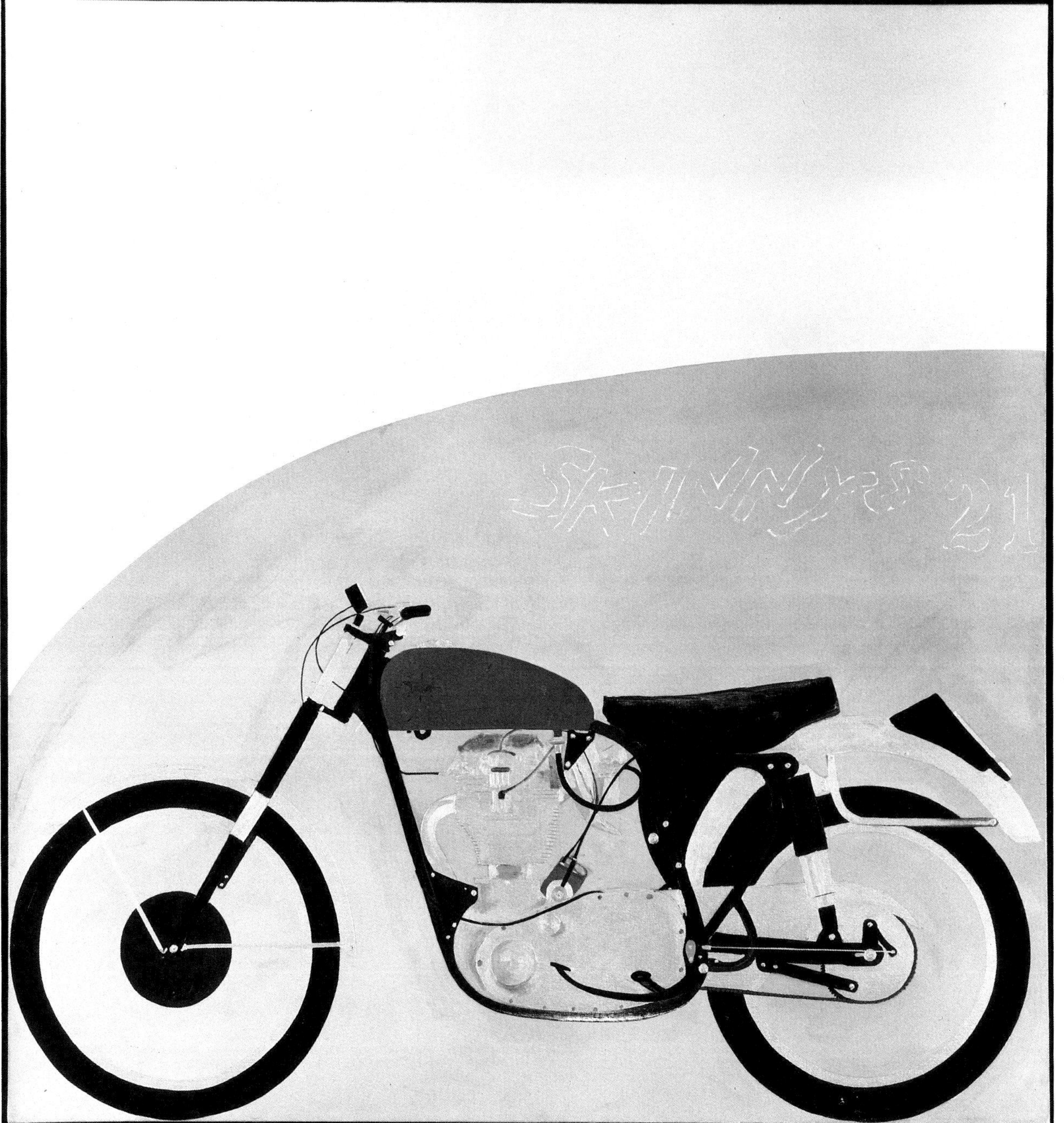

Fig. 4 Billy Al Bengston,
Skinny's 21, 1961, oil on canvas,
42 × 40″ (106.7 × 101.6 cm.).
Private collection.

prising that his work was so quickly linked to pop art. In some ways, Bengston's approach to painting closely paralleled that of the New York pop artists. Like Andy Warhol and James Rosenquist, Bengston advocated the use of preexisting images and minimized visible paint handling. But, Bengston greatly differed in his philosophy toward his subjects. His choice of motorcycle imagery was neither sarcastic nor ironic. Rather, he painted his bike out of true respect and appreciation for the machine's basic and honest styling.[16]

In later chevron paintings such as *Boris*, 1963 (pl. 7), Bengston continued to experiment, breaking free from the square format. Although the sergeant stripes remained centered in the paintings, the artist explored new compositions including circular, rectangular, and oval shapes. Often, as in *Tubesteak*, 1965 (pl. 8), which is painted on Formica, a flaunting of taste and an eccentricity that verges on garishness are characteristic. Bengston refers to these paintings done on synthetic boards and veneers as "woodies," which were intended to be installed flush to a wall of the same material, integrating the work into its surroundings. The name derives from the wood-paneled station wagons that were then popular among California surfers. Other artists at the time were similarly working with synthetic materials, exploring visual tensions between real and pictorial references. Among them were Richard Artschwager, whose hand-painted Formica furniture mimicked real wood grain, and Claes Oldenburg and his *Bedroom Ensemble*, 1963, a re-creation of a middle-class motel room made of wood, Formica, and vinyl. Although Bengston's woodies were never installed permanently as he intended, they introduced a concern that surfaces throughout his work: how a painting relates to·and integrates with its environment.

This inquiry was pursued further in 1965, when Bengston began working on dented sheets of aluminum. Collectively titled the *Cantos Indentos*, as a pun on Barnett Newman's *Stations of the Cross*, these paintings are now commonly referred to as "dentos." In *Holy Smoke*, 1966, and *Hatari*, 1968 (pls. 9, 10), the sergeant stripes remained in the center of the image, but Bengston would hammer, wrinkle, and sometimes even puncture the thin sheets of aluminum to create an irregular and misshapen surface. He then meticulously spray painted these metal sheets, creating a visual tension between the violated surface and the opalescent, vaporous atmospheres of softly layered colors. Successive sprayings caused colors to melt into one another, producing a brilliance as dazzling as sunlight or rippling water, or an atmosphere as buoyant as the sky and clouds. In the dentos, image, form, and color are transformed into a miragelike illusion that seems independent of the materials from which they are composed.

Although they hang from the wall like traditionally framed paintings, the dentos are meant to be seen under different lighting conditions and from different angles, like sculpture. In these pieces Bengston attempted to create works that dissolve into their environment by reflecting various aspects of their surroundings. As a result, the environment and its light become integrated with the pieces. In 1970 at the Mizuno Gallery in Los Angeles, Bengston explored this phenomenon by illuminating an exhibition of his dentos with only half a dozen candles. As the candle flames flickered and waned, the paintings manifested themselves with varying degrees of luminosity and color saturation. The broken surfaces revealed fragmented patterns of light and shadow and

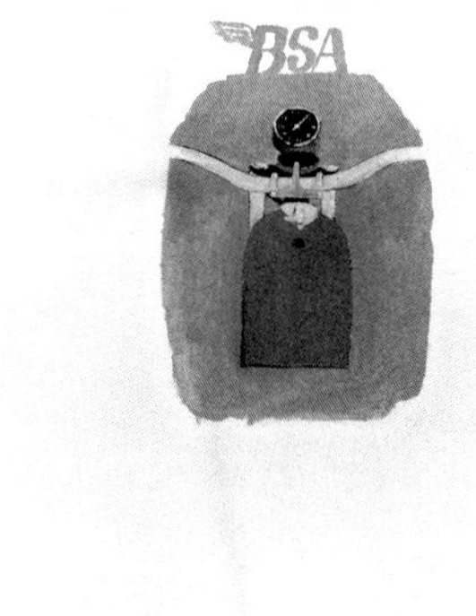

Fig. 5 Billy Al Bengston, *Gas Tank and Tachometer II*, 1961, oil on linen, 42 × 40″ (106.7 × 101.6 cm.). Edward Ruscha. Photo: Paul Ruscha.

reflected colors from the surroundings. As the viewer changed positions, the angle of view revealed new textures and patterns.

Because of the distorted quality of these paintings, some observers were quick to assign them a violent and malevolent symbolism. Discussing the dentos in 1968, curator James Monte wrote that "even after repeated viewings, there remains a large residue of pathos which illuminates the very center of the visual experience. Perhaps the pathos can be explained by a nearly inadmissible coupling of painterly pride and willful destruction."[17] For Bengston, nothing was further from the truth. The dentos were simply another vehicle that fused his interests in perceptual abstraction, color, and light.

A NEW MOTIF: THE DRACULA

With the seventies, Bengston began a new direction in his work. He changed his signature motif, his painting style, and the materials with which he worked. He also began to travel extensively, pursuing a growing interest in being outdoors with nature. Impressions of his travels abroad subsequently became an important touchstone for Bengston and his work.

In 1969 Bengston began to incorporate into his paintings the silhouetted shape of an iris, or dracula, as it is now known. His reasons for the change were twofold. First and most simply, Bengston had tired of the sergeant stripes. He also wanted to work in the more conventional medium of acrylic on canvas and felt the hard, geometric shape of the sergeant stripes was not compatible with the supple support of canvas.[18] He selected this image of the iris because it was a softer, more pliable form.

Bengston had worked with this flower motif for a brief time in 1960. At Barney's Beanery, an inexpensive cafe that Ferus Gallery artists frequented, he was intrigued by the logo on small sugar packets produced by the Iris Sugar Company; he subsequently adapted the image to his work. He completed three canvases, among them *Count Dracula II*, 1960 (pl. 2), that are distinguished by their iconic simplicity.[19] The silhouetted iris is placed in the middle of a square that sits in a larger square. When Kenneth Price saw the first canvases based on this flower, with its petals looking like extended wings, he commented that it looked like Count Dracula flying through the window as he metamorphosed into a bat. Bengston immediately responded to Price's impromptu observation and, thus, the iris came to be known as a dracula.

The simultaneous familiarity and enigma of the image, and its iconic placement in the center of the canvas, constantly intrudes on the consciousness of the viewer. The paintings refuse to become either wholly abstract or representational and provoke personal interpretation and analysis. Peter Plagens and Jeff Perrone, for example, who have written frequently about the artist's work, interpret the dracula as a sexual metaphor for androgyny. For Bengston, however, the dracula has no symbolic significance. Rather, like the sergeant stripes, it has a largely functional purpose, reinforcing or reiterating the formal problems of color and composition that Bengston addresses in his paintings. As he began focusing on more complex questions concerning color and space in the seventies, for example, Bengston placed the dracula at strategic points to reaffirm often illusionistic readings of space or the translucent layering of color.

When he resumed working with the dracula in the early seventies, Bengston continued the concentric arrangement of squares, with the dracula placed dead center. But his painting style radically changed, becoming more improvisational and spontaneous. This shift was largely prompted by the artist's experience in Colorado in 1969, when he was a guest instructor at the University of Colorado in Boulder. A house was provided for him in the Rockies, but he had no studio and was forced to paint outdoors in the fresh mountain environment. This exhilarating experience touched a wellspring of energy in Bengston and retapped his painterly, expressionist roots. These works, which measured on the average only twelve inches square, are distinguished by fluid paint handling and colors that dissolve in swirling, meteoric brilliance as seen in *Golden Dracula*, 1969 (fig. 6).[20] The paintings were intuitive and spontaneous, allowing Bengston to work more quickly and uninhibitedly than the spray-painting technique, which required at least twenty laboriously applied coats of lacquer.

The Colorado experience also instilled in Bengston an appreciation for nature that he began to explore through extensive travel. Among other places, he sailed, dove, and ran along the beaches in Florida, the Caribbean, and Hawaii. But most frequently he toured the Baja peninsula on his motorcycle, camping along the water's edge, exploring deserted hills, and swimming in remote bays.

The paintings Bengston completed between 1971 and 1974 record the artist's impressions of the light, atmosphere, textures, and colors of these different environments. From deep pools of saturated paint to almost frenzied splatters of pigment, Bengston cast a different mood in each canvas. In his hand, colors evoke the oily look of wet kelp or the glistening effect of sunlight as it strikes rippling water. The luminous white background and airy swirls and whips of paint that lace *Bahia San Luis Gonzaga Dracula*, 1972 (pl. 14), evoke a beautiful dawn breaking on the Baja peninsula.[21] The airiness of the painting contrasts with the density of *Honolulu Dracula*, 1974 (pl. 20), which was completed after Bengston's first trip to Hawaii. With its intense coloration—acid oranges, sumptuous purples, florid greens, and vibrant reds—and startling juxtaposition of patterns, the canvas vividly, though abstractly, evokes the opulent lushness of Oahu. The nearly smothering sense of pattern and color is alleviated by a centered white square in which a dracula floats. The white square provides visual relief, like a glimpse of open sky after a long walk through an overgrown, tropical jungle.

The role of environment was crucial to work that Bengston completed during a month-long stay in London in 1972. He had prepared an exhibition of his Baja and California paintings to be shown at the Felicity Samuel Gallery, but according to the artist, these canvases looked totally out of place in London, "like those garish toys made in Hong Kong or like the circus had come to town."[22] As a consequence, Bengston created new work for the exhibition based on his impressions of London and its light. *Jermyn Dracula*, 1972 (pl. 15), which is named after a street in London, evokes London's hazy and muted atmosphere and reflects the grayer and more subdued

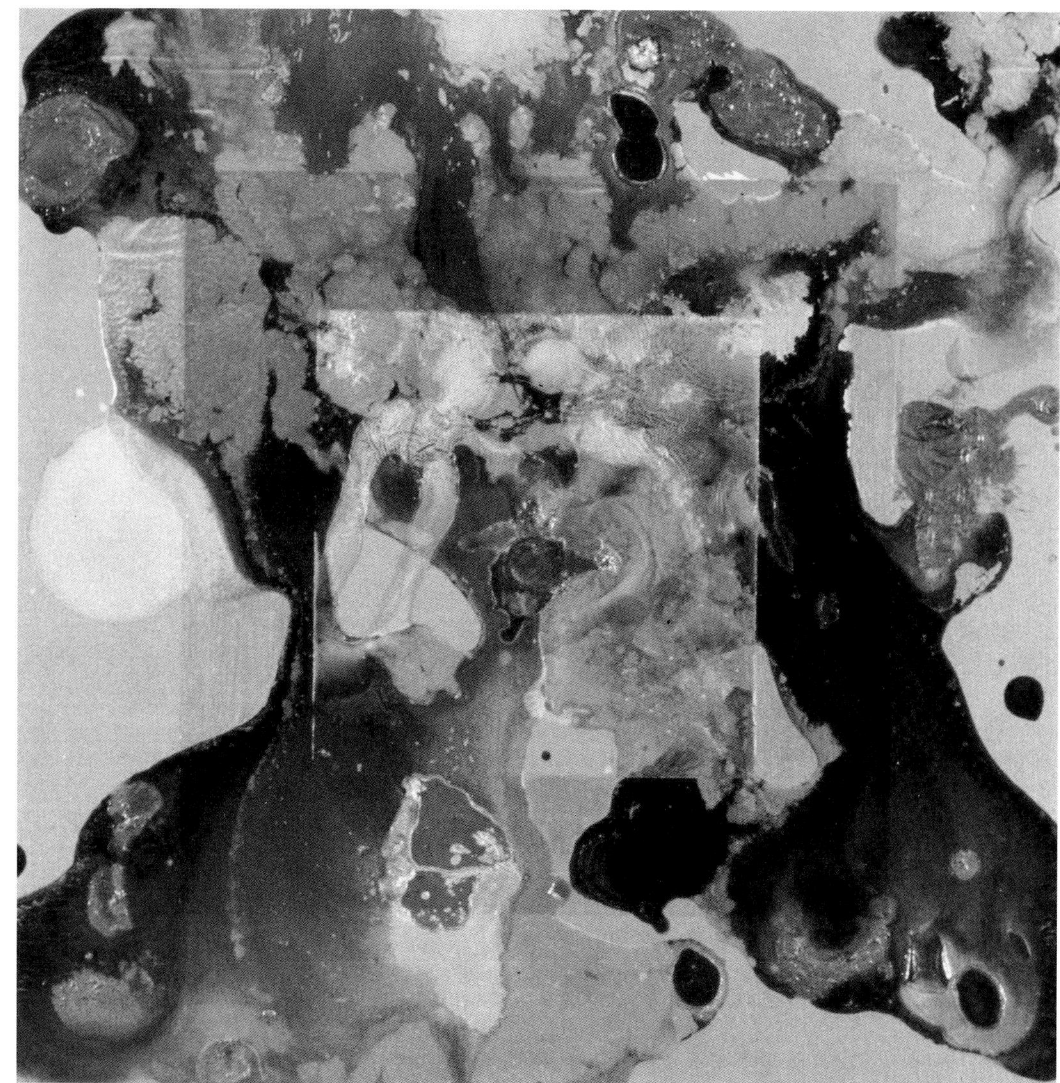

Fig. 6 Billy Al Bengston, *Golden Dracula*, 1969, oil on canvas, 12 × 12″ (30.5 × 30.5 cm.). Collection of the artist.

palette with which Bengston worked. A gray-tinted mist fills the painting, but the surface still shimmers with light, as though color were reflecting through layers of vaporous fog.

During his London stay Bengston also began to work seriously in watercolor, a medium he essayed briefly in the fifties. In London, the artist fully embraced its potential, as it provided a new and challenging means of capturing nature's many colors and changing light (pl. 16). Bengston's initial watercolors were based again on a centralized square format, but later within this fixed composition he explored exuberantly, sometimes recklessly, the fluid and light-filled beauty of the medium (pl. 17). Many of the watercolors are infused with atmospheric effects depicting soft light and colors that melt into a foggy mist. In others, the artist floods the paper with pigment, allowing it to luxuriantly bloom and swell, imparting a sense of natural, organic growth. Where line is used, it has a strangely living quality, as though it were growing out of the colored washes (pl. 18).

Although not merely studies, by 1974 the watercolors had assumed the role of introducing and clarifying ideas for Bengston's larger paintings. The portability of the medium freed Bengston from his studio so he could work while traveling, drawing on new experiences and environments to refresh his vision and invigorate his work. Its translucence helped him to record the changeable colors and light he observed while abroad. "A person who knows the territory can tell whether I've done watercolors in Puerto Vallarta, London, or Venice," he explains. "I might paint the same image in each place but I'm sort of a chameleon and I'll reflect the colors I see around me. In the same way, I'll paint winter colors different from those of summer, morning's colors different from evening's."[23]

In 1977, for example, the artist spent a month in Puerto Escondido, Mexico, on the rugged coast of the Pacific Ocean. He concentrated exclusively on watercolor, creating a rhapsodic medley of color and light. Based on his observations of sunshine and floral patterns seen through his louvered hotel window (fig. 7), these works are studies of light—jostled by the sinewy fingers of palm fronds, bounced off the glass louvers, and atomized into a prismatic array of hues. Set against the brilliance of the white paper, the colors are vibrant but fragile, revealing the artist's finesse and mastery of this elusive medium. The luminescent quality of these watercolors is also found in such predominantly white canvases as *Antaras Draculas* and *Capella Draculas*, both of 1977 (pls. 28, 29), and named after constellations and galaxies. These paintings suggest the iridescent and pearly interior of a shell, where colors subtly metamorphose as light strikes the surface at various angles.

VARIATIONS ON THE DRACULA

Throughout the seventies nature was a major source of inspiration for Bengston and was manifested in a broad range of rich, new work. Beginning in 1974 the artist directed his attention to the challenge of capturing the essence of water in his paintings. Since his surfing days, Bengston has been fascinated with the ocean and intrigued by the problem of depicting its colors, light transmitting and reflecting capabilities, and sense of continual flux. Many of the dentos and central-image dracula watercolors, for example, evoke the quality of light reverberating off the sur-

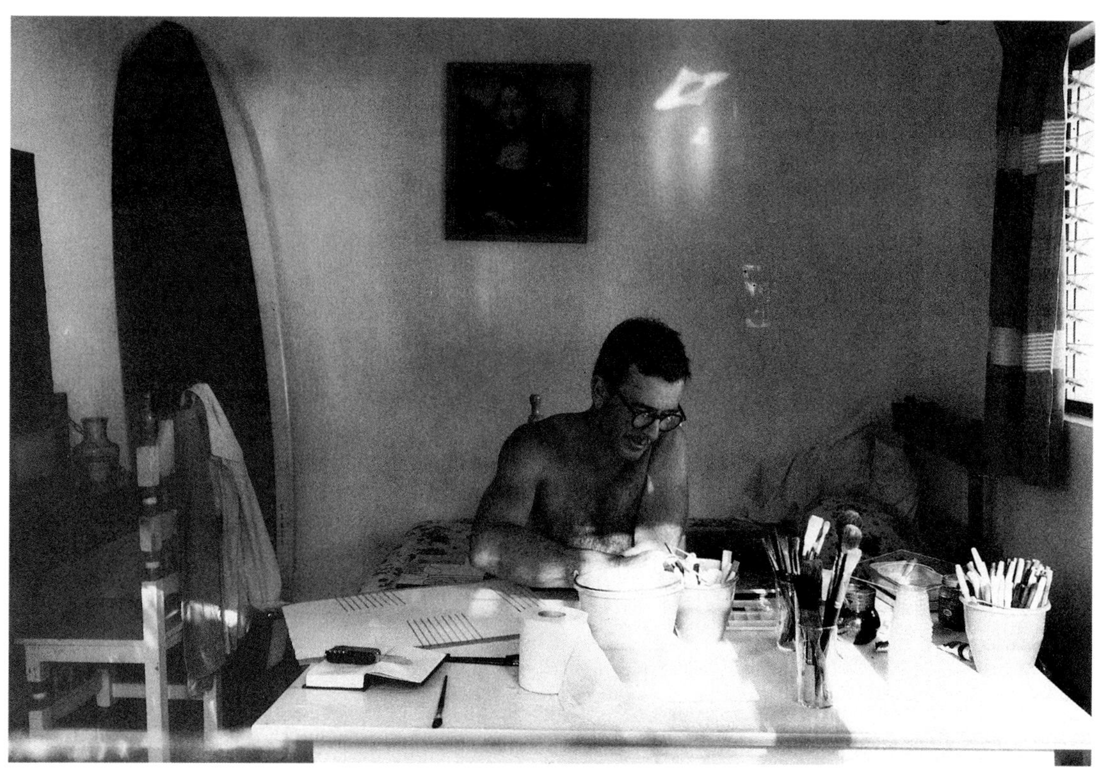

Fig. 7 Billy Al Bengston, Puerto Escondido, Mexico, 1977.
Photo: Jim Ganzer.

face of rippling water. Bengston turned his attention to the interior depths of the ocean when he began scuba diving in 1970. He was captivated by the microcosm of the ocean bottom and, as both diver and artist, has explored the Sea of Cortez and the local environs of Santa Catalina Island. "When I'm swimming in the ocean, I like to look at the bottom," he explains. "The most beautiful color is sand mixed with coral, seen through slightly agitated water —is it green or yellow? It creates a tranquil feeling."[24]

In his new work, Bengston abandoned the square canvas as being too static a format to evoke the feeling of water; he also freed the single dracula from its placement in the middle of the canvas. Instead multiple, overlapping squares or circles containing the dracula appear on painted canvas folding screens, bannerlike paintings suspended from the ceiling, and wide, unstretched canvases. While the format of these pieces was strikingly different, Bengston was returning to a familiar question he had posed in his earlier dentos—how a work relates to its surroundings and how it would be seen from more than one angle. He selected these new structures to engage the viewer visually in a three-dimensional environment, suggesting the experience of being underwater. Paradoxically, the critical and curatorial appraisals of these works bypassed perceptual concerns and more often placed them in a decorative context, aligning Bengston with the pattern and decorative—p & d—painters who gained attention in the late seventies.

The paintings on unstretched canvas, including *Garropa de Astillero Draculas*, 1974 (pl. 21), sometimes measured as much as sixteen feet in width, were tacked to walls without stretchers, and even extended around the corner of a room. An open-ended, sliding sense of space is created in which the painting no longer appears confined by the canvas, but expands to envelop the viewer in an environmental way. In these oversized works, Bengston enlarged the size of the draculas, which reduced their literalness, and shifted the location of them so that they rise or recede as positive or negative images on the painted surface. The translucent and liquid effects of the paint evoke the strangely moody but tranquil environment of the ocean's depths where sea blooms float in an ambient, fluid space.

Bengston's interest in creating an environmentally encompassing art that evokes the changeability of water is more daringly apparent in his paintings suspended in midair (pls. 23, 24). In these bannerlike works, which are titled after varieties of kelp, Bengston sought to convey the ambiguous and transient qualities of deep water, where distances are deceiving and colors and visibility are fugitive. They are painted on both sides with numerous circles, each containing a dracula, overlapping and converging with each other. Free to turn in space, the suspended paintings provoke different readings as light filters through the fabric from various angles and as the paintings gently sway and change positions. Because they move, the viewer's focus must be constantly readjusted within a relatively short depth of field, suggesting how vision is affected underwater by the constant movement of the ocean.

The screens that were created during the same period were a logical variation of the suspended paintings. Hinged and freestanding, the multiple panels of *Eagle Reef Draculas*, 1976, and *Iron Bound Cove Draculas*, 1976 (pls. 26, 27), can be set at angles to one another so the abstract patterns of circles and draculas change with the viewer's location. From a side view, the images are compressed, but then unfold, layer by layer, as the eye and body move by them. Like the dentos, the screens demand the physical participation of the viewer and reflect Bengston's persistent concern with the multiplicity of vision and the effect of motion on perception.

In subsequent but more conventional paintings that were stretched and hung on the wall, Bengston continued to explore spatial issues by creating conflicting references to two- and three-dimensional space. In *Brysselkex Draculas*, 1978, and *Trevapplinger Draculas*, 1978 (pl. 31), which are arbitrarily named after Swedish cookies, overlapping and converging fragmented, geometric forms appear to simultaneously advance and recede. The relative placement of partial circles and squares and lack of definition of positive object and negative background creates a puzzling sense of space. Bengston's use of transparent, reflective, and opaque colors makes these forms' relative positions unclear, compounding the spatial ambiguity. The powerful impact of the paintings depends on the viewer's knowledge that they are flat surfaces, which contradicts the illusion that the abstract shapes actually occupy three-dimensional space.

Many writers and curators have ignored the formalist underpinnings of these pieces, focusing instead on Bengston's use of brilliant colors and the stylized, repetitive image of the dracula that occurs in these canvases, screens, and suspended paintings. They have more frequently perceived the work in a decorative context, aligning Bengston with those artists—Joyce Kozloff, Miriam Schapiro, and Robert Zakanitch among them—whose works in the late seventies emerged as a new movement concerned with pattern and decorative painting. Bengston's identification with this style has been reinforced by his production of furniture, ceramic dinnerware, tapestries, and rugs.[25] Although he has frequently, in the last decade, produced such objects, Bengston makes a clear distinction between their production and his activities as a painter.

In many regards, however, Bengston's interests overlap those of the pattern and decorative artists, and his work has served as an important model for younger California artists such as Kim MacConnel, who also works in this mode. Like them, Bengston has placed visual pleasure ahead of aesthetic theory and has derived inspiration from other cultures, particularly that of the Orient. Bengston has frequently acknowledged that Oriental art, more than western tradition, has influenced him. His interest in Asian art dates to the fifties, when Bengston developed an enduring respect for Japanese teaware in which aesthetics and function are inextricably interwined. Bengston's screens, like the portable room dividers used in traditional Oriental residences, evoke images of nature through a highly stylized iconography. The repetitive patterning of the dracula and sensuous coloration that occurs in paintings such as *Trevapplinger Draculas*, 1977 (pl. 31), can also be traced to the richly variegated patterns found in Japanese kimonos.

To a large extent decoration itself became the subject of Bengston's work as he sought to create pieces that bridged the gap between the fine and applied arts. Bengston has always maintained that his paintings are made for homes and not museums—they are meant to be lived with and enjoyed. But decorative art can also be content laden, as indicated by Bengston's concern with the perception of space and motion. His work confirms the notion that painting can be both a vehicle for significant ideas and pleasing to the eye.

The parallels between Bengston's work of the mid-seventies and that of the p & d painters are marked. But while Zakanitch, Kozloff, and other like-minded artists have very specifically identified their art as a new mode of decorativeness, Bengston has remained aloof from such ideological discussions. Unconcerned with the burden of being avant-garde or of justifying his every move by theoretical or philosophical discourse, Bengston tenaciously clings to his freedom to experiment and explore new areas. Nowhere are these intentions more obvious than in his Hawaiian paintings.

THE HAWAIIAN PAINTINGS

In 1978, Bengston made a two-month visit to Hawaii and found there a landscape and climate compatible with his interests in both art and exercise.[26] A year later, he established a second studio in Honolulu, in which he very frequently works. The artist has explained that "the luxury of semiseclusion and quiet allows me to daydream and take care of the spirit."[27] Despite the relaxed atmosphere, Bengston's daily schedule is disciplined: he runs, swims, and rides his bicycle and puts in a full day in the studio. He largely confines himself to producing works on paper that introduce and clarify images and ideas that later appear in his paintings.

The first pieces Bengston completed in Hawaii were watercolors that captured his varied impressions of the islands (pls. 36, 37). In these works, the luxuriant colors and patterns of this tropical paradise announce themselves with unhalting exuberance: the splashy pink petals of hibiscus, the sleek green silhouette of palm fronds, the resplendent profusion of bougainvillea. Structurally the watercolors are composed of multiple, fragmented images and patterns that are overlapped and pieced together to form a visual whole. They combine the cinematic perception of running with the static sense of looking through a window frame that was first seen in the Puerto Escondido watercolors. "If it weren't for running I would have run out of images long ago," Bengston explains. "The images come from outside. My receptors are open, but I'm in a dream state. Sometimes I . . . come to a screeching halt and take a good look."[28] The paintings that immediately followed the watercolors, such as *Aloha Draculas*, 1979, and *Nakookoo Draculas*, 1979 (pls. 38, 39), continue to depict the artist's myriad observations and are characterized by the cutting and building up of space through superimposed planes of color. Patterns of shifting sand, the deep blue of the ocean, or the colorful patterns of aloha shirts are among the diverse but simultaneous impressions glimpsed.

In 1981, Bengston introduced a new element into his paintings and watercolors, a jagged edge that he refers to as "earthquakes."[29] In the watercolors, he literally cut the paper into saw-toothed pieces and collaged them together, visually implying a sense of physical disjuncture. Paintings such as *Ehukai Draculas*, 1981 (pl. 40)—*ehukai* meaning "red sea spray" in Hawaiian—similarly evoke this sensibility. Its crimson surface, subtly dusted with reflective paint, suggests, in a scintillating burst of color, the waves at dusk. The fragmented and serrated planes of color that tilt in different and oblique directions reinforce the sense of movement. The draculas appear upside down, on their sides, and nearly flying off the sides of the canvas, reiterating a sense of unrest.

During this period another important change occurred in Bengston's work: the stylized motif of the dracula gradually disappeared and was replaced by depictions of real flowers and other representational subject matter. In exploratory watercolor collages done in Honolulu in 1981, images of water and sky or foliage seen through louvered windows are very specifically described (pl. 43) rather than abstractly implied as in previous work.

By 1982 these collages gave way to outlandish and humorous imagery where fish fly in the air, joggers cavort in the dark of the night, and Hawaiian kahunas, or gods, converse with each other. They also evolved in increasing size and complexity, with some measuring nine feet in width or height. Bengston introduced a broad range of new imagery—sailboats, moons, and airplanes—subjects that are largely autobiographical and reflect his life in the islands.[30] From his studio in Oahu, for example, Bengston can see planes leaving the Honolulu airport almost every ten minutes. He has also built sliding doors with cut-out moon shapes that frame vistas of the island.

Bengston's turn to figurative imagery reflects his belief that change is crucial to any artist's inquiry; and the change that occurs here is marked. Collectively these vivid and fanciful collages are a world apart from the slick elegance of his spray-painted chevrons and the more ethereal watercolors of the preceding years. Whereas the earlier motifs of the sergeant stripes and draculas had no symbolic meaning, the viewer is now meant to read metaphor and narrative into Bengston's work. The artist's freewheeling and experimental attitude about making art and his exploitation of vernacular subject matter is not unique among contemporary artists. H. C. Westermann and John Altoon, two figures Bengston admires, similarly based their work on storytelling. But Bengston's audacious wit, combined with his brilliant sense of color and line, result in works that are uniquely his own. Appropriately, the collages are each titled *Ka'ao*, which in Hawaiian means a fictional or fanciful tale.

In these collages and the paintings that followed, the pairing of opposites is crucial, with one element depending upon the other to complete the whole, just as in Hawaiian storytelling. Frequently the earthy stories revolve around the eternal love triangle. Two men—macho man and the big-nosed stumblebum, or dork, as Bengston refers to them—vie for the attention of one woman. But as Bengston has observed, the two men are often one and the same, as he indicates in his painting *Ike Ole Ia Po*, 1983 (pl. 46). A two-faced personage, commanding the center of the painting, symbolically depicts such a compounded being and suggests the conscious and unconscious drives of the male.

These characters, as depicted by Bengston, are outrageously farcical—the woman has bouffant bangs and the stumblebum a nose that makes caricatures of Jimmy Durante look tame. Even the macho man does not escape Bengston's subversion: his face is finely chiseled to a fault; his aquiline profile is comically blunt and coarse. The artist himself often appears in these images as a thin, sometimes jogging, stick figure—a voyeur observing or participating in the scenarios (pl. 50). The droll quality of these pieces is sharply enhanced by florid contrasts of patterns, colors, and textures. In these paintings and collages it appears that Bengston has abandoned aesthetics to tell stories full of burlesque and slapstick. One collage, in which two kahunalike profiles flank the image of a fish, is a visual pun suggesting that the two men—and no doubt the artist—are telling fishy stories (pl. 51).

Despite the humor and whimsy that distinguish the Hawaiian work, Bengston has not abandoned formalist issues, particularly the visual tension between the readings of figure and ground and two- and three-dimensional space. The comic exaggeration of these images simply allowed him to explore such considerations without appearing ponderous. The artist has explained, for example, that the imagery in works such as *Ka'ao*, 1983 (cat. 61), was predicated by the question of how line could be used without suggesting volume. In the course of his exploration, the line came to define the female figure, free-floating in space but without three-dimensional form. The profiles of the two men are colored masses that underscore the sinuous linearity of the symbolic woman.

Bengston also manipulates line and color, as in the painting *Kipuka*, 1982 (pl. 45), to convey the saturated color and luminosity that pervades Hawaii, particularly its fiery sunsets and blue waters. The wavy hair of the woman, like glowing tubes of thin neon, suggest the man-made lights of Honolulu at night. The sky appears electrified with colors that may appear forced and artificial to those used to a muted world of smog and haze but which evoke the true experience of a Hawaiian sunset.

These intriguing images can simultaneously be read on different levels, thereby reiterating Bengston's interest in the duality of perception. Because the descriptive elements are radically simplified, they function as both referential images and purely abstract forms. The shapes also appear to occupy different and contradictory planes in space, as in *Kaukolu Hana Paewaewa*, 1983 (pl. 49). The eye weaves foreground, middle ground, and background together, moving erratically from the deep space of the sky to the flat planes of color that define the kahunalike heads. To assure this spatial ambiguity, Bengston deliberately provides contradictory information on the size and scale of the pictorial elements. In *Ka'ao*, 1983 (pl. 47), for example, an airplane and fish simultaneously float in a wash of blue, suggesting endless space; but does the blue describe sky or water? In manipulating images to convey two different backgrounds at the same time, Bengston plays with color and shape the way a punster plays with words. The collage is a visual, spatial maze in which he explores the quirkiness and ambiguity of perception. Freely composing visual jokes, Bengston has created a dazzling cosmic—and comic—scenography far removed from earthly affairs.

PAINTINGS OF THE MOON

Bengston's most recent paintings of moons seen through a mullioned window contrast vividly with his flamboyantly polychromed, figurative Hawaiian images. The artist has not totally abandoned narrative, but the story he unfolds is subdued and poetic, sometimes even haunting. The subject of the moon is still cosmic, but also personal and reflective. Bengston evokes a restrained mood of tension that, like a Japanese haiku, prompts a feeling of tranquility and contemplation. The paintings disclose yet another side of the artist, who now reflects upon the endless circle of life.

The motif of the moon and views from a window are certainly not new in Bengston's work. The ethereal Puerto Escondido watercolors of 1977, for example, were based on impressions of half-caught reflections of light on a window. A circular orb, suggesting a rising moon, was hinted at in such earlier abstract paintings as *Trevapplinger Draculas*, 1978 (pl. 31). Subsequently, the moon was very specifically described in Bengston's Hawaiian paintings, even when appearing as a mere sliver as in *Obake Madness*, 1984 (pl. 52). In his new paintings, the moon, in all its eerie, celestial magnificence, becomes the central subject. It appears that Bengston has telescoped his attention into this singular and solitary object.

The paintings, however, are not truly views from Bengston's studio window but evocative distillations of observation and memory. Occasionally he will paint a canvas that evokes a specific mood and then assign a title that corresponds to the work. Most often he will decide on a category of names and then randomly specify individual titles after the works are completed, as he has with such paintings as *Altoona* and *Portola*, 1987 (pls. 59, 60), which are named after small towns in California and Kansas.

In paintings such as *Agra*, 1987 (pl. 58), the moon dominates the canvas with commanding presence. Its size, magnified well beyond the power of the human eye, removes it irrevocably from the realm of observable phenomena to a domain incalculably remote in time and space and accessible only to a mythic imagination. Bengston's hand is evident in the built-up layers of the brush strokes, but a logic-defying glow seems to emanate through the transparent layers of paint. This phantomlike quality of light imbues the canvases with an otherworldly, even spiritual, essence. In their impersonality and restriction to a few silhouettes and shapes, the paintings possess a contemplative fixity.

The subject of the moon has been traditionally linked to mysticism, romance, and the spiritual. Bengston, however, is not comfortable with such discussions. Rather, for the artist, the moon is a vehicle for an in-depth investigation into light, color, and spatial perception—one of the continuous threads that weaves Bengston's varied oeuvre together. In many regards, the artist has come full circle, returning to the questions he first addressed in his chevron paintings some twenty years ago: how can a painting re-create a sense of luminosity and atmosphere? How can it provoke or alter perceptions of space and color? Bengston's answers do not rest on any scientific theory but are based on observation, feeling, and on the very nature of experience. In *Finland*, 1986 (pl. 55), for example, Bengston articulates the ephemeral quality of temperature. The icy blue coolness of the moon contrasts with the hot lemon-yellow bands that define the window mullions. The canvas imparts an almost palpable sensation, like placing a warm hand on a cold pane of glass.

The paintings of the moon are large, with some measuring over fourteen feet in width, and as a result they provoke an expansive quality. Like the dentos and suspended paintings, they are intended to engage the eye in a three-dimensional way and to reveal themselves differently in time and space as the viewer changes position. To heighten this sensation, Bengston uses metallic paints that reflect light in different wavelengths and intensities. The dusty, silvery hues in *Agra*, 1987 (pl. 58), for example, gradually warm to a pulsating coppery glow as the viewing angle changes.

Through these paintings Bengston seeks to slow the eye down, to provide an encounter for the viewer. "A work of art should never be wholly predictable," Bengston states. "If you know what you are going to see before you see it, then it isn't a work of art. . . . But if each time you look at it, you see something new, find that it means something more, something different, then you are on the track of art."[31] Time and movement are necessary to appreciate what is there to be seen, concentrating first on the entire canvas and then refocusing on smaller parts. Details, such as the tiny iridescent dots of paint that suggest stars that change color, must be integrated through extended viewing.

The paintings reveal themselves in a spatial continuum not only in reading from left to right but from foreground to background. Bengston manipulates color and composition to achieve strikingly contradictory spatial effects between figure and ground. In *Agra*, 1987, the dark blue background, contrary to normal perception, does not recede but asserts itself toward the viewer. This dynamic tension between the moon and the background is intensified by the moon's luminous depth of surface. Layering translucent glazes of color upon color, Bengston has created a sense of spaciousness that contradicts the relative flatness of the surrounding blue field.

The visual paradox in these paintings is accentuated by the compositional device of a window frame used in such paintings as *Altoona*, 1987, and *Portola*, 1987 (pls. 59, 60). A living sense permeates the canvases where multiple planetlike shapes float in an expansive universe. Bengston establishes an all-encompassing space not only by the large size of the paintings but by juxtaposing big shapes next to small ones. He also stains the canvas directly with pigment, using a technique that has precedent in the work of the color field painters and the ink paintings of the Zen masters. The areas of pure hue produce an atmospheric continuum and sense of infinity that is intensified by the use of closely valued colors and blurred transitions between different areas. The vertical and horizontal bands—which represent divisions of a window—interrupt the continuous field, giving it scale. Paradoxically, these flatly painted areas also limit the sense of expansiveness by asserting the two-dimensionality of the picture plane, thus creating an optical tension. This visual disjuncture is further provoked by the imbalanced use of vertical stripes—an abstraction of a mullion—in *Altoona*, where the middle stripe does not evenly bisect the large central moon and the stripe on the right adds weight to that side of the painting. The imbalance created by the opposing elements energizes the canvas, turning the painting into a field of dynamic forces.

From the sprayed images of sergeant stripes in the sixties to the recent paintings of moons, Bengston's work, when collectively seen, seems to have followed a circuitous and open-ended route. Adventuresome in life as well as in art, he has experimented freely with ideas. Although his art at times seems to have taken precipitous turns, the remarkable fact is that its essential content—painting as a response to nature—has remained intact. Intrigued by the changeability and richness of the world around him, he has sought to capture this quality in his work.

In essence, Bengston's paintings are about the perplexing dilemma of reconciling art and life. His interminable process of experimentation is a very private attempt to realize his impressions and ideas, regardless of the prevailing art world norm. His art represents a synthesis of the analytical and sensuous, derived from intellect and idea on the one hand and reverie and introspection on the other. Bengston himself has spoken of painting as an individual science of invention and discovery. The artist alone, he observes, invents his own formula in an effort to tell the truth to himself. His art is a search for a way of revealing a private vision based on his relationship to the world, as well as a perpetual testing of his inventive powers. His work affirms the persistence of artistic will as the source of creative impulse. It is an attempt to express inner experience more faithfully than a discursive explanation could do, to transfigure experience into an enduring image.

FOOTNOTES

1. Marshall Berges, "Home Q & A: Billy Al Bengston," *Los Angeles Times*, 23 November 1975, *Home*, p. 6l. Quote subsequently grammatically revised by the artist.

2. Bengston, interview with the author, 4 December 1986. Bengston had also studied ceramics under Kester at Manual Arts High School.
Unless otherwise indicated, quotations are from interviews with the artist conducted between October 1986 and August 1987.

3. Kenneth Price, who was also studying at the Los Angeles County Art Institute at the time, has explained that Bengston and he referred to the imperfections in their ceramics as "zens" (correspondence with the author, 4 May 1987).

4. Berges, "Billy Al Bengston," p. 53. Bengston has occasionally worked with ceramics since 1957, mostly designing and glazing prefabricated ware.

5. Jules Langsner, "This Summer in Los Angeles," *Artnews*, Summer 1958, p. 58.

6. Bengston credits the work of Craig Kauffman as influencing him to change directions. In 1957 Kauffman completed over a dozen paintings that introduced a sense of light and openness into his work, a direct contrast to the heavy, dark action paintings that Bengston and others were producing.

7. Jules Langsner, "Art News from Los Angeles: Bengston, Grant," *Artnews*, March 1960, p. 51.

8. Gerald Nordland, "Art: Valentines Etcetera," *Frontier*, February 1960, p. 18. According to this review, Bengston also painted images of flags, thus reaffirming the influence Jasper Johns had on the artist.

9. Ruscha, interview with the author, 9 February 1987.

10. In 1964 Bengston broke his back in a motorcycle race and subsequently gave up professional racing.

11. Quoted in Leo Rubenfien, "Through Western Eyes," *Art in America*, September-October 1978, p. 78.

12. The common interests that Bengston, Bell, and Irwin shared were confirmed in 1965 when the three artists were selected by Walter Hopps to represent the United States in the VIII São Paulo Bienal, along with Donald Judd, Larry Poons, Frank Stella, and Barnett Newman, the featured artist in the exhibition. In his catalog introduction Hopps wrote that these artists were "confronting critical issues of new space and structure in their art."

13. I[rving] H. S[andler], "Reviews and Previews: New Names This Month: Billy Al Bengston," *Artnews*, May 1962, p. 18. At the time, the Martha Jackson Gallery was exhibiting the work of artists soon to be identified with pop art.

14. Henry J. Seldis, "In the Galleries, 'New' Drawings an Old Story," *Los Angeles Times*, 16 November 1962, Part IV, p. 9.

15. John Coplans, "United States Section: VIII São Paulo Bienal 1965," *Artforum*, June 1965, p. 37.

16. Bengston once organized an exhibition, *Speed Sculpture*, shown at Montgomery Gallery, Pomona College, Claremont, California, in March 1968, which featured six motorcycles, a turbine dragster, sculpture by David Gray, and paintings by Bengston.

17. James Monte, "Billy Al Bengston," (Los Angeles: Los Angeles County Museum of Art, 1968), n.p.

18. Bengston reintroduced the dracula motif into his work in 1968 when he received a fellowship to create prints at June Wayne's Tamarind Lithography Workshop in Los Angeles. He selected the flower shape because he felt it was more appropriate for the softer medium of paper. Bengston also gave up painting with polyester resins and lacquers because of the health hazards they posed.

19. In addition to these paintings, Bengston completed several small, realistic ink drawings of the iris, rendered in a delicate Morandi-like crosshatching.

20. In Colorado, Bengston also decorated a group of prefabricated ceramic plates that he calls his "Colorado diary."

21. Bengston also completed several paintings that he collectively refers to as the "Motel Draculas." These canvases, among them *El Cortez Dracula*, 1971 (pl. 13), record the artist's impressions of the inexpensive Baja motels in which he frequently stayed.

22. Peck, Stacey, "Home Q & A: Billy Al Bengston," *Los Angeles Times*, 10 August 1980, p. 25.

23. Berges, "Billy Al Bengston," p. 61.

24. Quoted in Fredericka Hunter, "Artist's Dialogue: A Conversation with Billy Al Bengston," *Architectural Digest*, January 1984, p. 146. Quote subsequently grammatically revised by the artist.

25. Over the years, Bengston has frequently worked in other areas. In 1971 Bengston created his version of "tea tables," in which the artist's chevron paintings were imbedded in thick slabs of clear resin, then bolted to a variety of supports such as old packing crates and roughhewn tree branches. In the seventies he designed rugs, tapestries, and ceramic dinnerware that incorporated the motif of the dracula. Most recently he has produced furniture based on the playful themes found in his Hawaiian paintings.

26. Bengston first visited Hawaii in 1974 to escape an especially cold winter in Los Angeles. He visited all of the islands but did not respond favorably to Hawaii, largely because he was on a prepackaged tour. He visited Hawaii again in 1978, staying in Maui to work on his watercolors, train for the New York City marathon, and participate in a rough-water swim. During this extended visit he became enamored of the environment.

27. Quoted in Hunter, "Artist's Dialogue," p. 150.

28. Ibid., p. 146.

29. Bengston decided to incorporate this serrated element into his work after experiencing an earthquake in San Jose in 1979.

30. For a time in 1986, Bengston also began to include images of his pet Manchester terrier into paintings such as *Moses*, 1986 (pl. 57).

31. Berges, "Billy Al Bengston," p. 61.

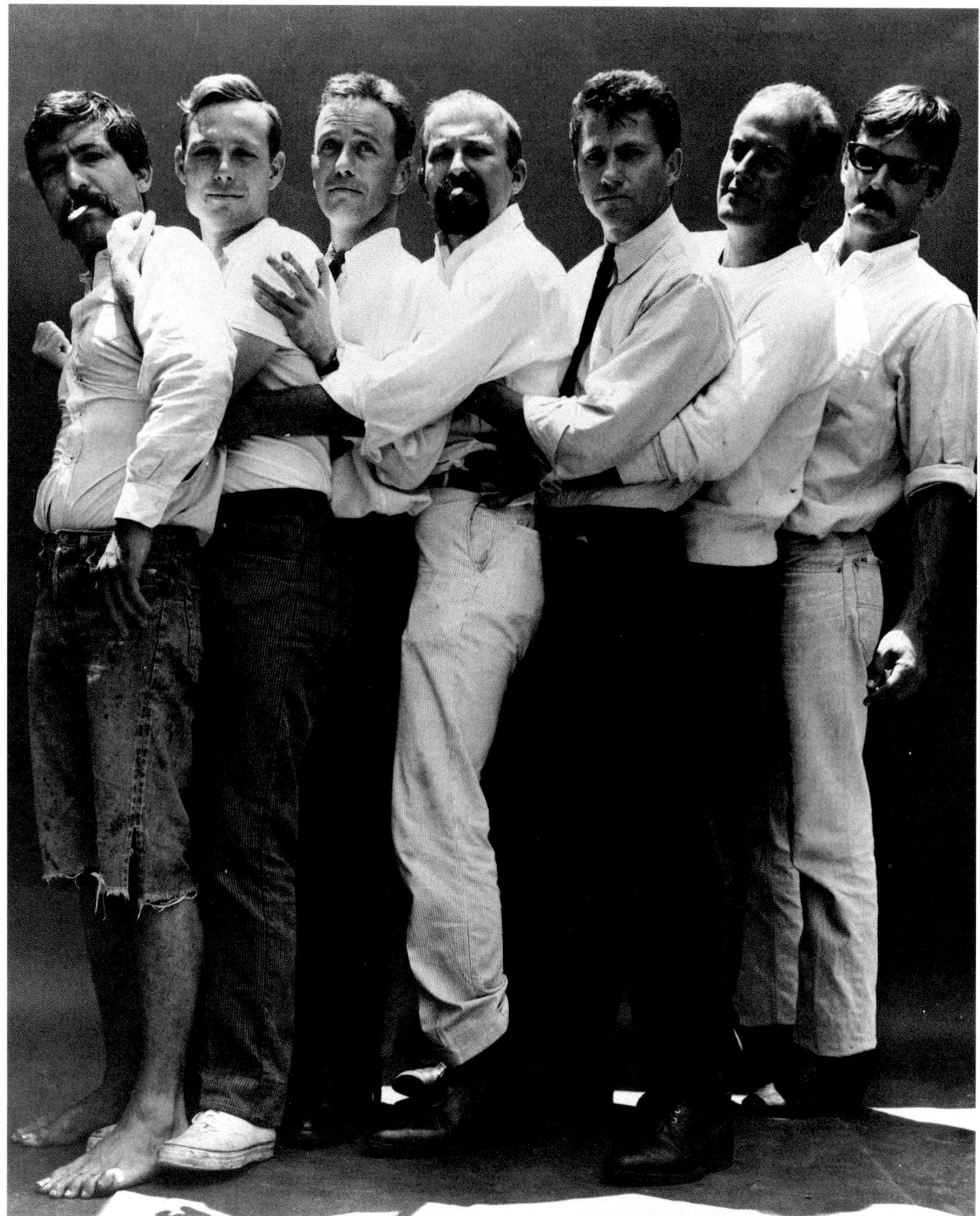

Ferus Gallery artists (left to right): John Altoon, Craig Kauffman, Allen Lynch, Edward Kienholz, Edward Moses, Robert Irwin, Billy Al Bengston, 1959. Photo: Patricia Faure.

A Remembrance of the Emerging Los Angeles Art Scene

by Henry T. Hopkins

In the late fifties, a group of artists evolved in Los Angeles who radically altered local understanding of art and who had significant impact upon the emergence of Los Angeles as a center for independent action, creativity, and originality. The influence of these artists, identified at that time with the Ferus Gallery on La Cienega Boulevard, continues into the eighties, as each new generation of Los Angeles–trained artists borrows from an awareness of their early struggles to gain acceptance for their art in a culturally conservative community.

At that time, the only Los Angeles artist who had anything like a national reputation was Rico Lebrun, whose Picasso-derived expressions of a maimed and crippled post–World War II world appealed to the romantic psyche of that theatrical city. Lebrun, at the peak of his influence and supported by the local press, founded a whole school of disciples who came to dominate the art faculties of southern California universities. Unfortunately, this Lebrun mania allowed the budding art community to ignore a number of extraordinary modernists, such as Oskar Fischinger and Lorser Feitelson, who continued to live and paint in Los Angeles even though it was not in the best interest of their careers.

That era, the homey and bland Eisenhower years, coincided exactly with the lamentation of transplanted New York gallery director Irving Blum that "living in Los Angeles was like slowly sinking into a bowl of warm farina." Another art dealer, James Corcoran, has identified Los Angeles in the fifties as "Omaha with a beach."

Until 1965 the city's only art museum was one unit of a tripartite museum of science, history, and art. Most of the trustees were history and science oriented and desperately conservative, especially considering that Los Angeles was touted to be the city of dreams. In the mid-fifties, chief curator of art James Byrnes was allowed to purchase a tiny Jackson Pollock painting and a Josef Albers, *Homage to the Square*, only if he promised to use them for educational purposes and not to hang them on the museum walls.

Clearly, conditions were perfect for rebellion and, in retrospect, it seemed inevitable. Young, idealistic artists studying and hanging around the professional schools—Chouinard Art Institute, The Art Center School, and Otis Art Institute—had little to be *for* and much to be *against*: the gloomy art of Rico Lebrun, a retrogressive museum, and no art gallery support system to speak of.

The little Pasadena Art Museum, out of the way and housed in a faux-Chinese pavilion, offered some stimulation with the Galka Scheyer Collection of Wassily Kandinsky, Paul Klee, Lyonel Feininger, and Alexej Jawlensky, and a sympathetic director in Tom Leavitt. The posh Frank Perls and Paul Kantor galleries in Beverly Hills showed work by accredited European moderns and even the New York school. But, for the most rebellious artists, a more compatible street life began to emerge on North La Cienega Boulevard, where the youthful Esther Robles and Felix Landau galleries began to show some work by California artists.

For example, Landau represented Peter Voulkos, a Californian and an acknowledged American master of clay art, who was a seminal influence on young Billy Al Bengston, both as teacher and peer-group leader. After gallery openings, they would amble up the street to Barney's Beanery to spend time in animated conversation with compatible types.

The Barney's of those days was a congested, dimly lit bar with inexpensive drinks, scarred tables, and congenial bartenders. The bar adjoined an even less expensive eatery where the food budget of a struggling artist could be stretched. Billy Al Bengston insists that while the Beanery's location (a few blocks from the galleries) was helpful, it was "because Barney was the only barman who was willing to carry a tab" that the Beanery became the premier Los Angeles art world hang out. So popular did it become, with the artists and the art crowd that wanted to be identified with them, that Edward Kienholz memorialized it in its entirety in a major tableau piece now owned by the Stedelijk Museum in Amsterdam.

Bengston recalls that "since no one in his right mind ever thought that he would make a living from his art, Barney's was an absolutely necessary link in keeping our spirits up. All we did was paint, go to the galleries, and do whatever we could to make ends barely meet. We didn't have the support of the WPA as in the 1930s and the NEA hadn't happened yet, so talking to each other for moral support was critical."

Bengston recently expressed his thoughts concerning the artist's life in Los Angeles: "The big change in American art took place about twenty years ago; before that there was no reason to be an artist—there was no reward, at least as far as young artists knew. It probably happened before that in Europe—Matisse must have had some kind of notion that being an artist was a career. But in 1960, I can assure you that none of us in California knew it was a career. Here, you always had to have another profession. 'Well, you're a painter—now what are you going to do for a living?'

"I guess I was a leader for others in saying that 'I am going to be an artist for a living, whether I die of it or not—I am not going to take another profession.' My friends were doing a variety of things to stay alive—John Altoon was doing illustration; Ed Moses and Craig Kauffman were teaching; Ed Kienholz was surviving by bartering—but there wasn't a tradition of somebody being an artist for a living.

"At that time we talked about how incredible it was that Willem de Kooning sold out his gallery show in New York and made something like twenty thousand dollars. De Kooning then was fifty-two—my age now—so at least I had something to shoot for in twenty years if I got to be as good as de Kooning."

During this early period, the young radicals found their own local hero in John Altoon, whose grand Armenian profile recalled Arshile Gorky, but who in reality looked more like a reborn Paul Gauguin. His ribald and generously encompassing life-style, peppered with bouts of severe depression, combined with his immense talent as a draughtsman and his absolute compulsion to paint, gave artists a focal point to gather around and from which to draw strength.

One evening after a Peter Voulkos opening, Bengston and Voulkos visited the NOW Gallery, which was operated by artist-entrepreneur Edward Kienholz. Here Bengston met another artist, Craig Kauffman, who would become a lifelong friend, as well as sometime art dealer Walter Hopps. Los Angeles art history was about to be made.

Kienholz and Hopps merged their major talents and their modest incomes to establish the Ferus Gallery (its name derived from a Latin root word misapplied to mean ferocious or unbearably intense) as an homage to the Fauves and as a commitment to the avant-garde. Ferus Gallery has been written about extensively—often to the neglect of other important art activities going on in the city at the same time—but if you were young, idealistic, and rebellious, that gallery was the only act in town. It became a social center for the artists as much as a showcase, with openings becoming occasions for "Can you top this?" activities, including Klieg lights and fancy dress.

It remains difficult to pinpoint exactly why this gallery was of such immense importance to the artists and to the community. The proper encompassing word is ambience, but then that needs to be defined.

First, the erratic brilliance of gallery director Walter Hopps, for whom the words "art" and "mission" are inseparable, cast its aura. He was supported in this unsupportable task by his wife, Shirley Neilson; his first partner, Edward Kienholz; and his last partner, Irving Blum.

Second, the gallery interior was carefully organized, handsomely white, immaculately clean, and beautifully illuminated. The Hopps-Blum team were great believers in "less is more," and each art work was given room so ample that it suggested Shaker spareness. The effect was often spiritual. To understand its impact fully, consider that the standard for the time was burlap wall covering and a desire to get as much merchandise on the wall as possible.

Third, the gallery carefully selected its artists—each of whom showed signs of the capacity for absolute invention. Their work did not, and still does not, look like that of each other or anyone else. In addition to the gallery member artists from Los Angeles and San Francisco who dominated the schedule, the gallery also offered special esoteric exhibitions, which reflected a pattern of perfect intent: Josef Albers, Giorgio Morandi, and Kurt Schwitters. Their exhibitions put immense pressure upon the young locals to compete—not so much with each other as with art history. As Bengston still remembers it, "The only way to know my work was any good was to hang it mentally between the work of two artists I admired; if it held up in that context, it was okay. There was no other test."

By 1960 Ferus Gallery had become the command post of the "other" Los Angeles art world, and the local artists who were represented there became heroic in the eyes of a new art audience. There was never a written manifesto of gallery guidelines but there were clearly unspoken common desires that bonded the group, even though they were very disparate types. Each opening was a cause for celebration and an opportunity for many to see what new standard might be set.

A classic example of the type of exhibition that established the artist, the gallery, and the attitude that would dominate Los Angeles art for the next decade was Billy Al Bengston's "valentine" show. The exhibition, which opened on February 14, let it be known that New York's second generation of abstract expressionists held no fascination for the new Los Angeles artists.

Bengston's paintings rejected large scale in favor of measurement by inches rather than feet. They were so carefully painted that he remembers wearing out dozens of no. 1 red sable brushes on a single painting. The images were centralized in the manner of Josef Albers and the subject of each painting was a heart, personalized in homage to a great heroine of the silver screen. *Brigitte*, for Brigitte Bardot, was a great favorite of the time. The colors were clear and the construction precise.

How conscious Bengston was of his total rejection of abstract expressionism and the prevailing national aesthetic attitude is open to question. But clearly, these paintings could not have been produced anywhere but in Los Angeles, nor would they have been produced in any environment other than the one surrounding Ferus Gallery, which begged for invention of the highest quality.

The Installation of *Billy Al Bengston* at the Los Angeles County Museum of Art, 1968

by Maurice Tuchman

THE 1968 INSTALLATION AT LACMA THAT SURVEYED BILLY Al Bengston's paintings to date was an intriguing event. Organized by James Monte, then assistant curator in the department of twentieth-century art, the show comprised forty-six paintings made between 1958 and 1968 . It continued a series of one- and two-man exhibitions organized at the new museum, which opened in April 1965, and followed shows of Peter Voulkos, Edward Kienholz, John Mason, Robert Irwin, Kenneth Price, and Wallace Berman. Monte's insightful text, sensitively recording the origins of Bengston's work, remains a basic document in the interpretation of the artist's work. Ed Ruscha designed the catalog, which quickly became notorious for its sandpaper cover, and which reflects his own deadpan artistry, albeit with more affectionate humor than is usual: the penultimate and last pages portray Billy on his bike, at first racing with machismo, then losing it, about to spill. But the installation, designed by architect Frank Gehry, was perhaps most striking in effect, rivaling even the power of Billy's paintings. The viewer entered an unusual space, filled with old furniture, reused walls from previous exhibitions, domestic-style lighting, and a new volumetric ordering: within the fifty-by-seventy-foot overall space was, for example, a cube that housed a single painting. Throughout there was a flow-through sense of fluid space that was emphasized by raw, unfinished wooden beam structures. The creators themselves—Billy Al and Frank Gehry—had instigated a process that ended up surprising them. Their unusual collaboration also initiated a genre in contemporary art. It was prophetic, establishing new parameters for contemporary display of art. It also addressed issues in the emerging California light-and-space movement, and influenced certain manifestations of "installation art" that were to dominate much of the seventies. Many artists conceived of their studio work after this exhibition with fresh ideas about their work per se and about its presentation. Arguably Frank Gehry's most far-ranging architectural insights were born in the dynamic interaction with Bengston in creating this environment. Yet, the Billy Al Bengston installation at LACMA has not even been alluded to in later critical consideration of his work.

Billy, sensitive to the "futility of talking about abstract art," desired instead to "talk about all the things *around* it—the ambience."[1] Bengston has done entire exhibitions that were lighted only by candles, exhibitions that were hung exaggeratedly high, others ground-huggingly low. He commented, "Now, you can *talk* about the light source that illuminates a work of art or the room that surrounds it, but hardly anyone does. They get right to talking about the painting as if it didn't make any difference whether it's displayed in a dark hallway or the Guggenheim Museum. It just doesn't make any sense to me. They only see the painting one way.

"For myself, I'd be much more interested in talking about the way it's displayed, since it's inevitably displayed badly. I may seem to be a little overly obsessed with lighting, but there's a reason for this obsession. Lighting is either the most important thing, or it's of no importance at all. If you have to have a painting lit in a certain way and that lighting has to remain constant, then you aren't doing a painting, you're doing a light-piece. Personally, I'd be satisfied to have my pictures seen only by daylight. In fact, I'd prefer it. I don't like light fixtures.

"A painting doesn't really have a chance in a museum, although you can't blame the people who work there. Start with the assumption that museums are designed by architects, who invariably hate artworks that disturb their designed space, add the fact that the surface skin that the paintings are hung on must be durable, throw in a building code, and you have a set of circumstances that doesn't allow even the most conscientious people the freedom they should be allowed in terms of display. Probably this has contributed to the rise of nonmaterial art—when the environment you are working with is so bad there's no sense trying to put anything worthwhile in it."

I asked Billy whether the installation concept traced to an earlier experience. His response sheds light on the special character of Los Angeles as an emerging art world center in the early sixties.

BAB: My whole social life in the early sixties was built around the gallery opening and one day Irving [Blum] came in and started cutting back on that and decided that we weren't going to have an opening. Kienholz had a key to the gallery, so he and Craig Kauffman and I got into the gallery and we just went around and raided all the trash cans and stuff like that, just stuck it up, and opened the gallery like business as usual and everybody came in and had a great time. That was our party. I mean we'd *done* that. I think that's when I met Joe Goode, he came in, he was really knocked out by it. So we'd done that but we hadn't modified the gallery in any way. We put it together in half an hour to forty-five minutes; it was good exercise.

---

1. I interviewed Billy Al Bengston in my office on 28 January 1987; later that day Frank Gehry and Ed Ruscha joined us in this reminiscence. Several sections from the solo interview with Billy have been incorporated into this essay, as have interviews with Larry Bell, Irving Blum, Laddie Dill, Joe Goode, Robert Irwin, James Monte, Ed Moses, Ken Price, and Nick Wilder conducted by telephone in March 1987.
  Richard Morris, secretary, department of twentieth-century art, Los Angeles County Museum of Art, and Julia Roessler, an intern from the University of Southern California, prepared typescripts from interviews with the artists and art dealers interviewed for this manuscript. I want to thank them for their exacting and timely assistance.

Catalogue cover with sandpaper designed by Edward Ruscha for 1968 exhibition at Los Angeles County Museum of Art.

MAURICE TUCHMAN

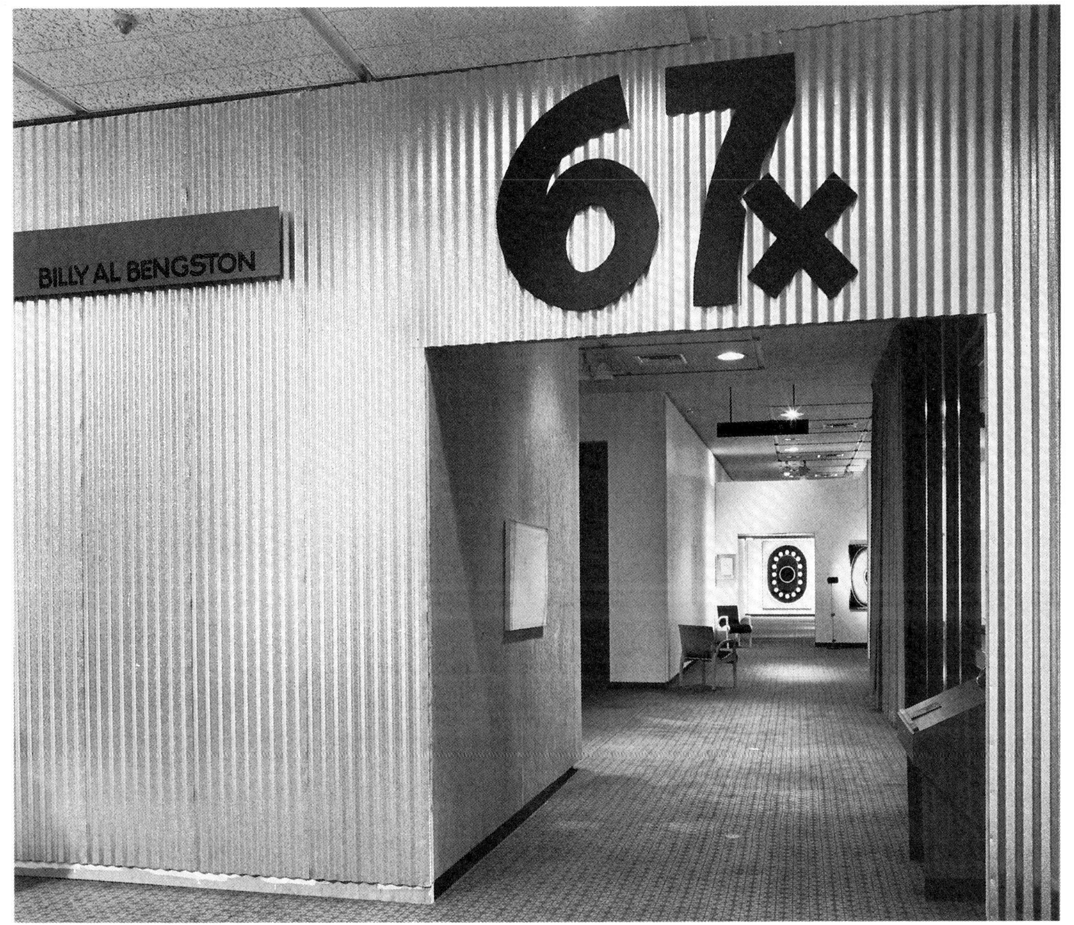

Entrance to exhibition, *Billy Al Bengston*, at Los Angeles County Museum of Art, 1968. Installation designed by Frank O. Gehry in collaboration with the artist.

MT: A scavenger hunt became a social and artistic event. In the museum's 1968 installation people were encouraged to sit on couches and turn off the lamps or turn on the lamps or read magazines and just sit around. . . .

BAB: That was a social event in that I figured you should get the idea in an ambient way, you don't have to be inundated by the pictures. You don't have to stand there. You and I, we forget we're privileged people, we get to look at paintings in a privileged fashion most of the time. The common man doesn't have that luxury and this was sort of my concession to the regular person who got to come to the show: they could look at it in kind of a regular way.

MT: How did this influence your concept of the show?

BAB: I think that the installation reflects that the pictures were painted to be seen in a familiar environment, in an environment that's flexible and not the standard museum environment and to function correctly they had to have that kind of environment.

And at that time I felt pretty smug about the idea of the dentos because I felt that I had taken the concept that we understood as abstract expressionism to the end: in other words I brought the environment in. If viewed correctly you lose the edges—the painting goes forward, the painting goes back, the painting is in flux. It was everything that I think that we had to think of as modernists at that time.

MT: How much did the museum installation look like your studio at the time?

BAB: It was originally conceived to look a little bit like the studio. My studio was an irregular rectangle; it had angular walls in it. This is where the angles in the museum installation came from.

About the gallery walls, you may remember one was blue, one was gray, one was made up of all these museum colors and Frank said, "Well, we're going to paint it and then we'll put the baseboards in," and I said, "No, it looks great. Let's leave it as is." So that's where the idea of collaboration came in. I looked at it and I said, "This is great, I mean this looks terrific." As a matter of fact, I still think it does when you look at these photographs [of the museum installation] and you see all these studs and facings. I mean I've never seen that before. It gives a kind of mystery that you don't see in installations. Also the installation illustrates process. The paintings are finished, the paintings can go any place, they could go anywhere. If people wanted to expend the effort to look at the pictures, they're there to look at: you don't have to do anything more to them.

MT: What about the colors? Isn't it absurd, for an artist as sensitive to colors as you are, to put his work up against colored walls?

BAB: Well, I would never consider these to be *colors*: they were museum colors or *office* colors, which are the colors we have in here now, your office. This carpet gray is made with red and green mixed together, and white—red/green/white actually—but maybe a little purple gray, too. It is a color but it's *not* a color. The beige wall is not beige: that's three or four different colors mixed together.

All the galvanized metal: that was Frank's innovation. It was the beginning of his career; I mean he became famous for galvanized siding on houses. Nobody did that. Since then he has turned to chain link. He's not doing that anymore either. That's an awareness of materials. I was aware of materials, he was aware of materials: why not, we said, have two heads instead of one. The furniture came about the same way. I told Frank what I wanted was only regular furniture and what he did, and this was the only thing that really got me mad at him, was that he went to Hertz or someplace like that or Abbey rents and rented all this God-awful motel furniture. I said I wouldn't have that junk in my house or anybody's house, so I said send it all back. That was the weekend that I went out in my truck and borrowed all my friends' furniture. I can go through the pictures and tell you whose furniture all this is. And then I borrowed plastic boxes from Art Services and made these tables. It was a roundup to make it look like—and this sort of basically looks a little like—an artist's studio in that it's barely, sparsely chaired. That's Ruscha's chaise: he still has that, by the way. I wiped out a lot of peoples' homes at the time. Nobody had any place to sit for a while. This is one of my old tables, that's one of my rugs. I built that thing. These chairs, I don't know—oh, those were Ruscha's. The lamps, I borrowed those table lamps, most of them from Ed Janss. This furniture is from Larry's house—boy, Larry was wiped out. I don't know who we borrowed the TV set from but that might have been left over from the rental—that's one of my old rugs I owned, this is Larry Bell's chair, that's one of my chairs, that's my lamp.

MT: The photographs and posters on the walls?

BAB: Just a bunch of photos. Things I was interested in at the time, a little bit of my history.

MT: Gallery announcements, your portrait drawing by Don Bachardy, the poster of Eldridge Cleaver for President . . .

BAB: At this time Eldridge Cleaver was the cause célèbre. You know that poster got me more credit in this museum than anything.

MT: With the staff?

BAB: Preparatorial staff and the guards. I could do no wrong here.

MT: This raw beamed wood opening, open spaces by Gehry . . .

BAB: That was completely Frank's idea. I was racing at the time. You've got to realize he wanted to make a statement and he made a statement. Very comforting isn't it? I mean, it was all Frank's interpretation of my life.

MT: In this installation do you think there were successful parts and less successful parts?

BAB: Oh sure. The successful part was that it got done. The fact that there were no windows in the gallery was not a success.

I didn't go out and borrow lights, but lamps. I think one of the main problems with show places now is that all our light comes from "twelve noon" and that is not the way light is. Light comes at us from all directions and that's the beautiful thing about light during the day. You get it from all directions.

MT: You haven't done another installation like it since. Why?

BAB: I guess I just became bored with it. I knew what it was doing and it always seems to me that if you really know exactly what you're doing it's no reason to do it. You always have to have a certain degree of mystery. If I know what I'm doing, then somebody else is liable to know. And if they know what I'm doing then why would they want to look at it? Why would they want to be involved in it? It seems to me you should want to do something that is different, something that fascinates, not something that someone can figure out.

Following this part of our conversation, Billy Al and I were joined by Frank Gehry and Ed Ruscha, who had contributed their talents to the installation and catalog and shared their memories of it. Ed Ruscha designed the catalog for the exhibition, which became as notorious as the installation and is now a collector's item. I asked Ruscha about his flocked, beribboned, sandpaper creation:

ER: Billy is very easy to be around these days, but back then, there was only one surface that described him and that is sandpaper.

MT: Obviously, the flocking pertains to his other side.

ER: Yeah, he was multifaceted: he had coarse grit and fine grit. He had a religious side too; that's why we put the ribbon in there.

MT: [to Frank Gehry] We've been chatting about the installation and looking at the book of photos of your design. Why don't you turn some pages and reflect on how you got involved with this. Tell me, how did it happen?

FOG: Billy asked me to do it and then Jim [Monte], I guess. I asked him how he wanted his paintings hung. And he said that he wanted to put them in carts and just leave them in the middle of the room so people could just look at them. Do you remember that?

BAB: I don't remember that. Good idea: let's do it next time, okay?

FOG: And then we all discussed the [museum] carpet: I'll never forget this carpet. The ceiling was also hard to deal with, in terms of the aesthetic imposition. I remember those were the issues we were trying to do something about, to change.

MT: Change the floor and the ceiling?

FOG: Neither of which we could. Anyway, we made a layout of the thing and I wanted to do it all in natural plywood.

MT: That was your first, immediate reaction?

FOG: And then we were going to paint some and somebody—maybe even you [Billy Al]—objected to it, to not having the natural plywood.

BAB: No, I remembered that they had that used plywood downstairs [in the museum shop].

FOG: I know, but then, all I remember is that the used plywood was brought up and I thought I'd have to paint it. I said, when we put it up, that I liked it the way it was, with the changing colors . . .

BAB: But you wanted to put a baseboard in, I remember that, and I said no, no baseboard.

FOG: And then we wanted it to look like Billy's studio, kind of. To have that kind of aesthetic. And we thought that would change the feeling of the room and get rid of the institutional quality of it, with the carpet and the ceiling. And then I remember there was a problem because I made too many rooms, and the guards wouldn't work it, so we decided to put TV sets in the rooms the guards wouldn't otherwise enter, and that's the way we got them to go in the rooms.

BAB: So they would go in there and guard that room. That's how the decision came for the open walls, so you could look at the TV from the other rooms.

FOG: And then we decided to go out and rent furniture; this got to be horrific. Because Billy wouldn't get involved with that. He said, "You do it." So I went out and rented furniture at the furniture rental place and it came in and it was the toughest thing I've ever seen. It looked like some hotel in Kansas. Billy walked in and started yelling at me. He called me all kinds of names. It was awful.

ER: You made it look too much like home.

MT: So the furniture was sent away and Billy started scavenging among his friends.

BAB: I rented a truck.

FOG: You were working in anger, you were furious. You worked best in anger. He pulled all this stuff in and it was beautiful.

BAB: One day, overnight, I worked straight through.

MT: Were you there much of this time, Frank?

FOG: I was there part of the time. He hated me. I couldn't stand in the same room with him.

In retrospect, the rental furniture was awful. I don't know if you remember it, Maurice, but I walked in and saw it. I said, "Don't let Billy in here," and Billy walked right in.

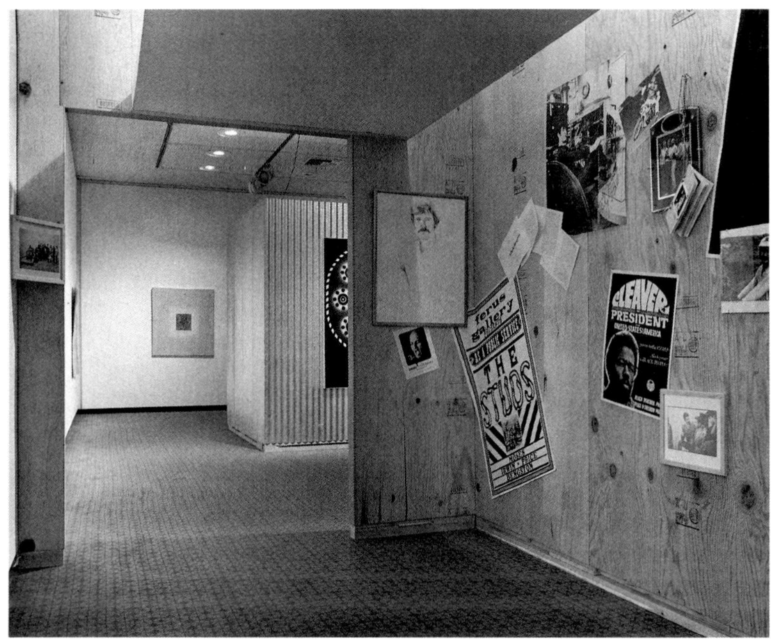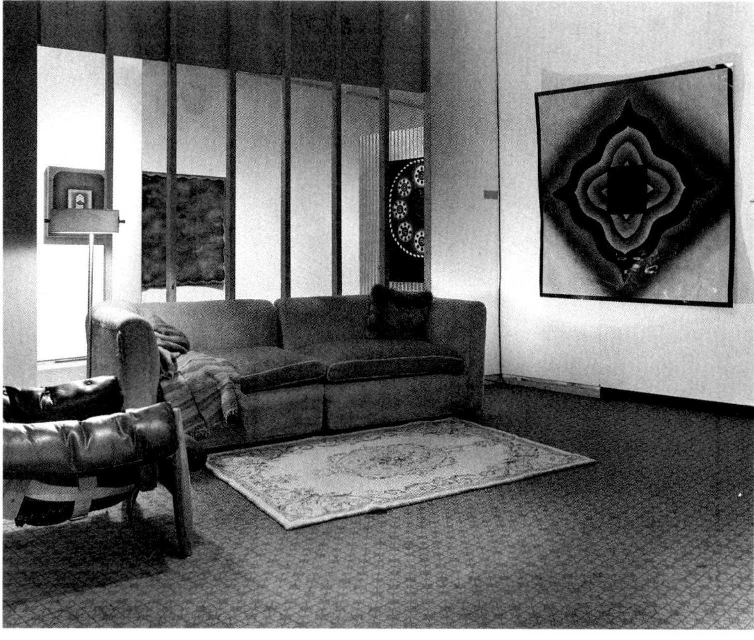

Installation views of exhibition, *Billy Al Bengston*, at Los Angeles County Museum of Art, 1968. Installation designed by Frank O. Gehry in collaboration with the artist.

MT: So as this transformation took place in Billy's hands by borrowing from Ed Janss, Ed Ruscha, Larry Bell, and other people, you were sort of watching it happen: it looked to you as if something interesting was happening?

FOG: It was great.

MT: What did you like about it?

FOG: It was what we were trying to do. It was the right mood. It was part of the art. It seemed like a true collaboration between us, even though it wasn't.

BAB: It was, it was before they knew about the word collaboration. We didn't know the word before.

FOG: We really got into each other's head in a way. I made a move and Billy made a move—even though it was done in anger and threats and worry and all that. It was terrifying to me because it was the first time I had been asked to do something. We had done the museum's Japanese show, *Art Treasures from Japan*, in 1965, and had a very big success here with that, but that was very straightforward. But *this* for me was really loaded. I mean, I revered this guy—and I still do, I love him—and I felt a double whammy: I had to really produce, and make it nice for him. I had to work, produce and make it something I could like and feel comfortable with.

I think this thing alone changed all my work after that. I felt a lot of people raised eyebrows about me doing this. But you can look at what I did afterwards; I did more stuff. I did the Donn O'Neill haybarn with the galvanized metal and which had telephone poles and a piece of metal in it, so I loosened up. I did Ron Davis's studio with the galvanized metal.

MT: Can you go on with that?

FOG: There was an attitude about it that became part of my work . . . using the metal and the material. Up to that time I think I was working very traditionally with refined workmanship and all that stuff. Trying to get it but never getting it.

MT: What triggered you to use galvanized tin and raw wood? How did it happen?

FOG: It provided the most contrast with what was there, the institution, the character of the museum. It seemed to fit with his stuff. I mean making that little room out of galvanized tin and putting that black painting in it was spectacular.

MT: You intended to contradict the somewhat "offensive" space of the museum?

FOG: We were just trying to humanize it, make it more comfortable for his work.

MT: How did you feel when it was finished?

FOG: I loved it, I was really excited.

MT: What did it mean to you?

FOG: Well, I felt like I was part of it. The team, the group, that I had contributed to it. I knew that it was going to raise some eyebrows and it did. I remember [then museum director] Kenny Donahue coming through there. He didn't like it at first, but in the end he got used to it, he realized it.

MT: What about during the course of the show? Do you remember any reactions of any interest?

ER: Well, it was unorthodox, it just wasn't like you say, institutional. I'm frankly surprised that you don't see more unorthodox installations of art, period. I think artists when they came and saw this thing . . . I mean, you didn't see anyone copying it. Of course it would be a little hard, without sticking out like a sore thumb. But artists get a little funny when it comes to collecting all their past works and putting them in an exhibit. You have to call upon something deep inside of you to get something like that done, and usually artists will go for the refined look.

FOG: Well, it's hard because the museum represents a kind of symbol of acceptance; it's the temple of art.

Back to the installation: I think I've always wondered about and marveled at the way Billy has done interiors. He's changed his studio there on Mildred. I used to go there every month or so for dinner and every time I'd get there it was a different place. Is that right? I'm probably exaggerating.

BAB: No.

FOG: It was pretty changeable and phenomenal. I try to get architectural magazines to do articles on you.

MT: And the raw-beamed, open spaces in the installation?

BAB: That was something you always found in my studio. I was always in the process of putting up walls and taking walls down. So I think that's part of his flow-through concept; my concept was that this is in flux, let's just keep it that way. Also to illustrate that this exhibition is not etched in stone, it's here today gone tomorrow. This is all to keep you from being embarrassed while you're looking at pictures. Just in the last five years I began to knock down walls—that's a financial consideration.

FOG: I always thought that it had something to do with your feelings—that you had to shake up the place to move on.

BAB: Well, that was part of it too. It's also because you're doing these tight-ass paintings and you want to do something that doesn't take a lot of thinking.

I now think the installation was pretty tight; I think we could have made it a lot looser.

FOG: I think he was pretty brave—now in hindsight—to let me do it. But then it sounded so right.

The statue [of Billy Al Bengston, motorcyclist] was all my thing, wasn't it?

BAB: It was all yours, one hundred percent.

FOG: It was something I contrived and I live with it now, too. I thought that the Hollywood Wax Museum would want it. After we paid for it, I told them we were going to donate it to them, but the guy in charge said, "Well, the kind of people that come to the Hollywood Wax Museum probably don't know Billy Al." The statue was a crazy idea. I thought somehow the motorcycle thing was a big aesthetic piece of him. I wanted Bob Graham to make a Billy statue and Graham wouldn't do it. He said, "I don't do that kind of art." When I ran into a brick wall there Babs Altoon, who was working for me, she found this guy, Spoon Singh, and he had a white turban. Babs arranged the dinner with Spoony Singh at his penthouse apartment at the Hollywood Roosevelt Hotel, and John Altoon and Babs and I went to talk to him about this project and he said if we could get him a mask and hands of Billy, he'll do it. We had to get Billy a mask without him knowing what we were doing. We didn't want to tell him too much. Billy liked the Hollywood scene then a little bit, so we sent him over to Westmore, the makeup artist, and told him we wanted to get a face mask made. We got a face mask and sent it to the Hollywood Wax Museum for fabrication. Then the thing was naked. We thought, what are we going to do now? We borrowed his uniform, his boots.

BAB: My leathers.

FOG: Nobody told anybody that in order for this thing to stand up they had to bore a hole through his best racing boots, which made it impossible for him ever to race again . . . we got this whole thing, and then we asked if we could borrow a bike for the opening and we made this whole tableau with 67x, his AMA Pro number. I'll never forget the statue was standing there and Billy saw it for the first time. It's pretty awesome to see yourself.

MT: How did he react?

FOG: He turned white, or something.

BAB: I don't remember either.

FOG: It was a pretty ghastly experience for him, I think.

MT: It happened just before the show opened?

FOG: Yes, it was the first time he saw it. It said a lot about him, and a lot about where the stuff came from. It put out a lot of explanations.

MT: How did it explain something about the art or about him? Other than the personality or the myth about Bengston as a cyclist. What did it explain about the art or about the installation?

FOG: The use of materials. The sense of the paintings, the dentos, where they came from—the metal, the dents, the motorcycle, it all came out of that somehow.

Recalling the Bengston installation today one realizes that factors of exhibition design were basic to the discourse of the Ferus artists and constituted a major element in their rapport. Each artist prodded and poked the other. "So much had to do with these [Ferus] artists playing to each other," Irving Blum reflected. "There wasn't a vast audience, as you very well know. The audience was first and foremost themselves and they would extend themselves in every imaginable way in order to send a message to the rest of them. That was really their audience, that is who they played to, that was a big concern for them. As you know, there weren't people batting the door of the gallery down in the fifties and sixties. So the audience was really an audience of their peers and if they could secretly and sometimes not so secretly send a kind of covert little message—through installation—they wouldn't hesitate to do it. Bengston is central; Ed Moses had absolutely the same kind of mind, and Kenny Price too. A certain kind of naughtiness is involved and the desire to shock and be somewhat sensational, which I remember the show as being. And wanting to make it all kind of homelike or even a little tricky, the opposite of high style."

A "sensitivity to odd spaces and to 'theme' rooms—Hawaiian scenes, jungles," as Ken Price remarked, was shared by Bengston's peers, especially Ed Moses and Larry Bell. Moses at this period was continually reconfiguring the spaces in his studio, employing a wide range of building materials and creating strange, short-lived environments: all the Ferus artists responded to this ever-changing phenomenon, analogous to Schwitters's *Merzbau*, but always fluid rather than iconic. Claes Oldenburg's frequent presence in Los Angeles in the early sixties, and especially his creation of the *Bedroom Ensemble* in Los Angeles in late 1963 (based on a theme-style motel near Malibu), also established the background for the museum installation, perceived as a work of art in its own right.

Ken Price recalls that the installation added to the impact of the show: "Confronting ordinary stuff, such as furniture and carpets and regular everyday things, may be a better way to get into the art than a standard museum installation. It created additional energy. And there was an abrasive quality too—including those sandpaper covers [of the catalog]."

"It was real impressive," recalls Larry Bell. "Each room in that installation was like a tableau, loaded with stuff personal to him: it was complementary but subordinate to the feeling of the imagery. Of course, the painting skill was awesome. I didn't understand exactly what he was doing, but it was filled with spontaneity and feeling and intuitions about space. It was aimed at humor and to shorten the distance between humor and the value of the paintings."

For Joe Goode, Bengston's paintings succeeded in the museum installation precisely because they remained the artist's work. "They were still his pictures, you knew the artist's intentions and how they were made. Here, you felt his painting was being with you as well as that you were being with it. Billy was the first artist to make a showroom out of where he lived, which influenced all artists' studios in Los Angeles. I think it also affected the development of living environments as art forms."

If the 1968 installation at the Los Angeles County Museum of Art was ignored by critics, it was remembered vividly by artists and influenced their subsequent work.

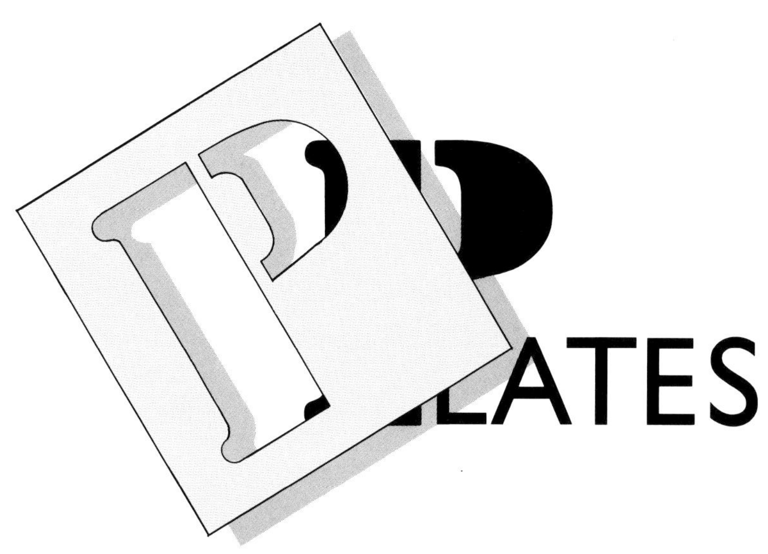

PILATES

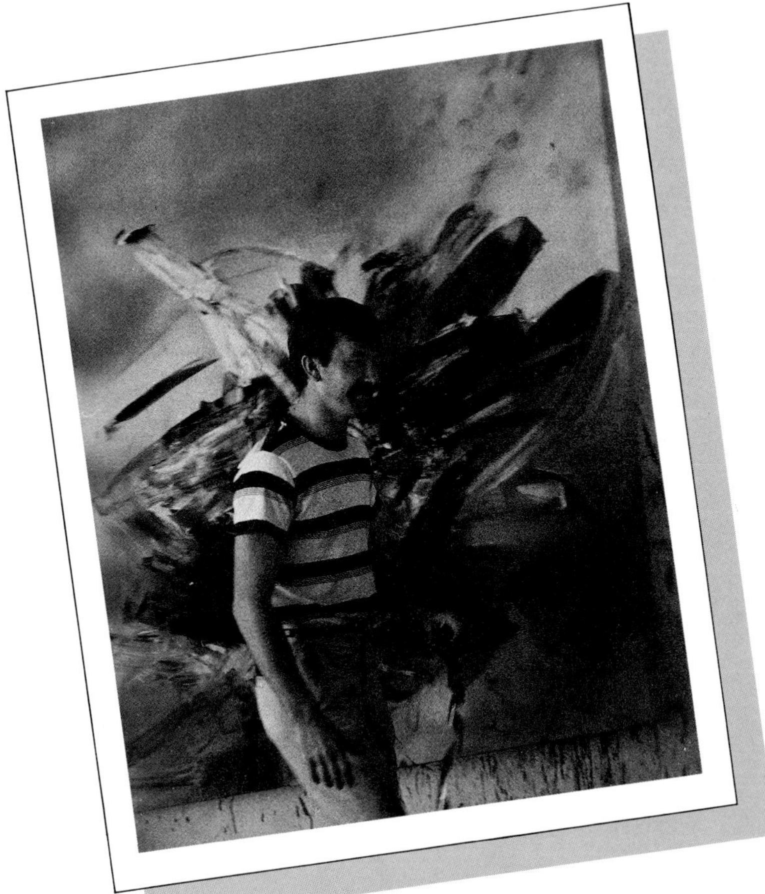

Billy Al Bengston, Los Angeles studio, 1958.

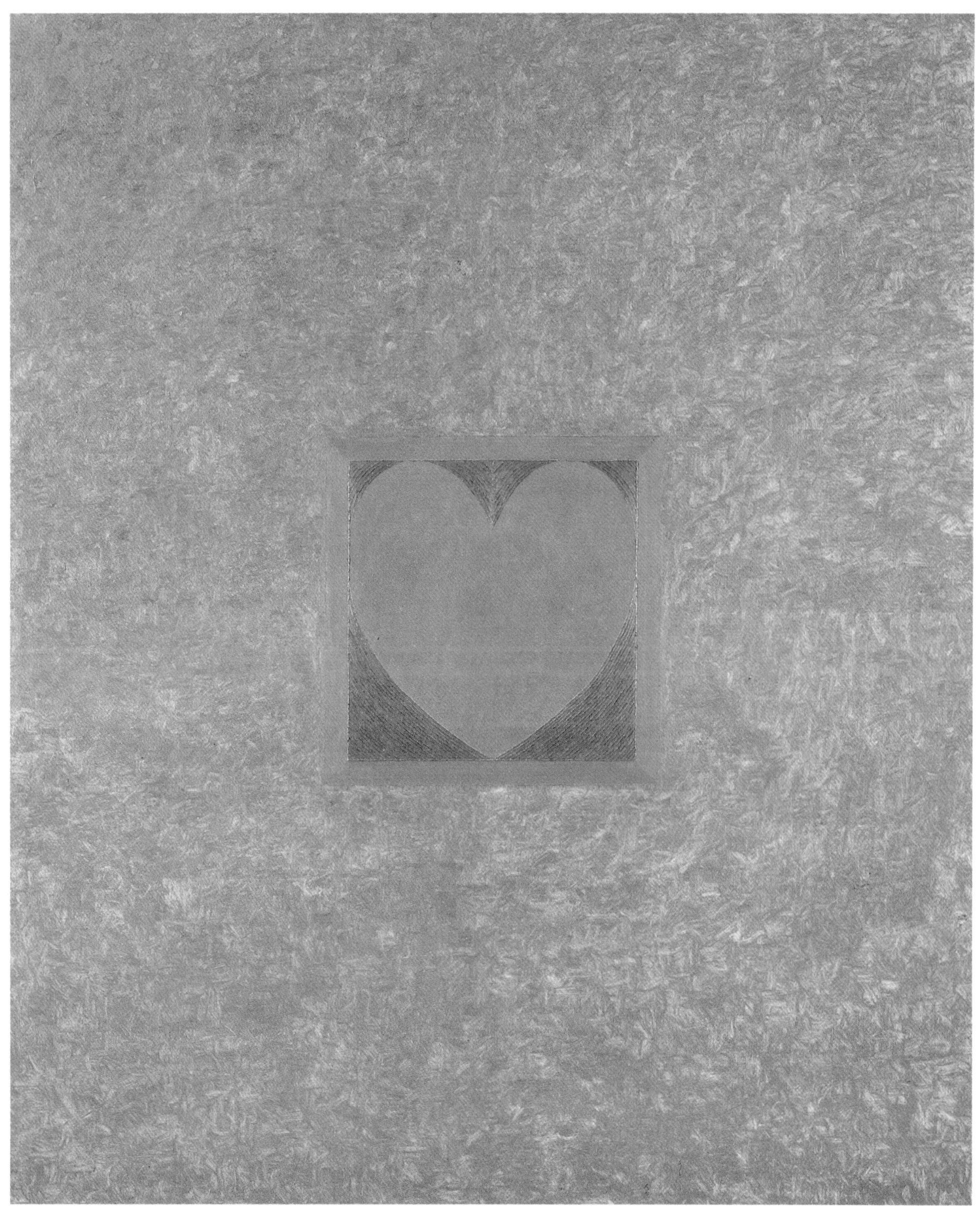

PLATE I
GRACE
1959

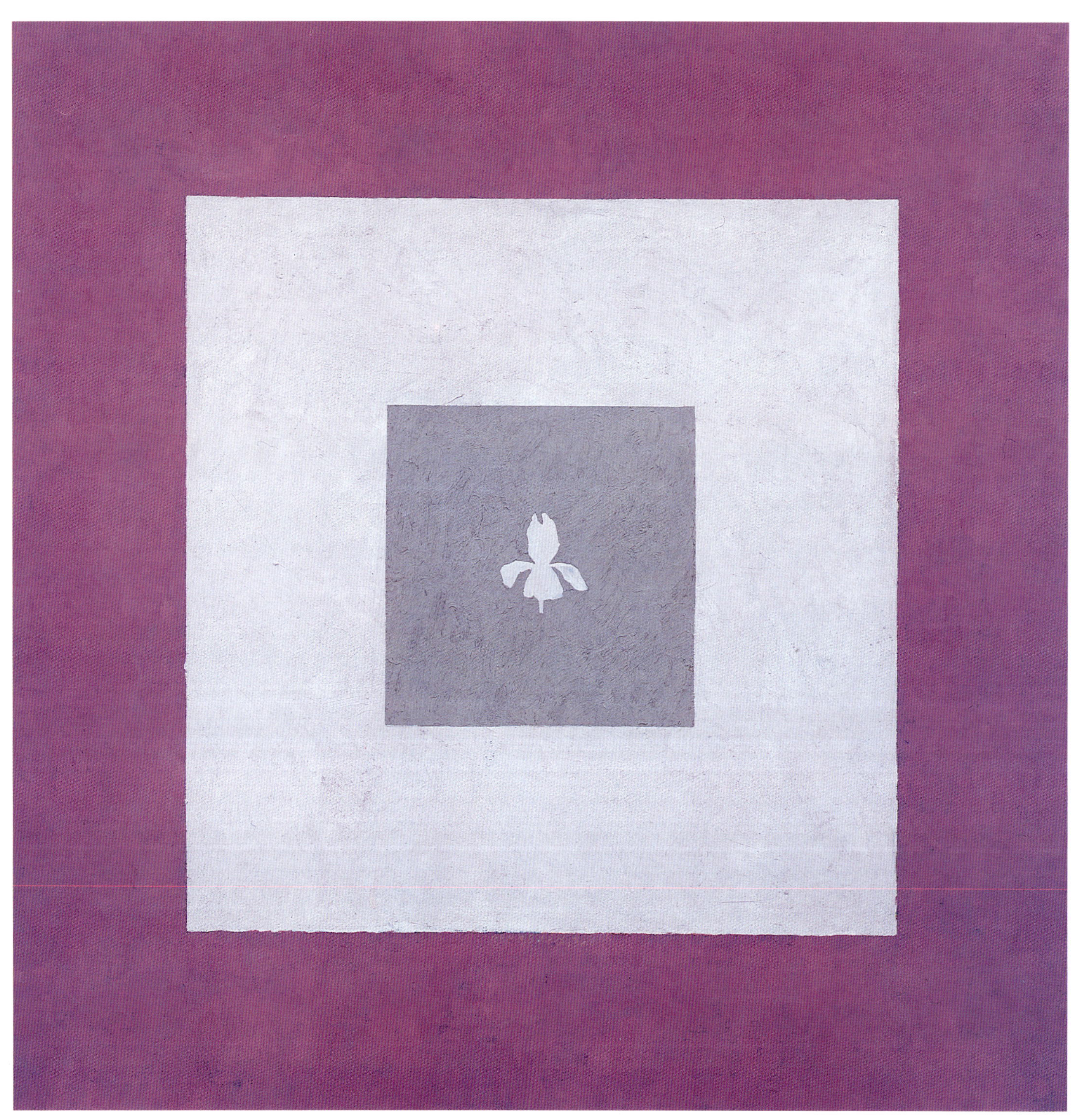

PLATE 2
COUNT DRACULA II
1960

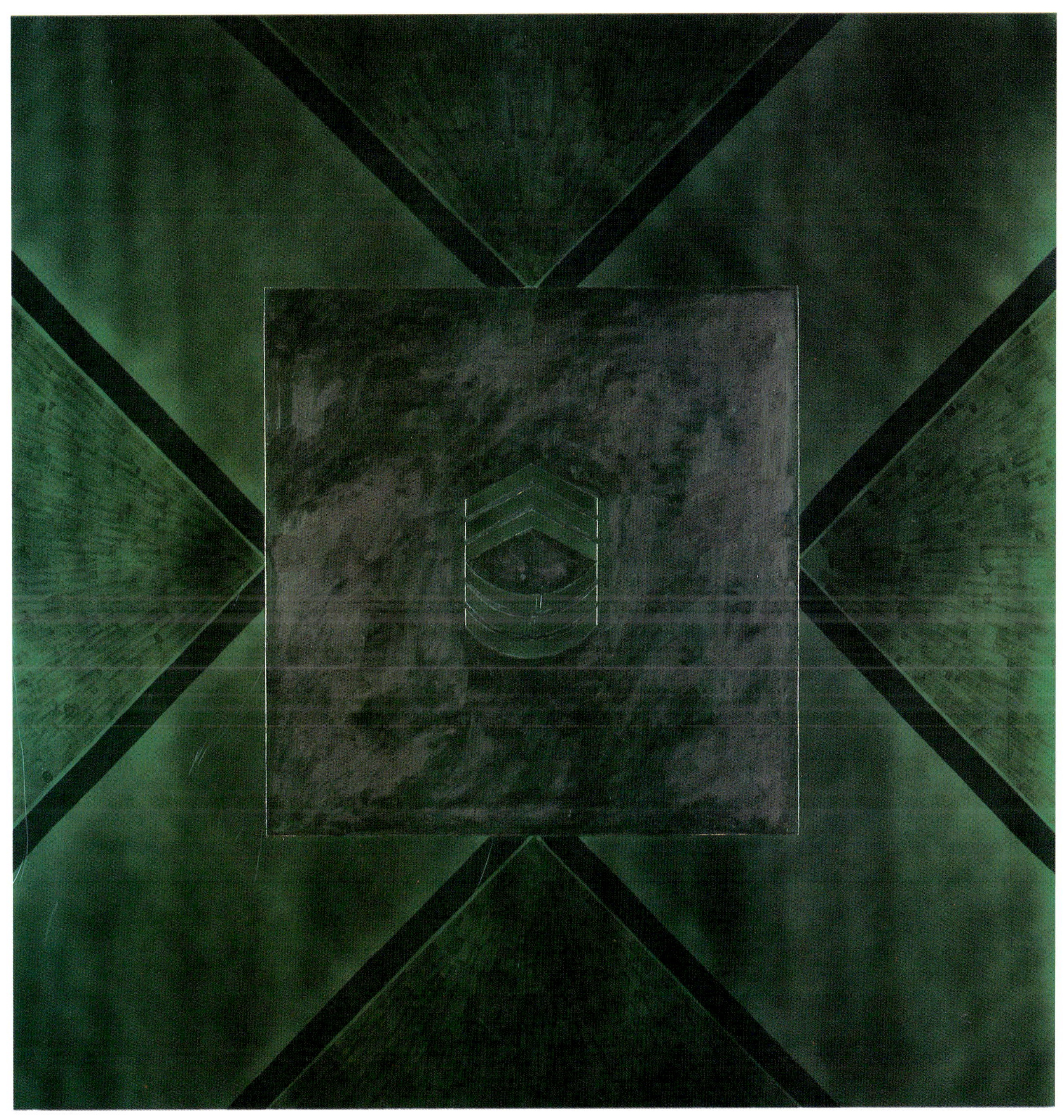

PLATE 3
MR. BRITT
1960

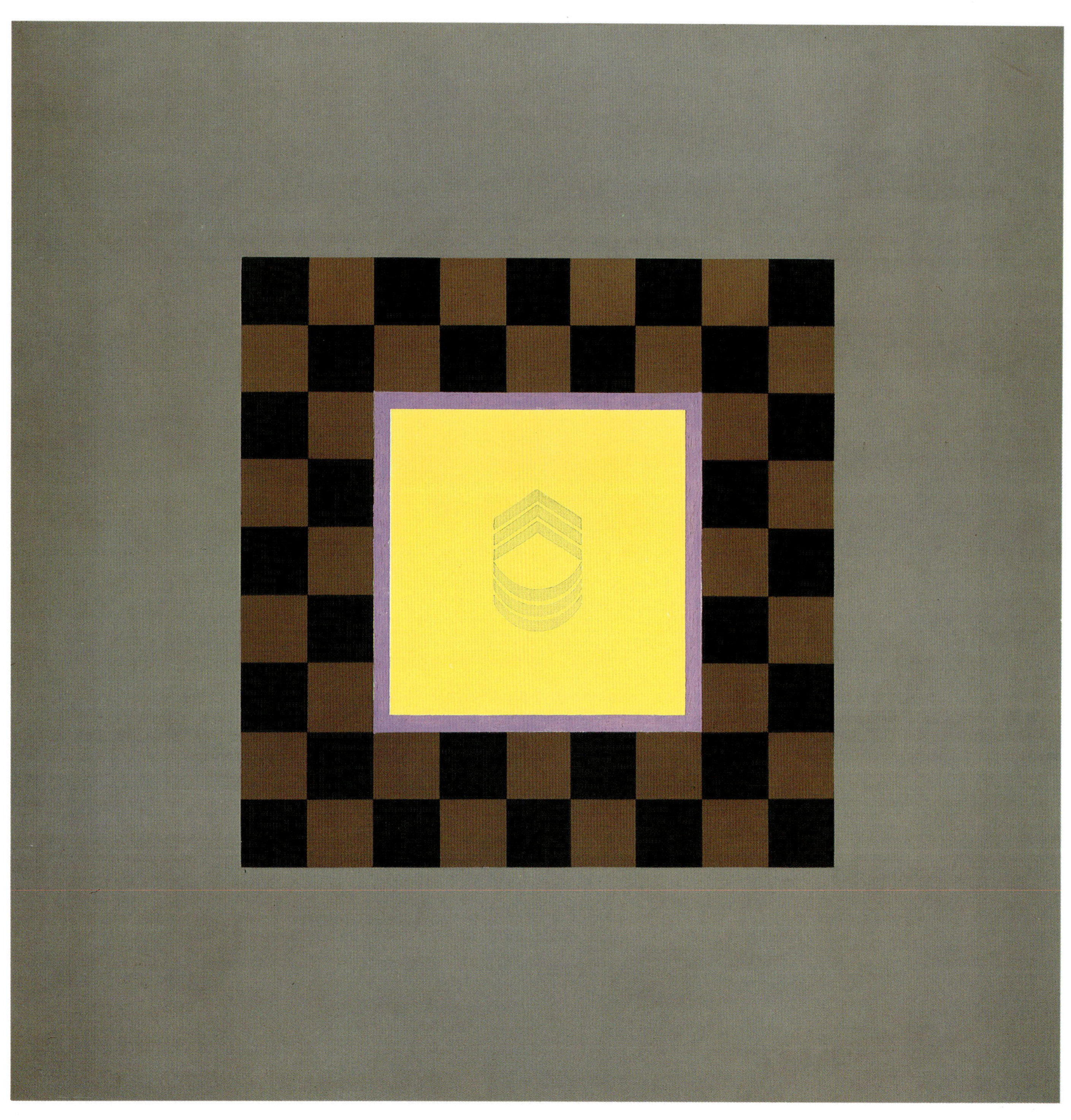

PLATE 4
STAINLESS BOB STEEL
1960

60

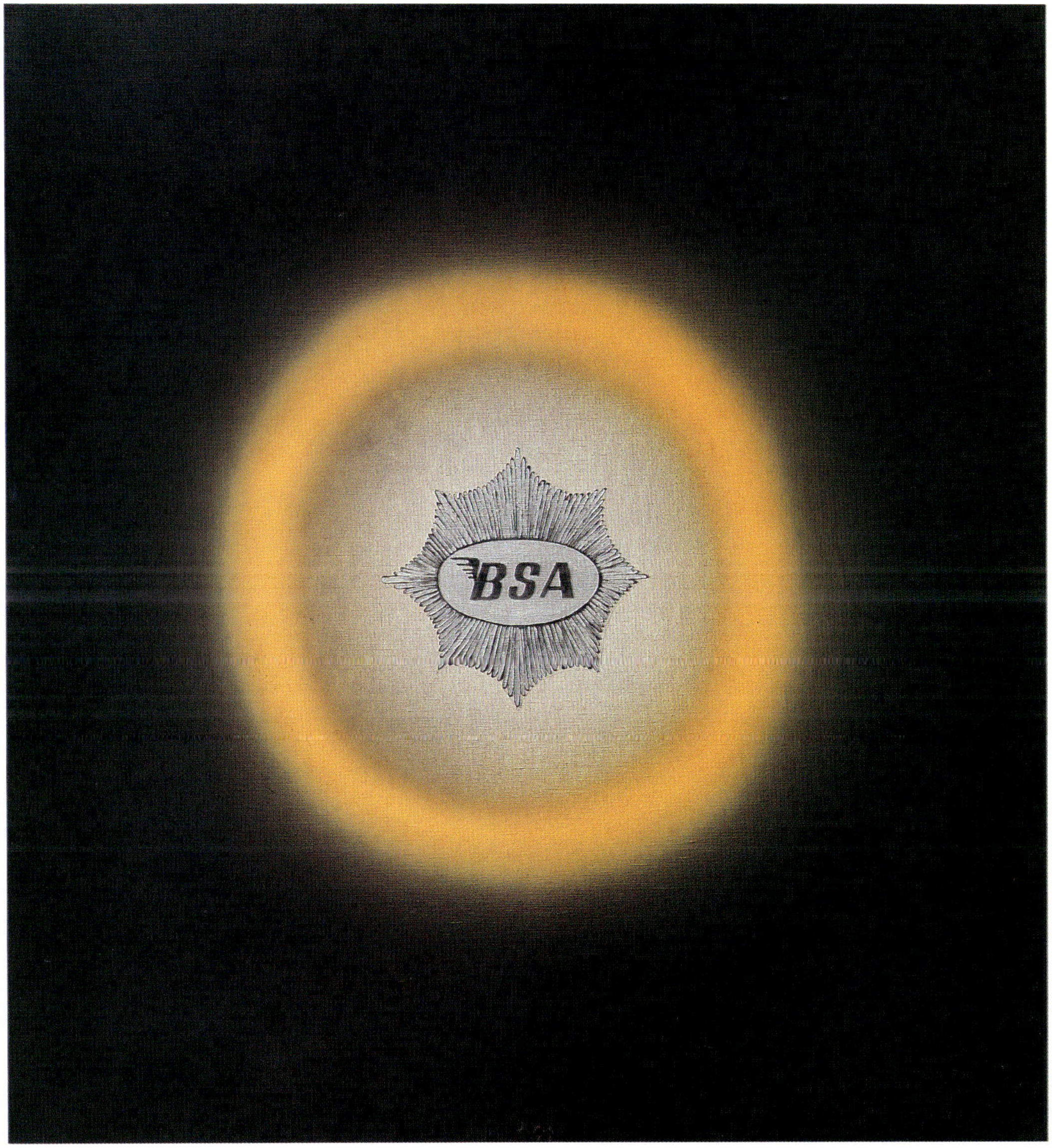

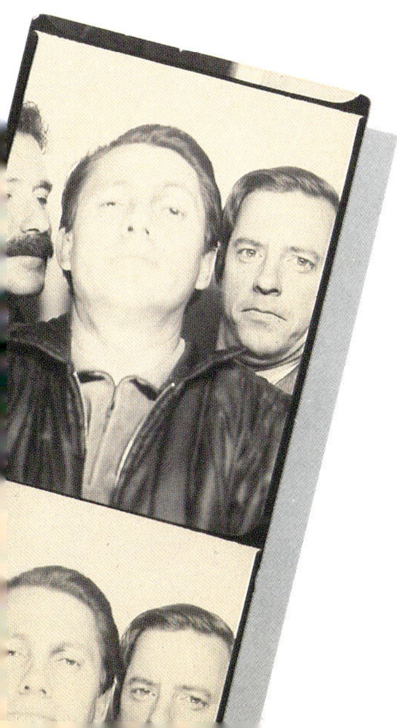

PLATE 5
BSA
1961

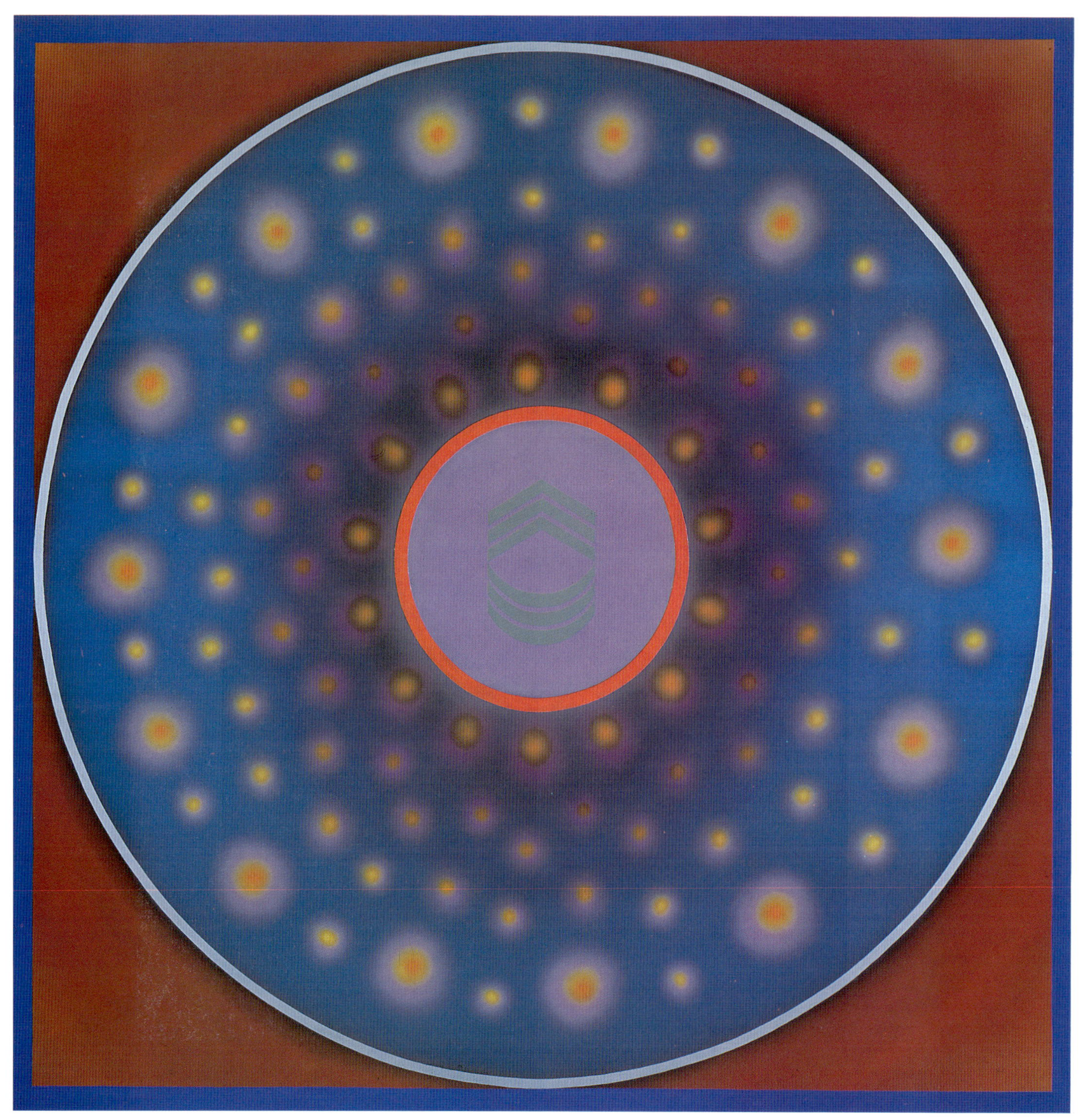

PLATE 6
BUSTER
1962

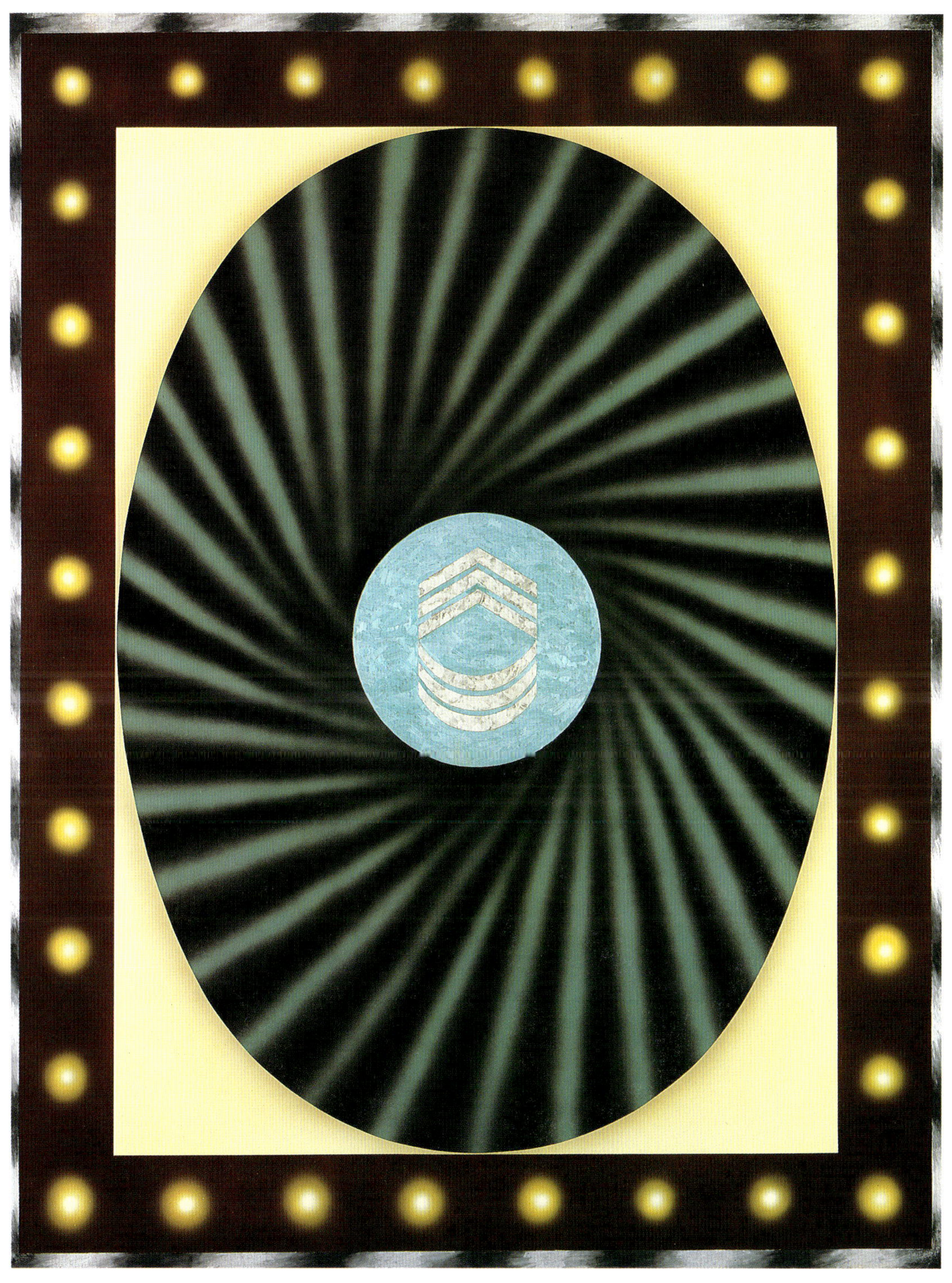

PLATE 7
BORIS
1963

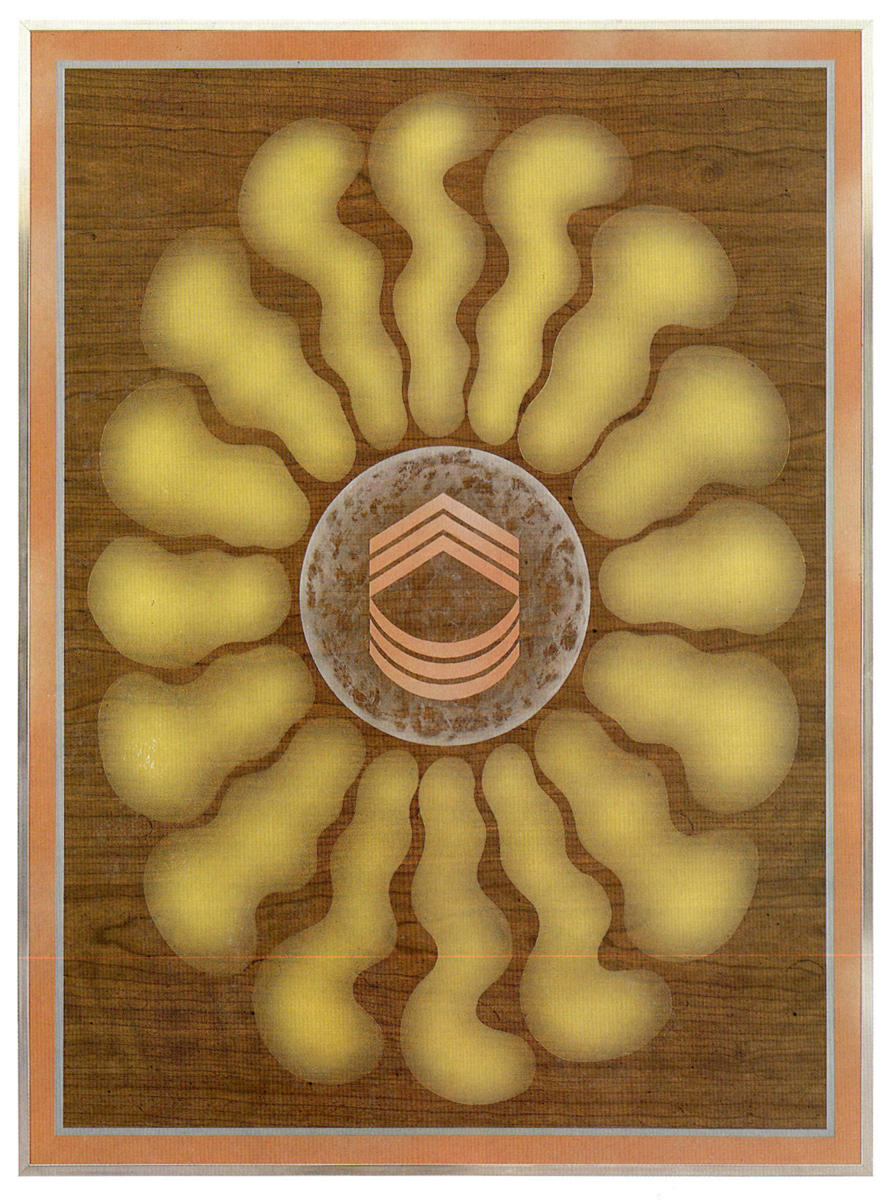

PLATE 8
TUBESTEAK
1965

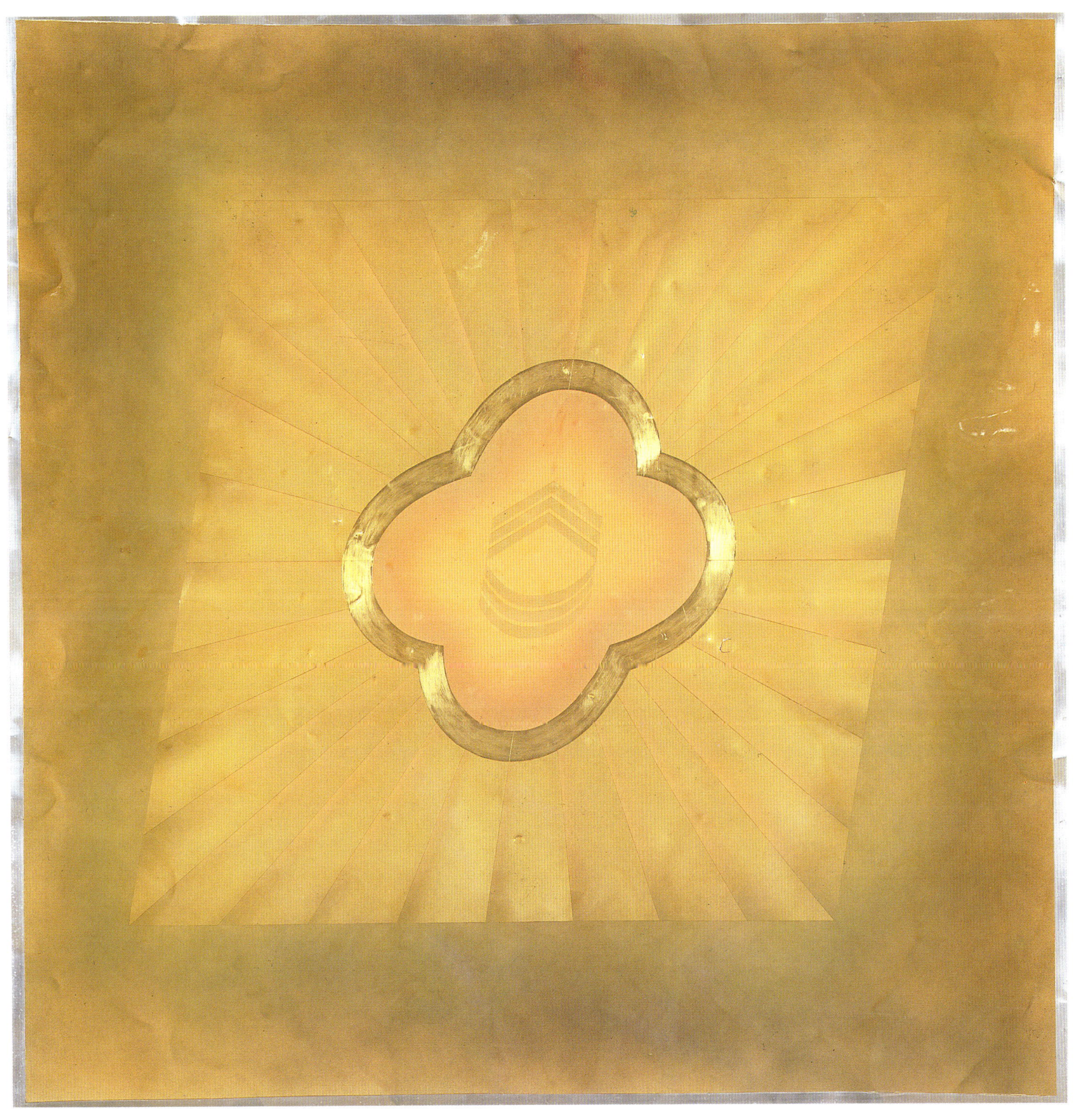

PLATE 9
HOLY SMOKE
1966

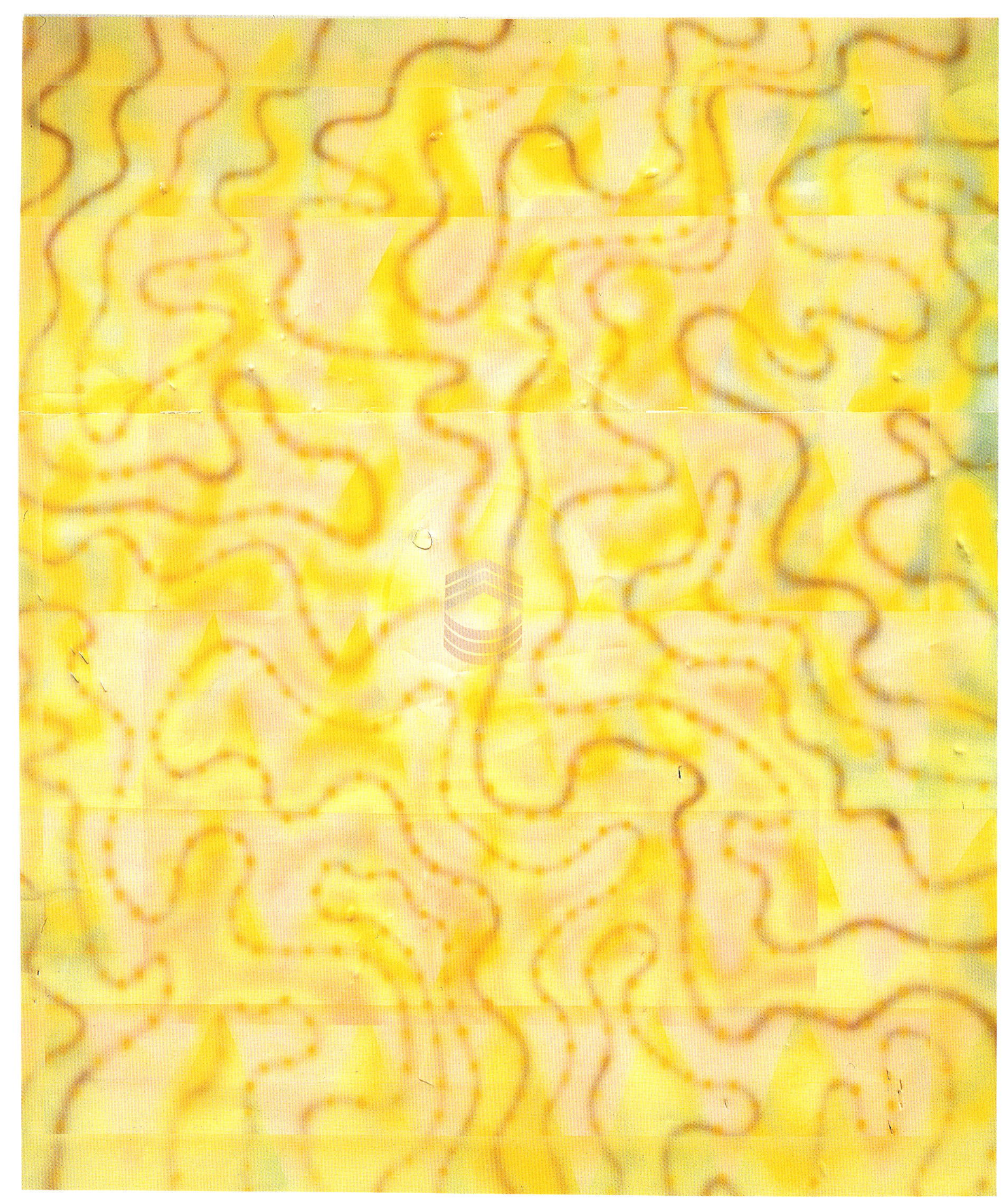

Joe Goode, Billy Al Bengston,
and Edward Ruscha
(left to right), 1968.

PLATE 10
HATARI
1968

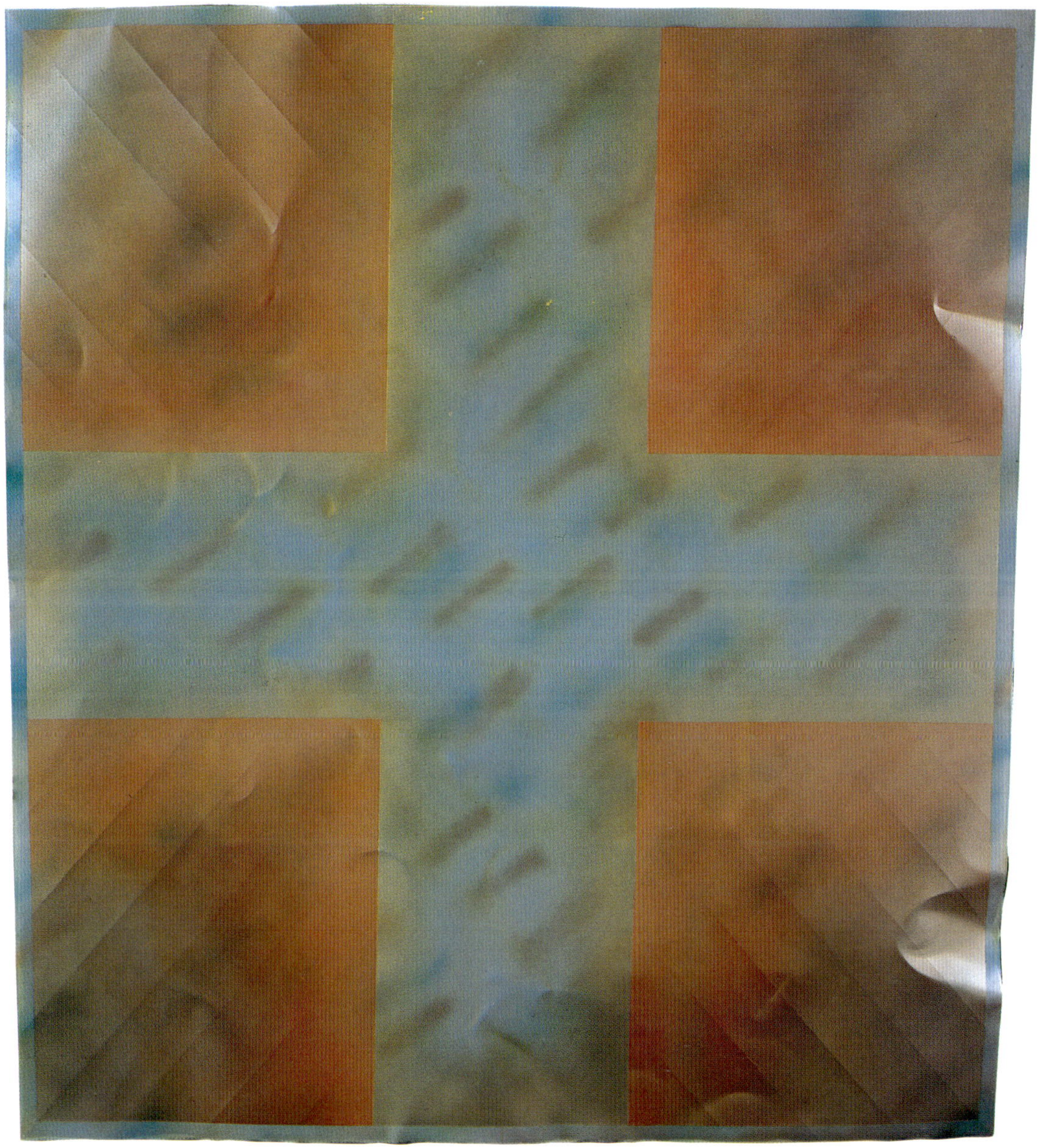

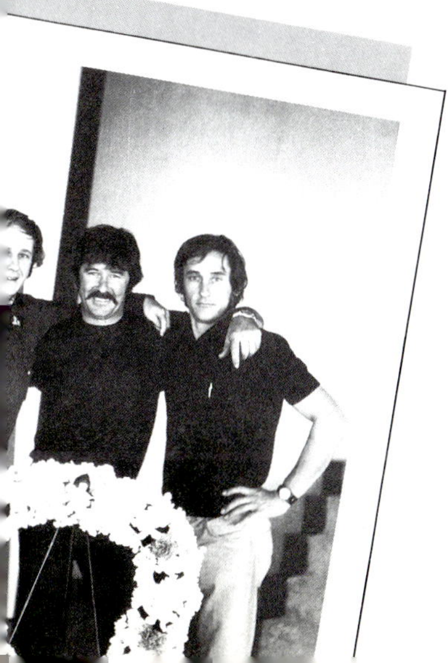

PLATE 11
PARADISE CANYON
1969

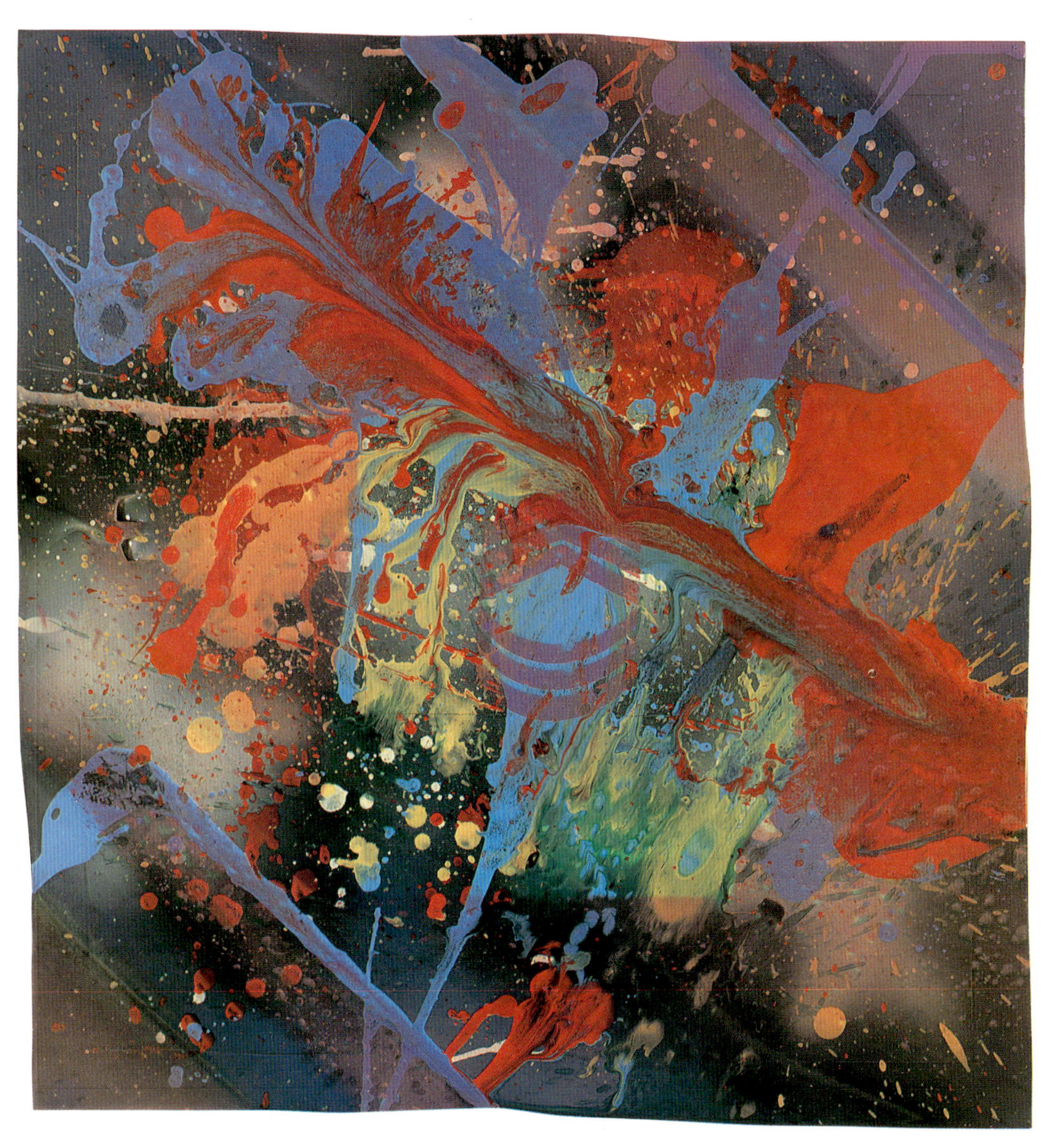

PLATE 12
BLOOD ALLEY
1970

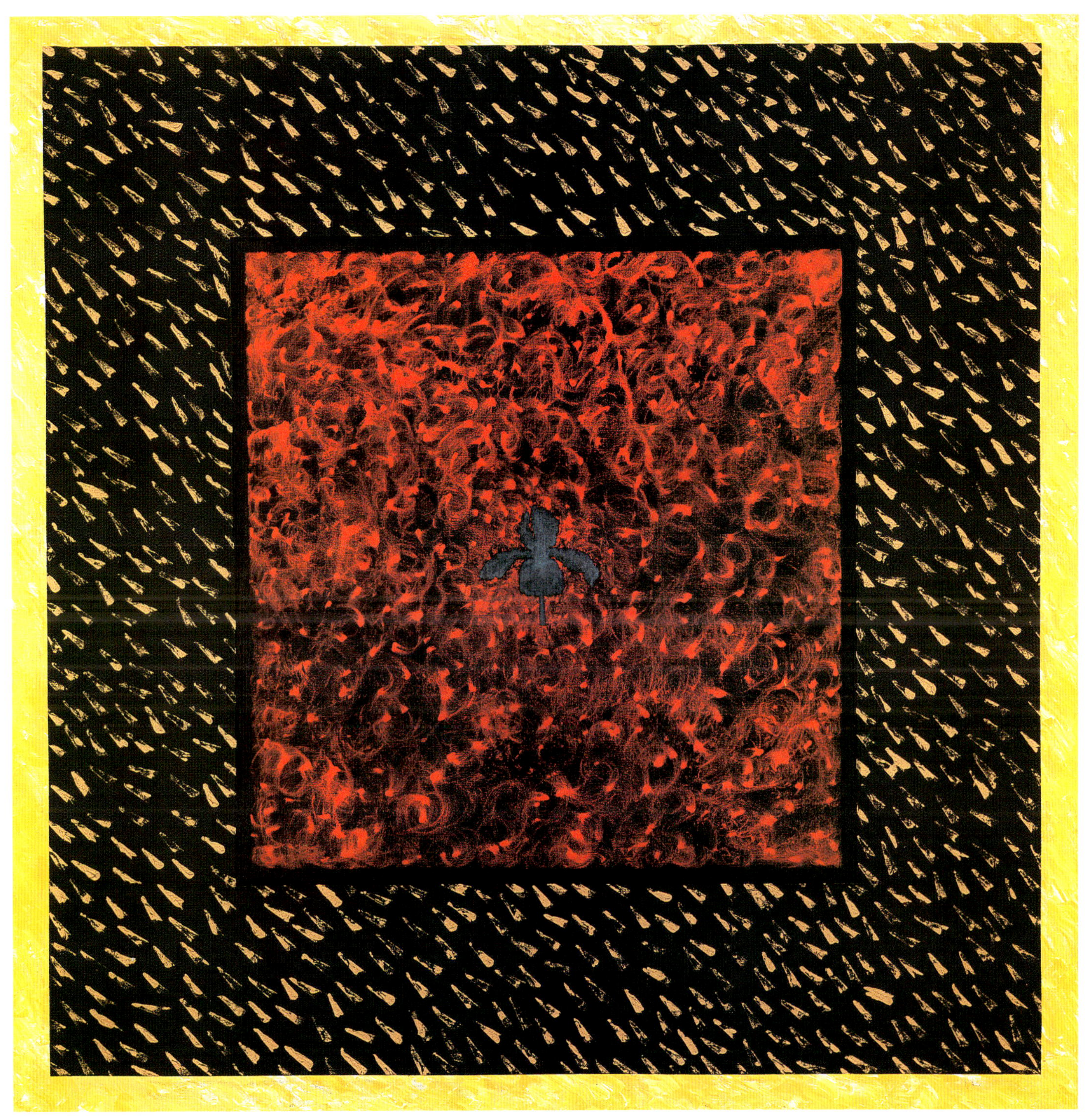

PLATE 13
EL CORTEZ DRACULA
1971

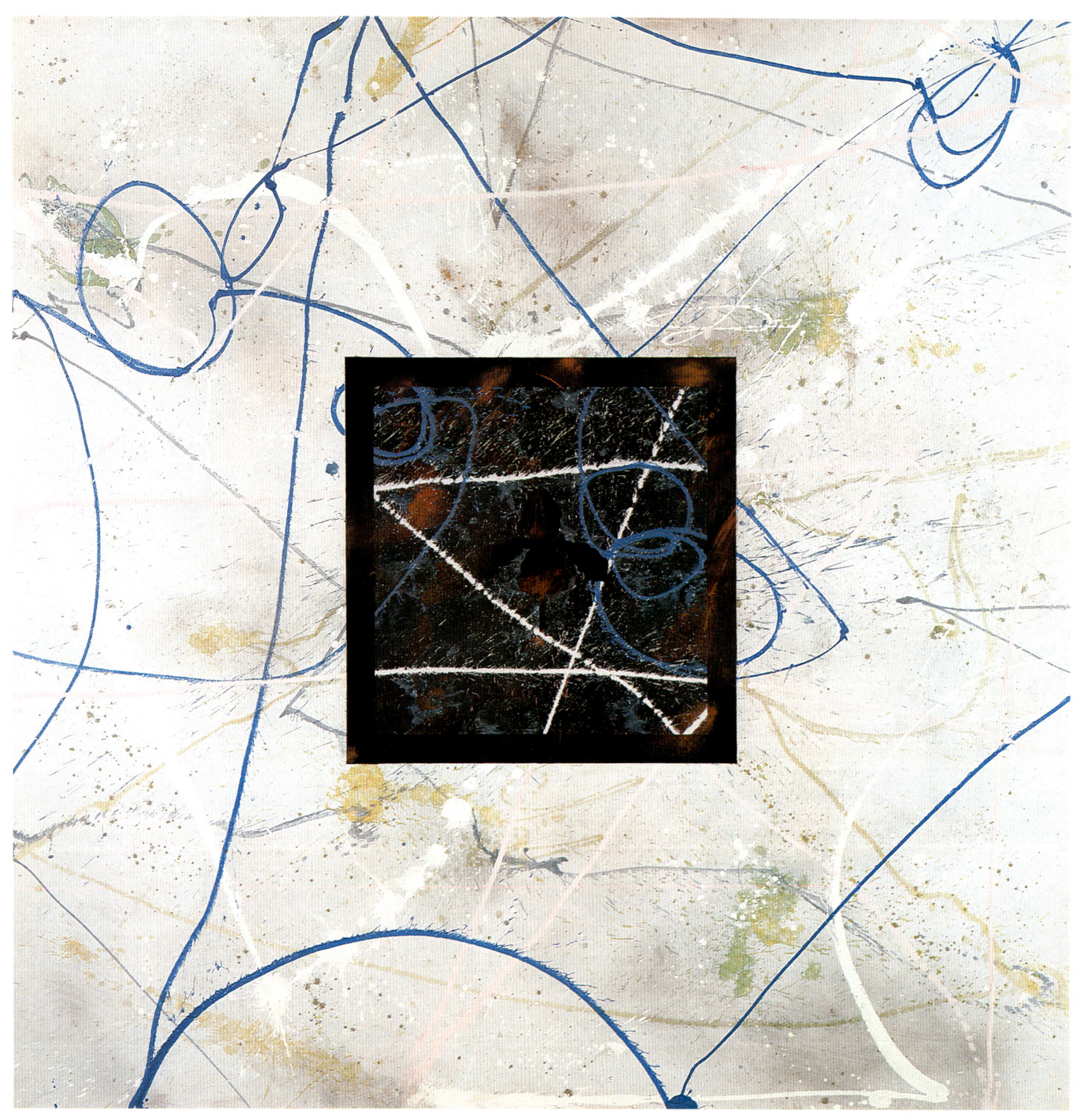

PLATE 14
BAHIA SAN LUIS GONZAGA DRACULA
1972

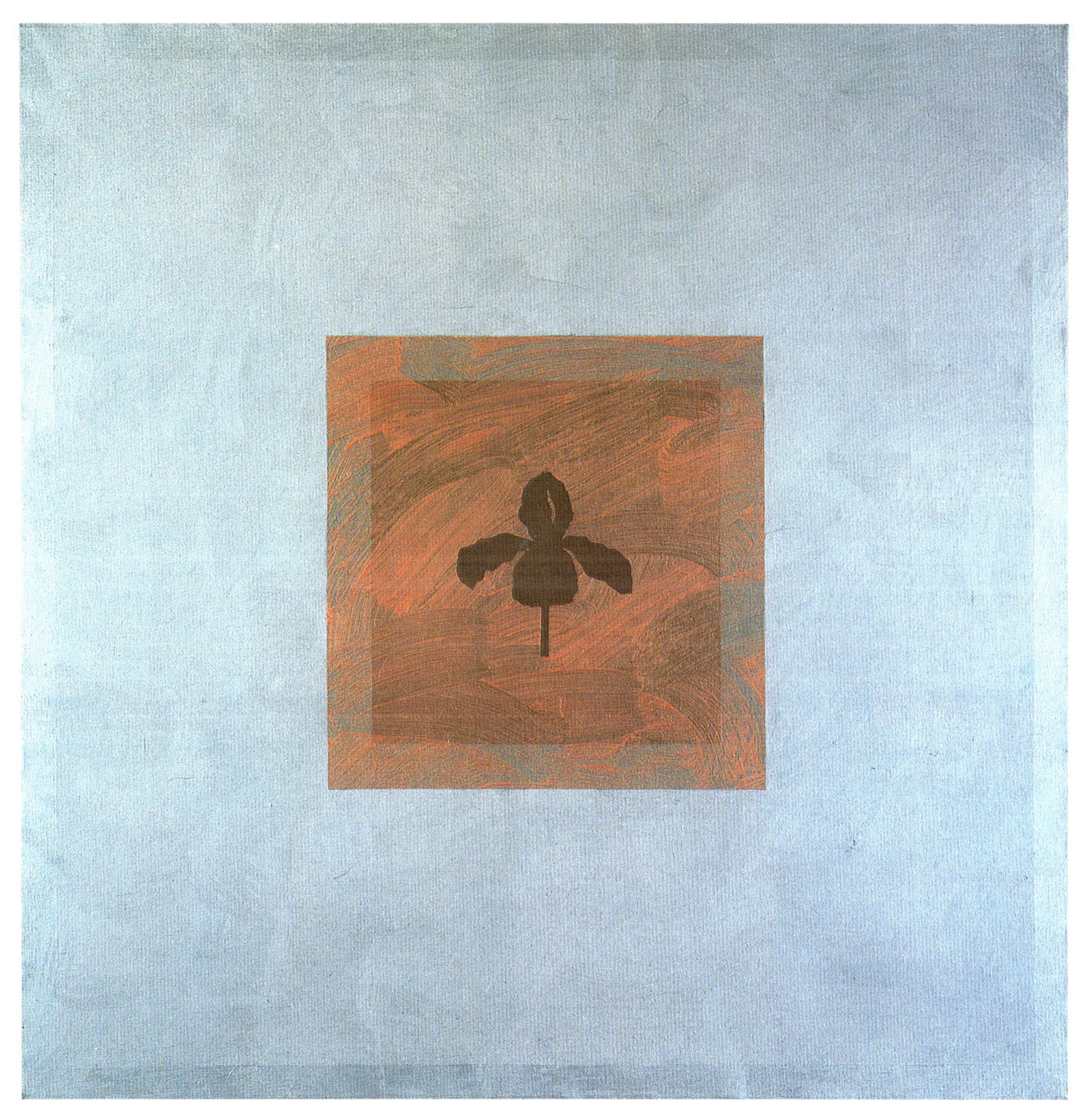

PLATE 15
JERMYN DRACULA
1972

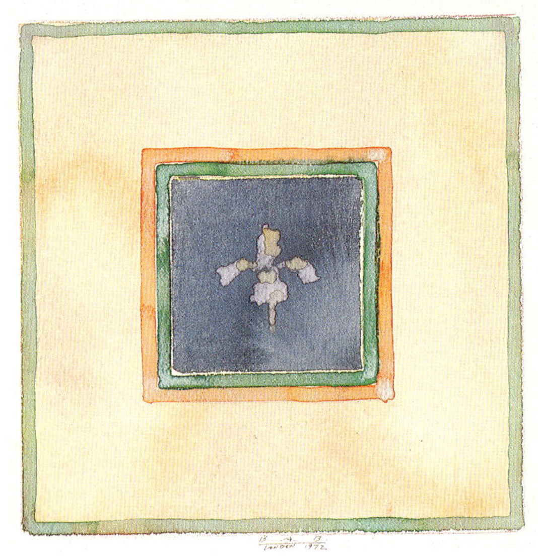

PLATE 16
UNTITLED (LONDON)
1972

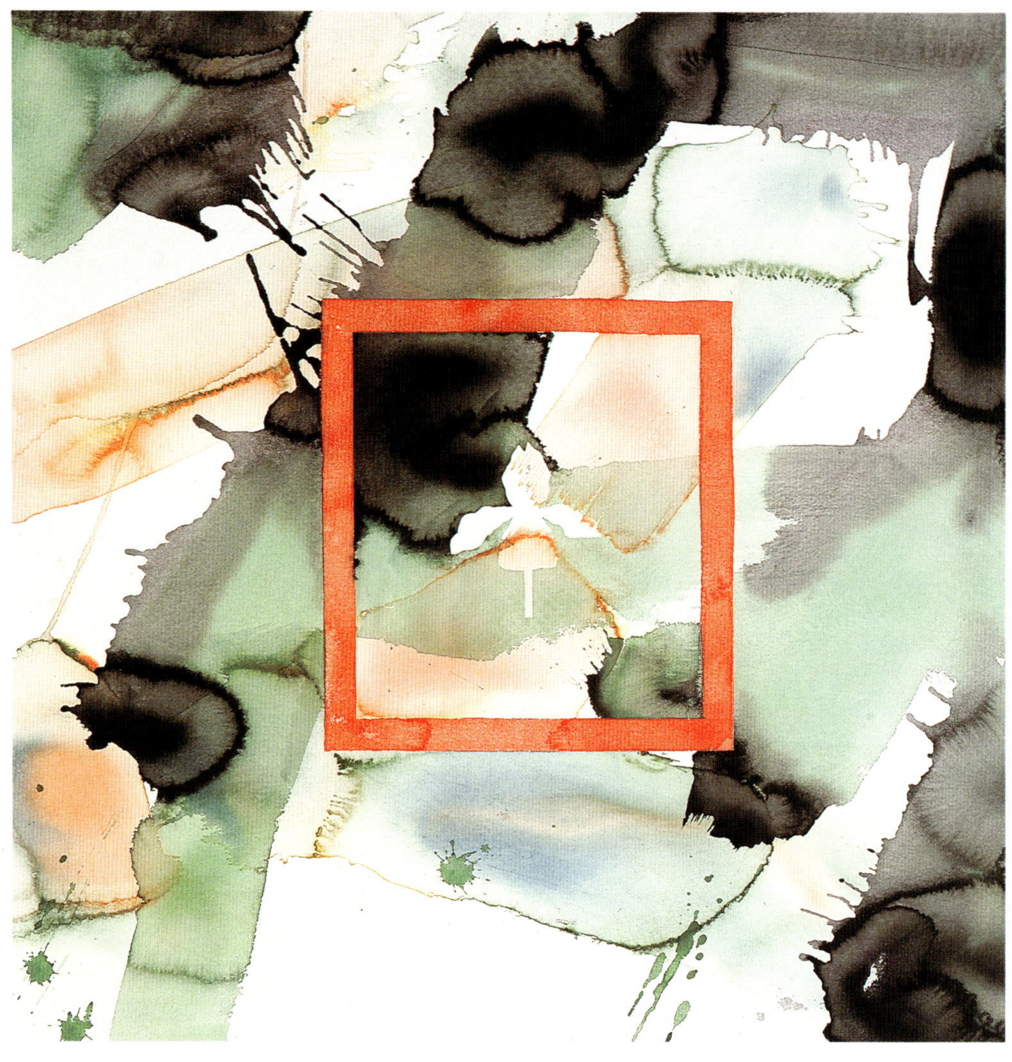

PLATE 17
UNTITLED (VENICE)
1972

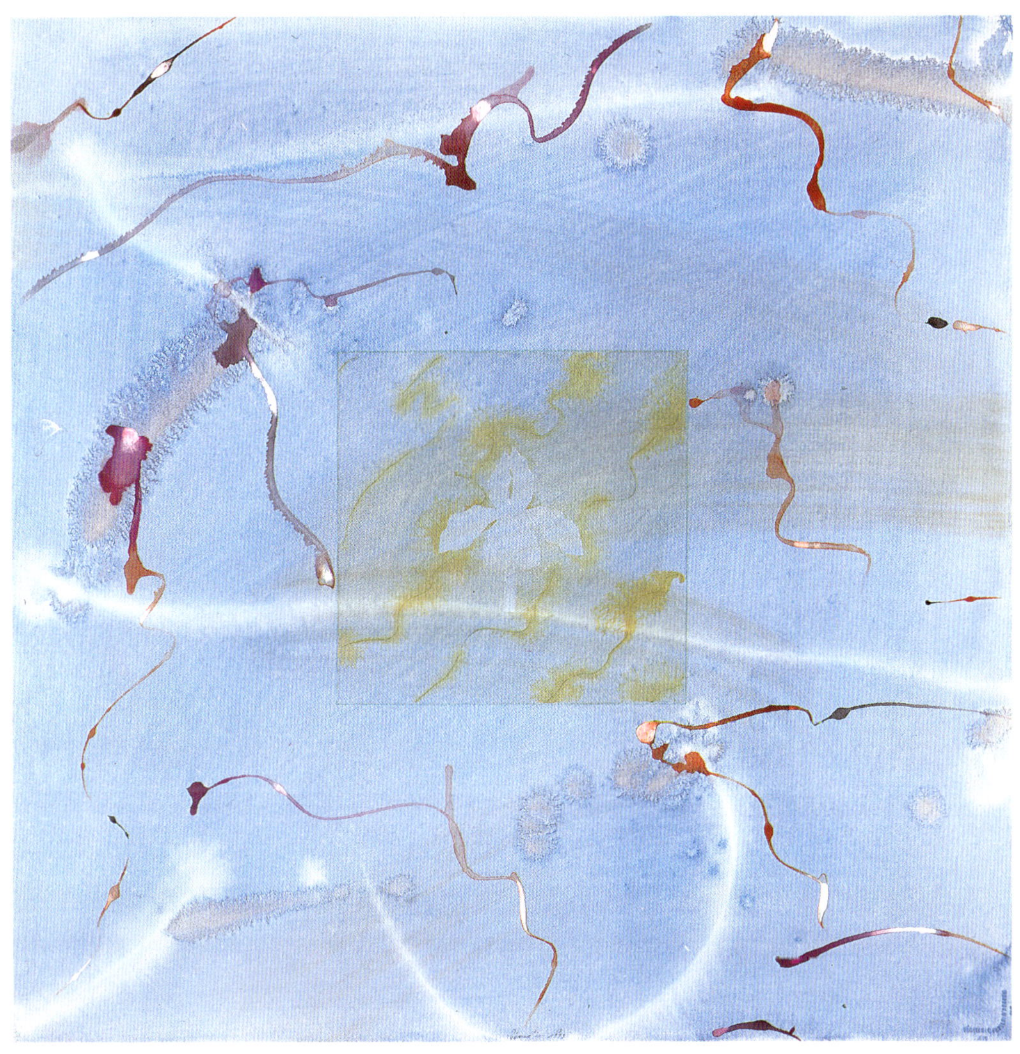

PLATE 18
UNTITLED (VENICE)
1973

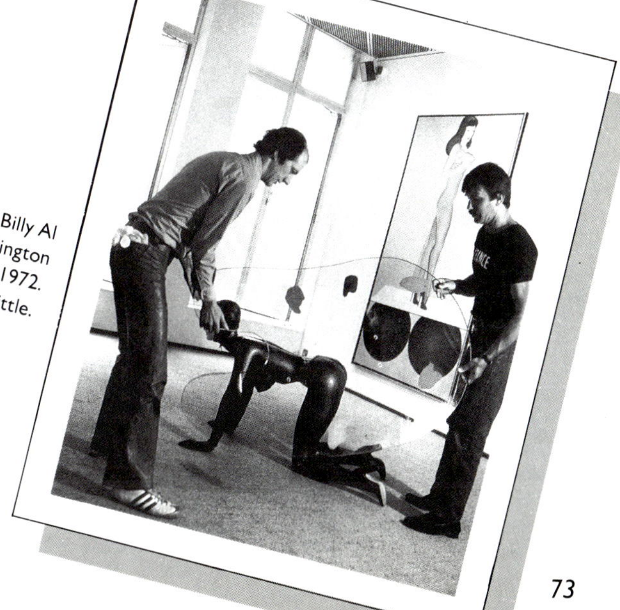

Allen Jones and Billy Al
Bengston, Waddington
Gallery, London, 1972.
Photo: Penny Little.

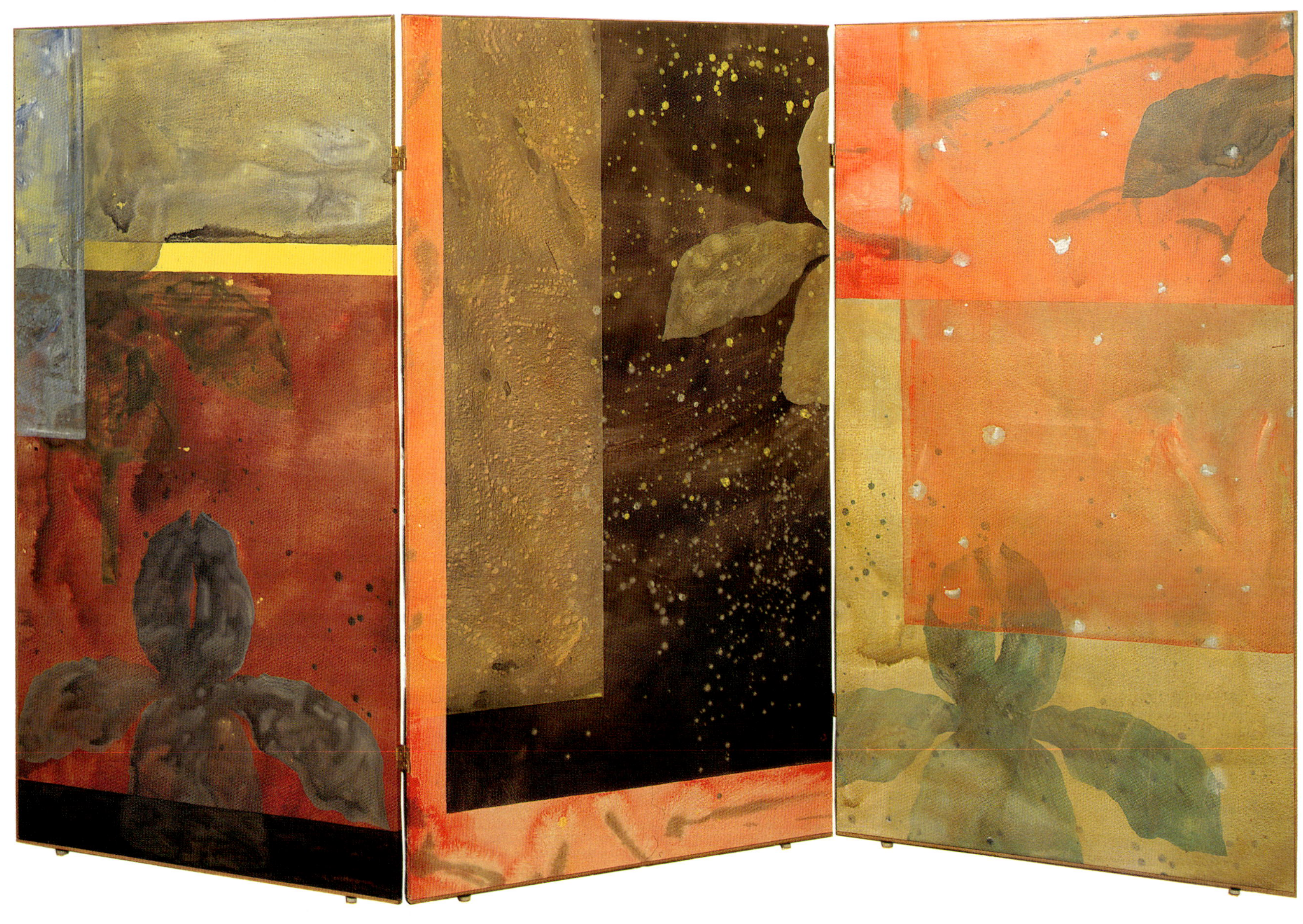

PLATE 19
EL LIMONA DRACULAS
1974

74

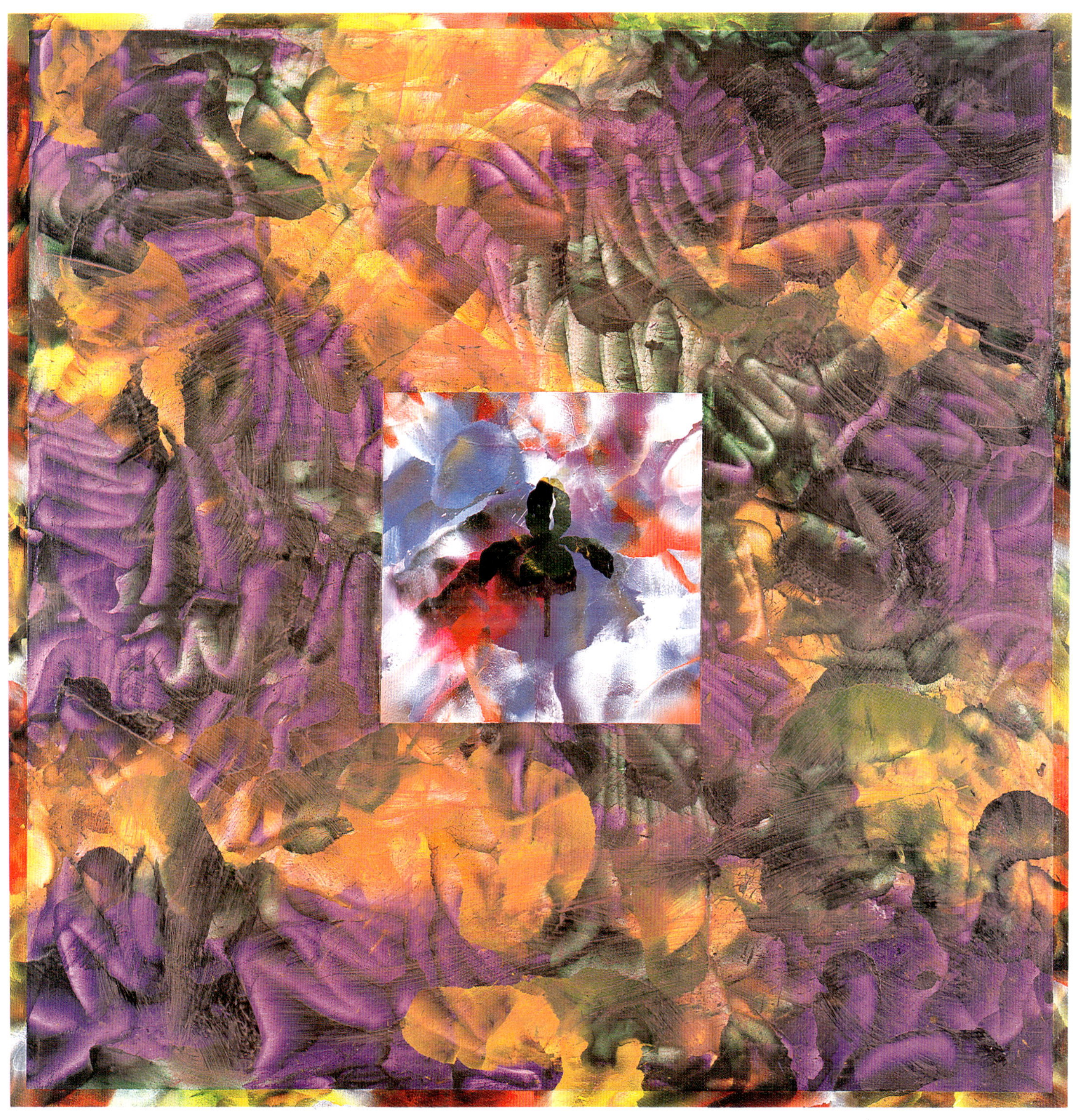

PLATE 20
HONOLULU DRACULA
1974

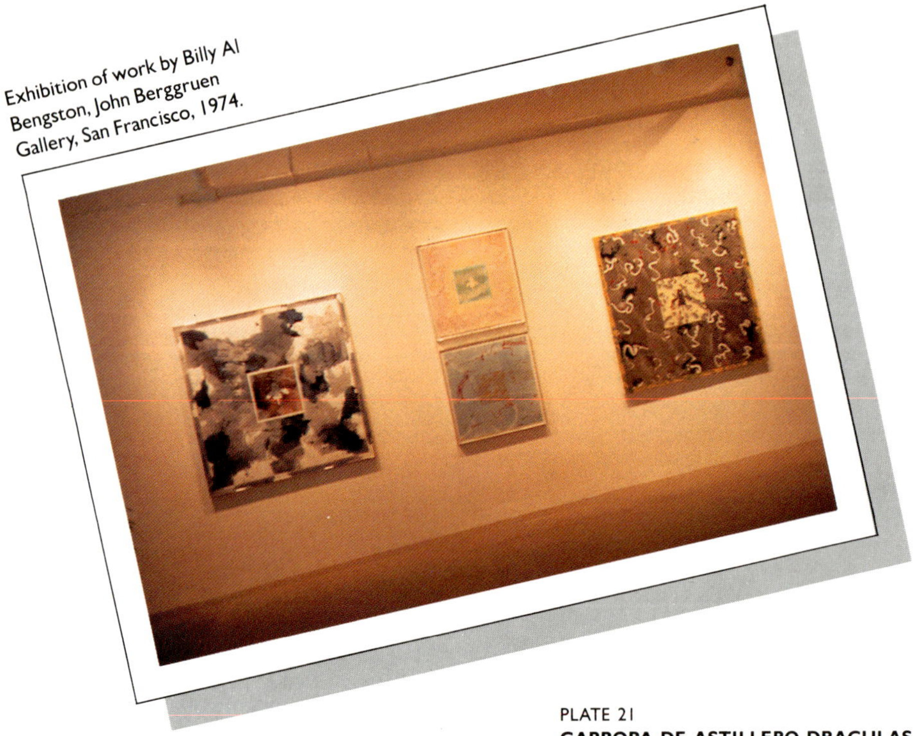

Exhibition of work by Billy Al
Bengston, John Berggruen
Gallery, San Francisco, 1974.

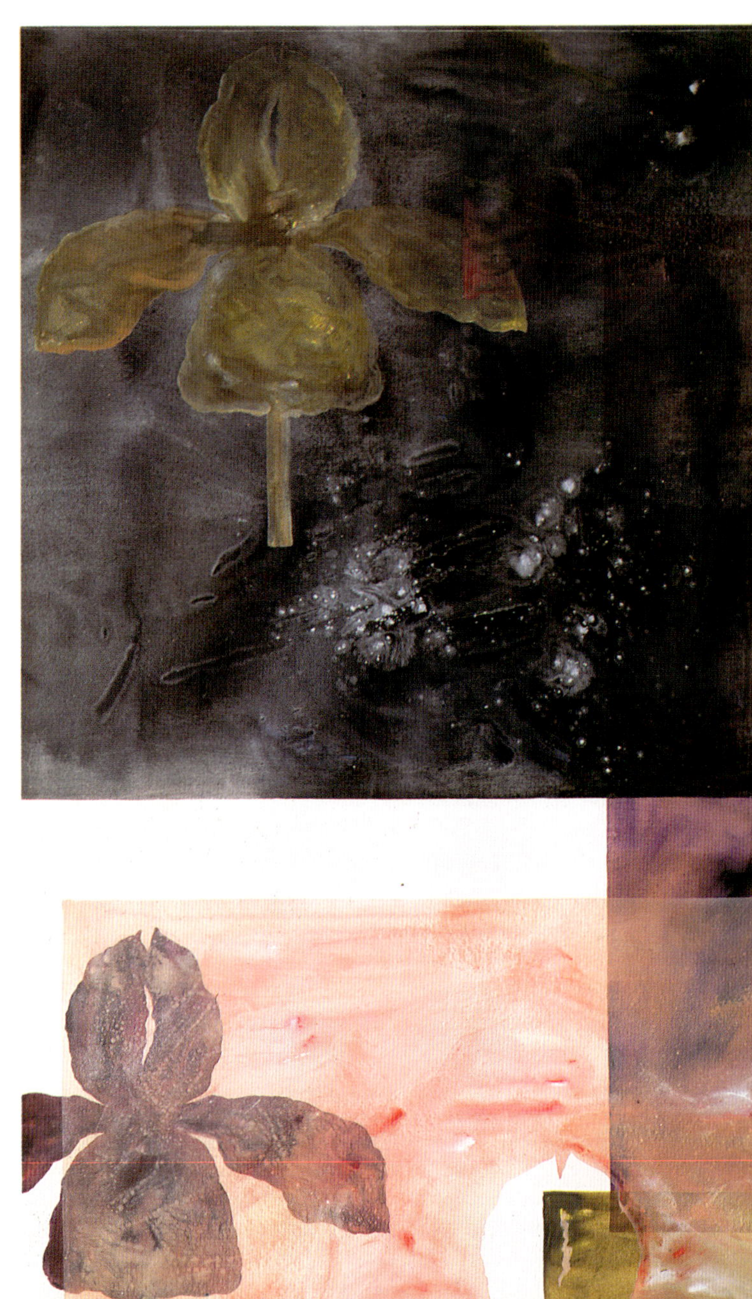

PLATE 21
GARROPA DE ASTILLERO DRACULAS
1974

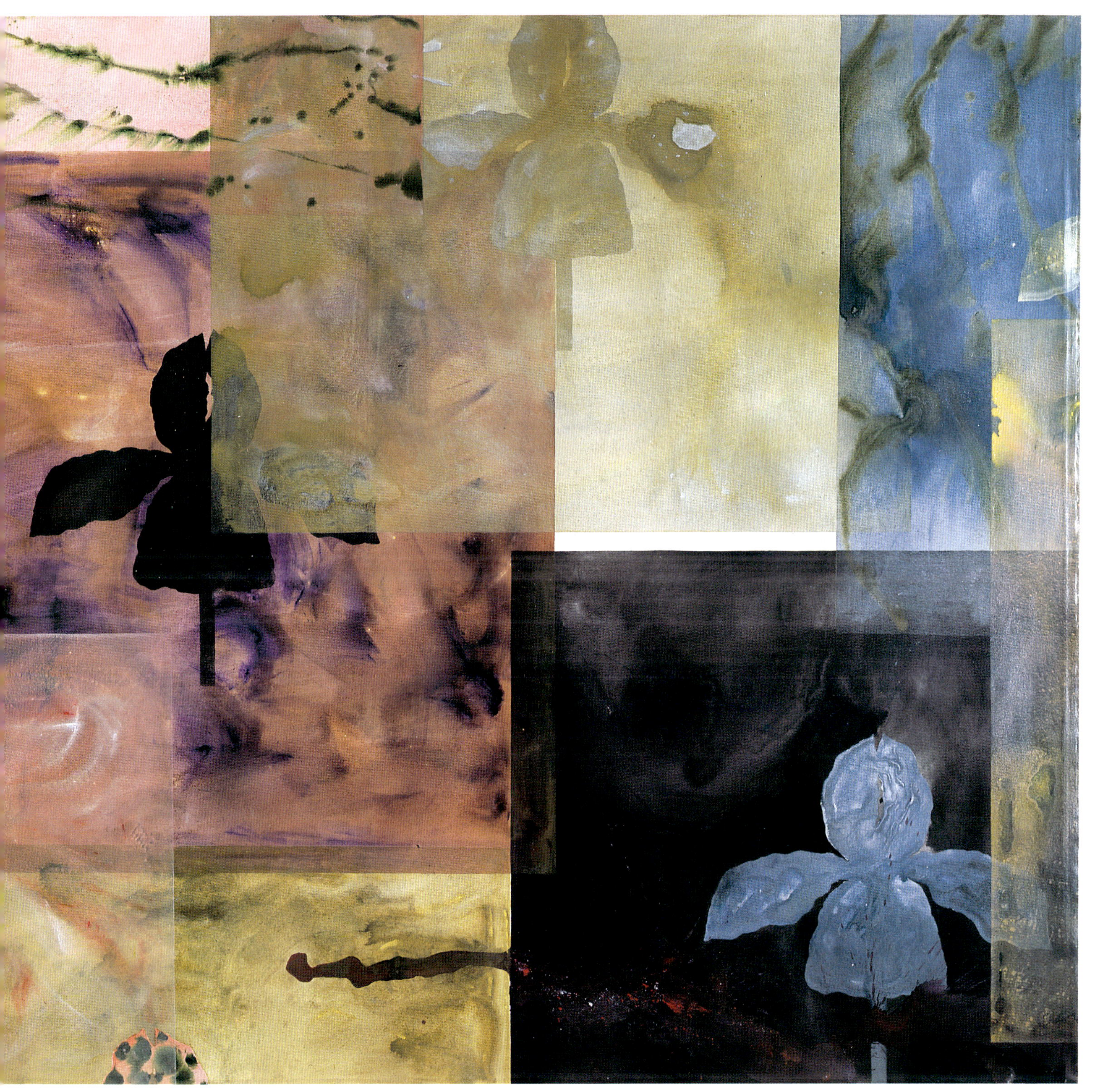

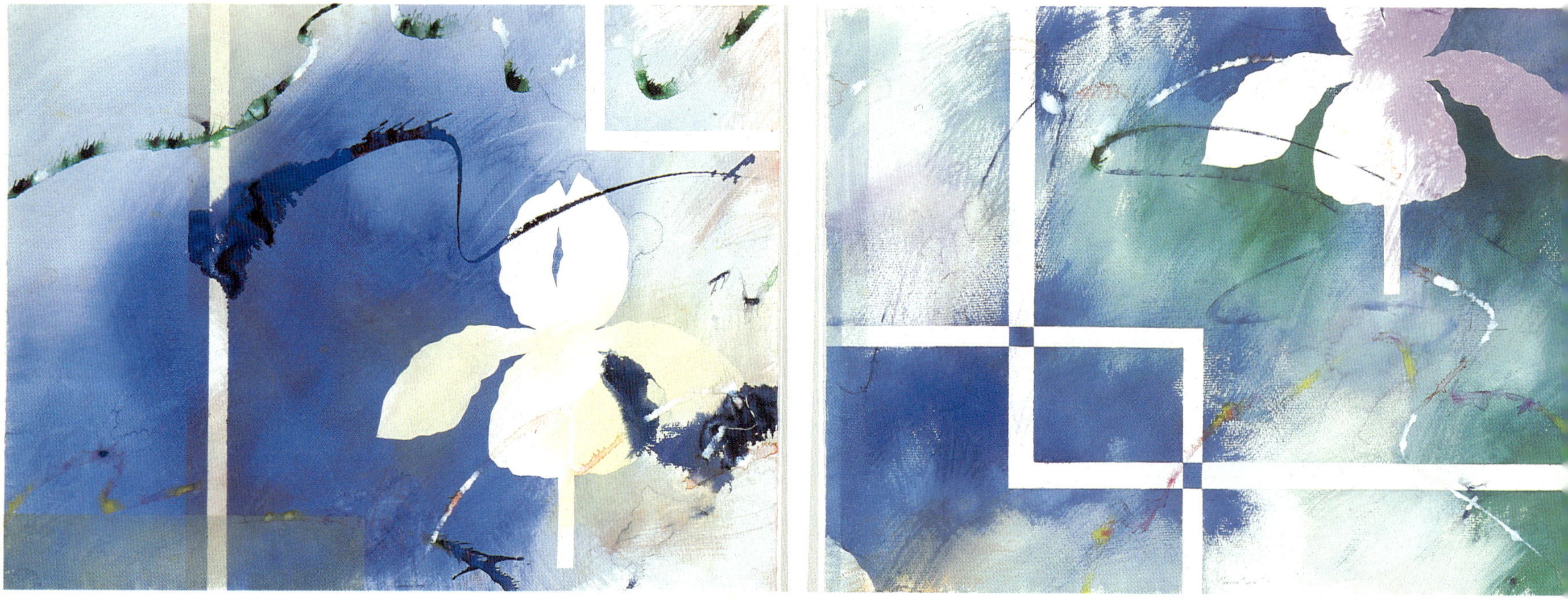

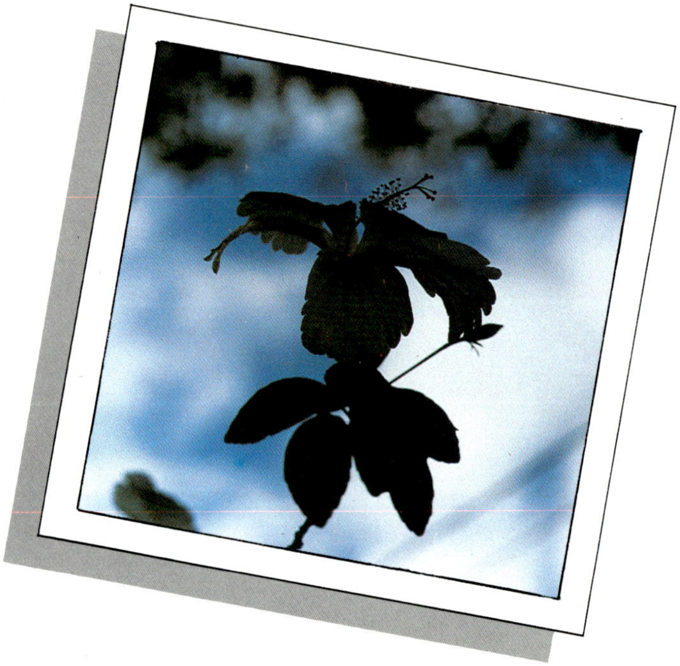

PLATE 22
UNTITLED (VENICE)
1974

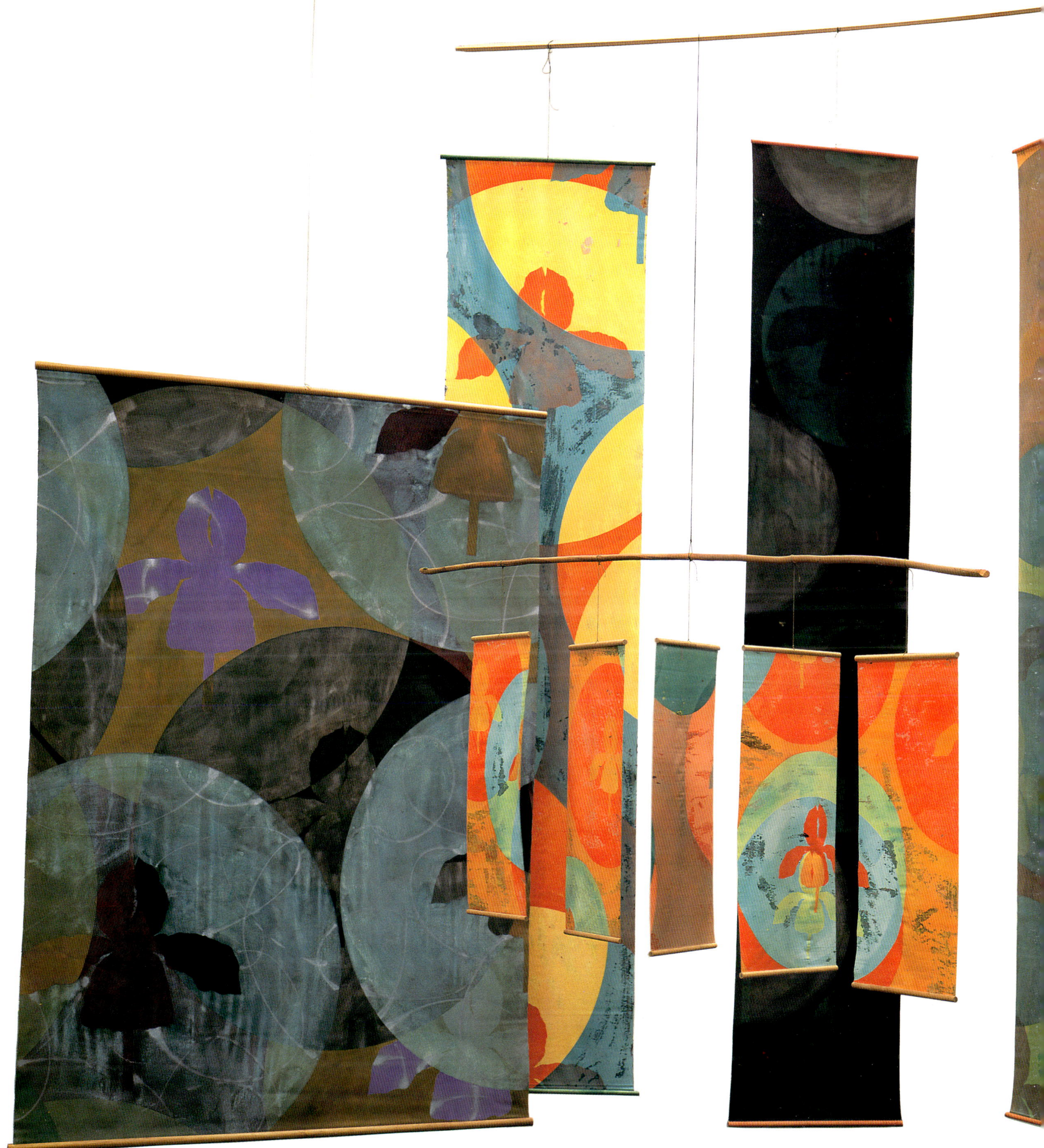

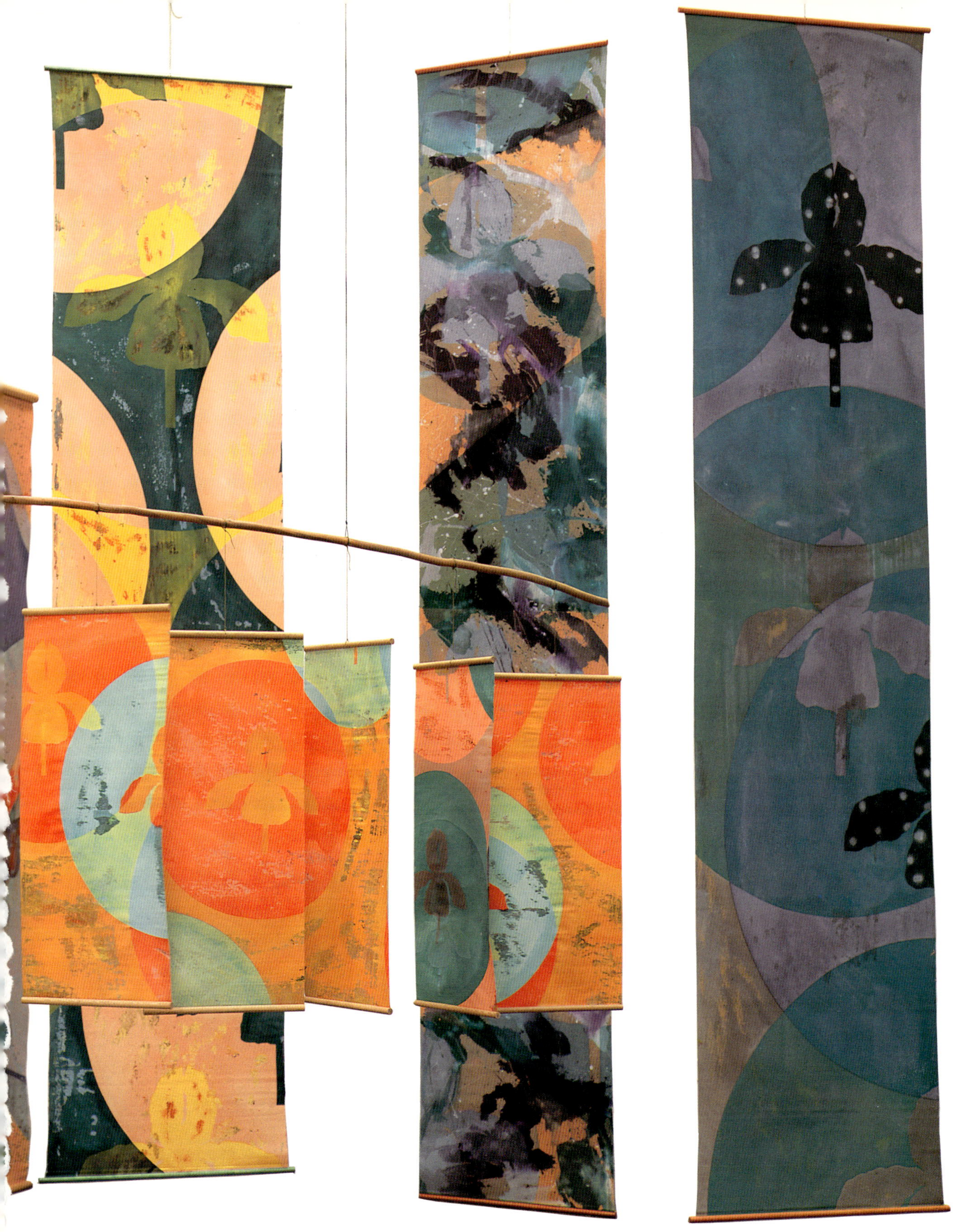

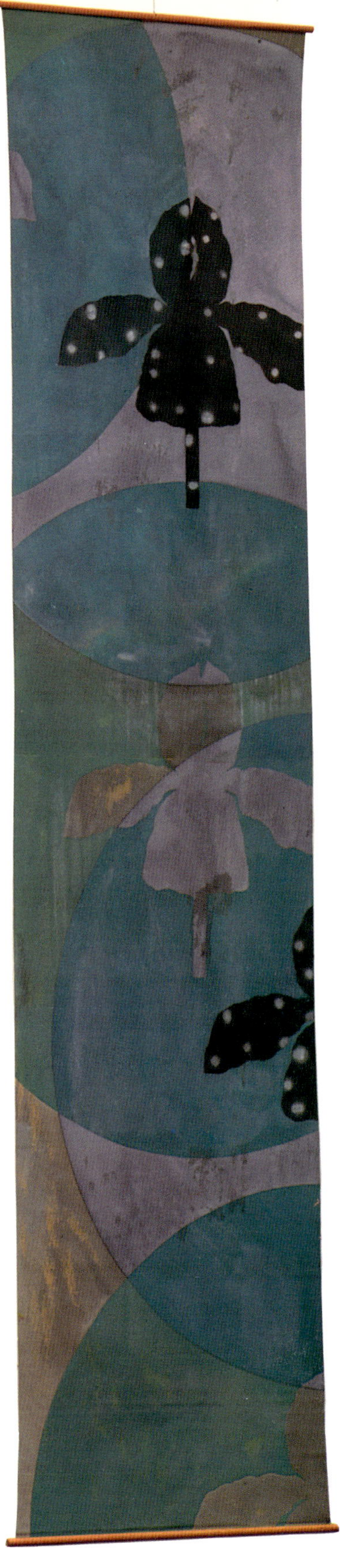

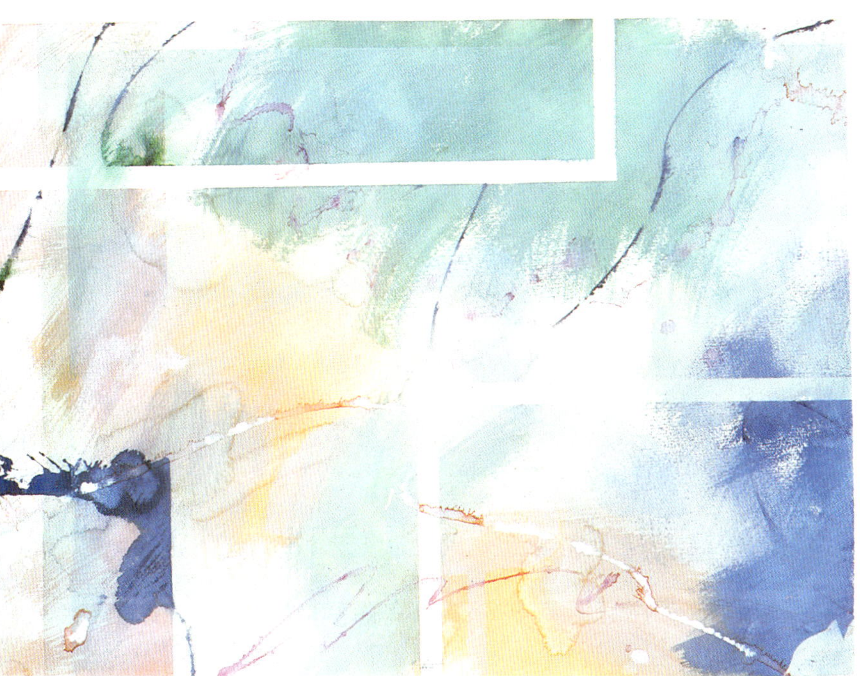

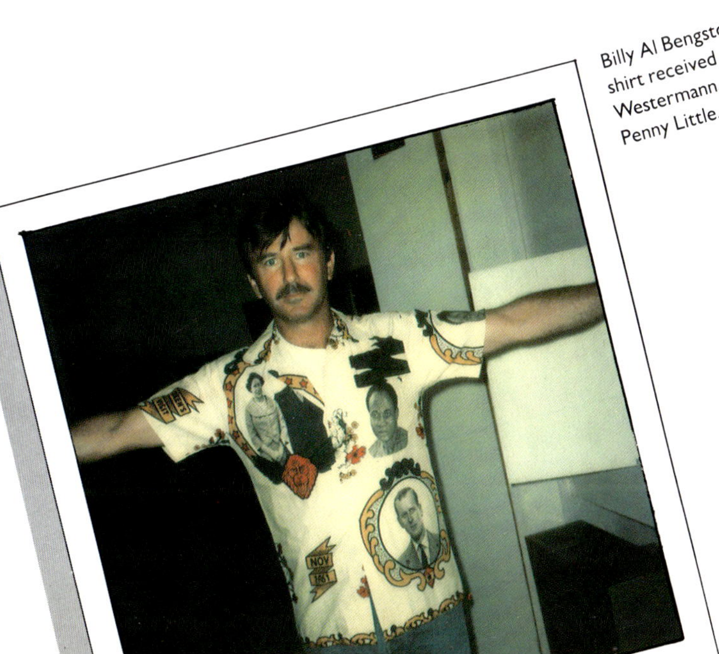

Billy Al Bengston modeling shirt received from H. C. Westermann, ca. 1970. Photo: Penny Little.

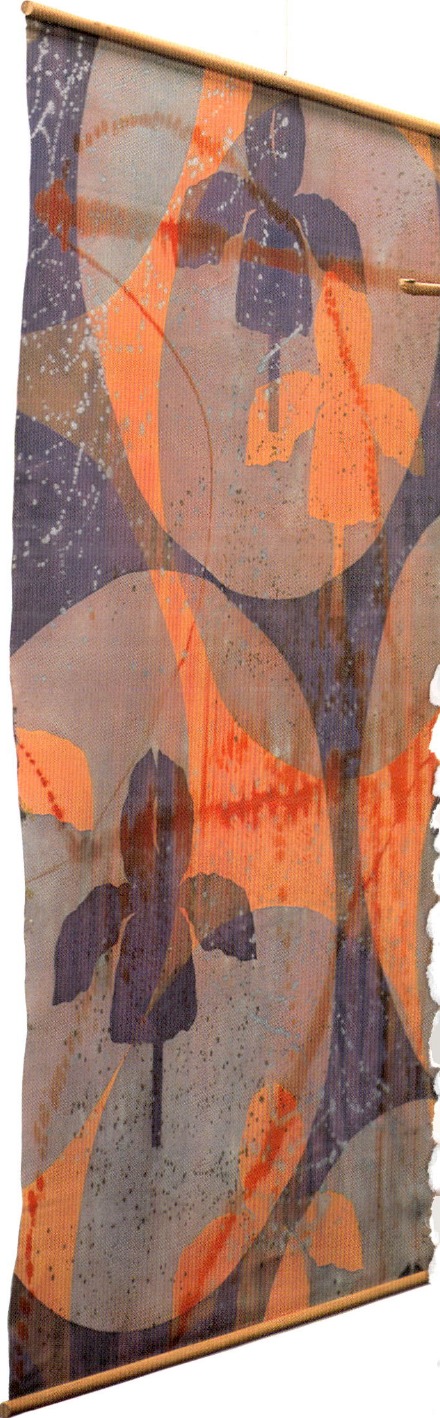

PLATE 23
Front:
BOSSEA DRACULAS
Left to right:
HYMENENA FLABELLIGRA DRACULAS
DELESSERIA DECIPIENS DRACULAS
IRIDOPHYCUS DRACULAS
ALARIA VALIDA DRACULAS
1975

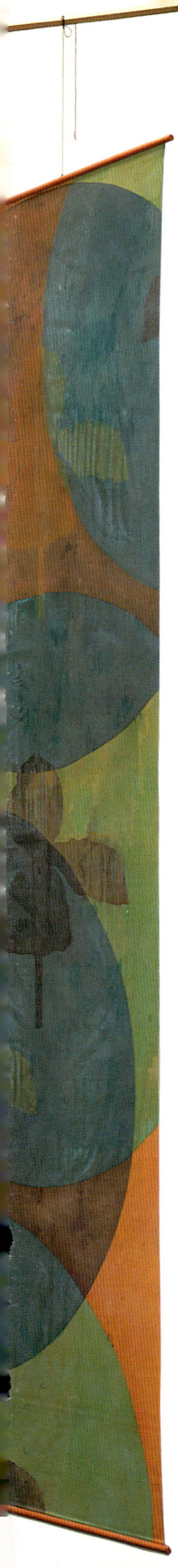

PLATE 24
Back view of Plate 23
1975

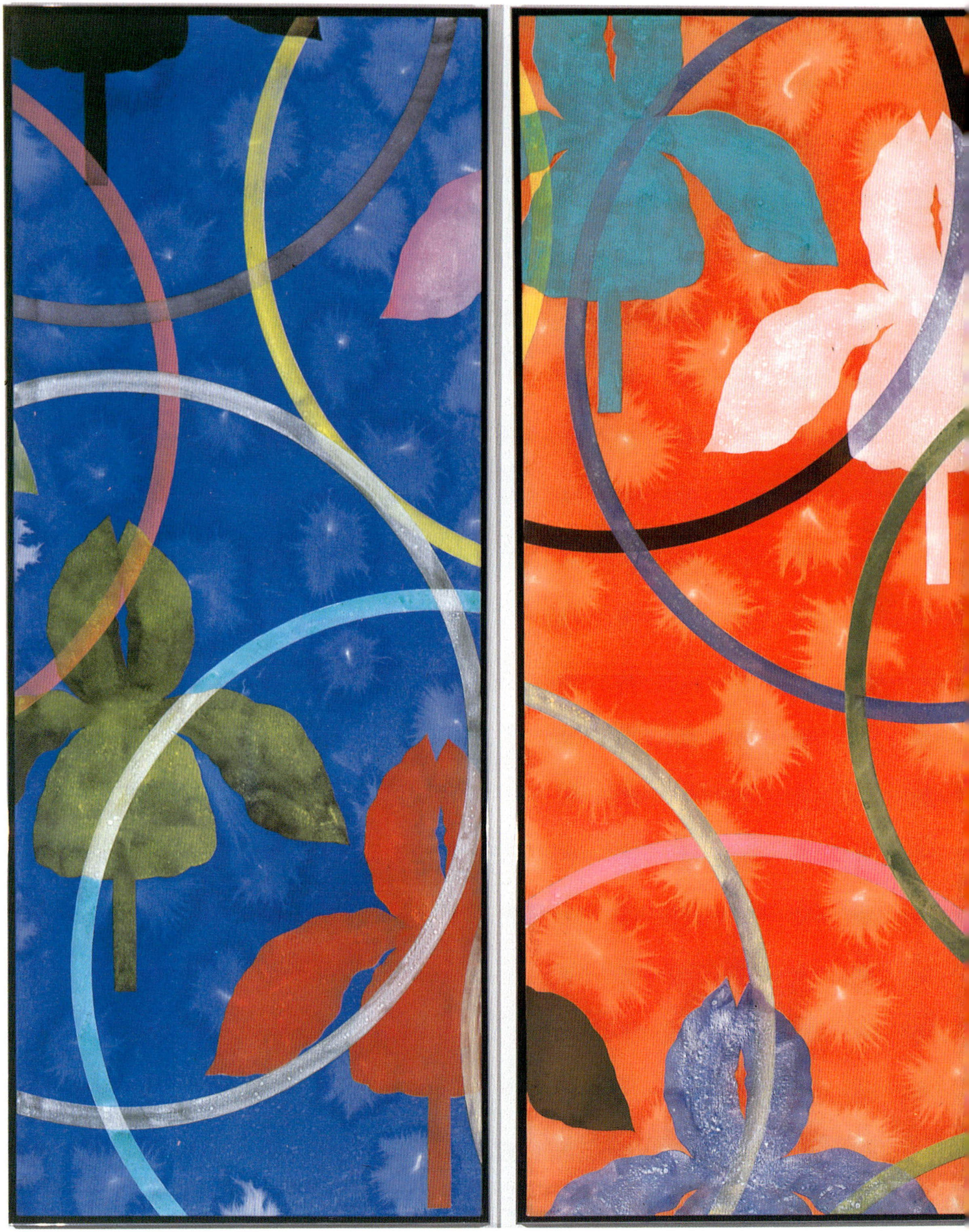

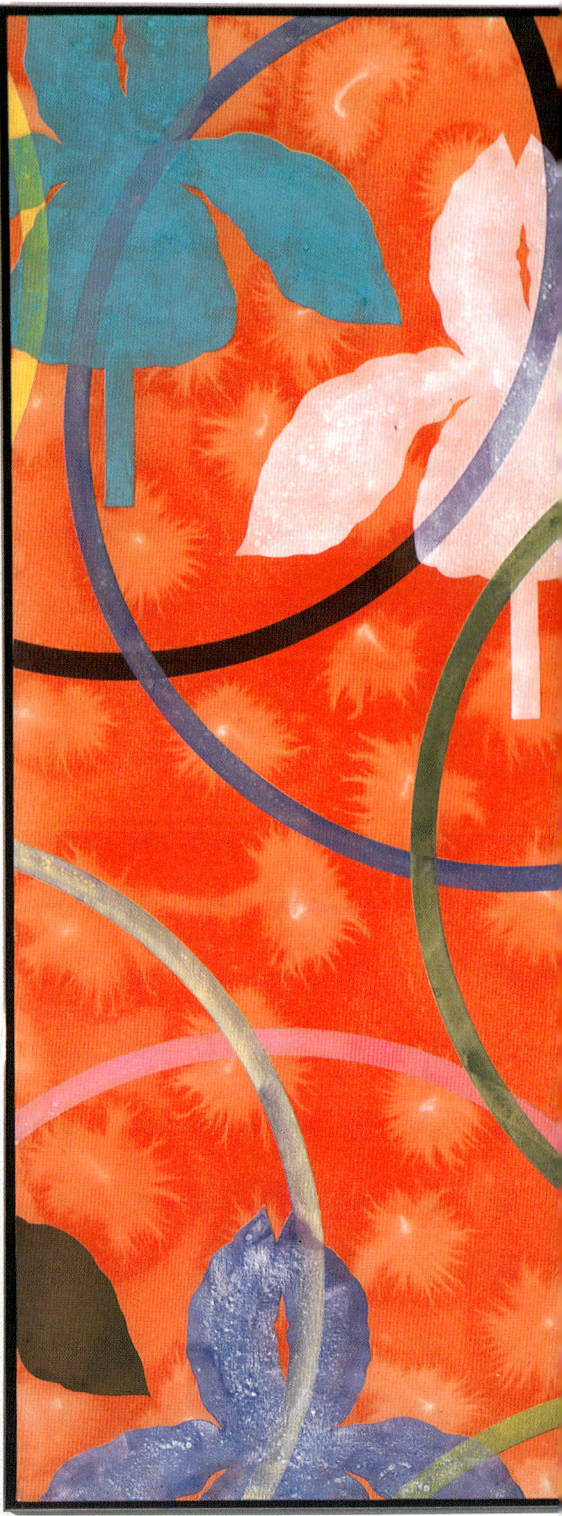

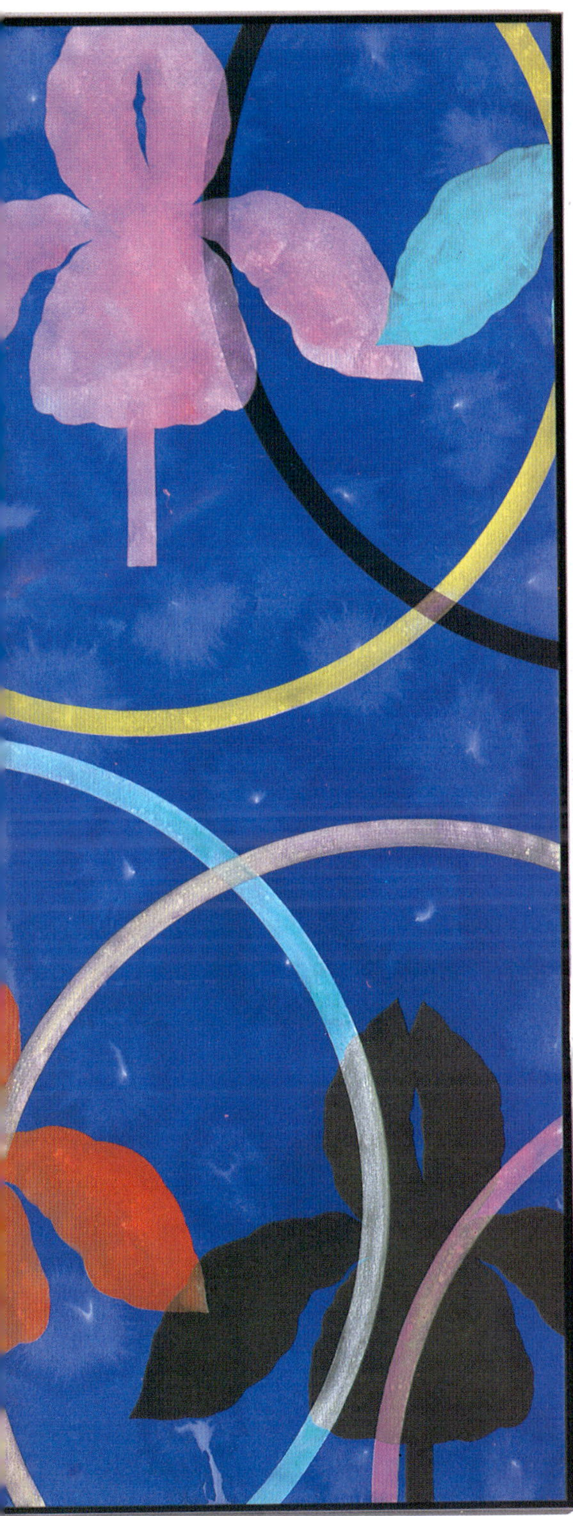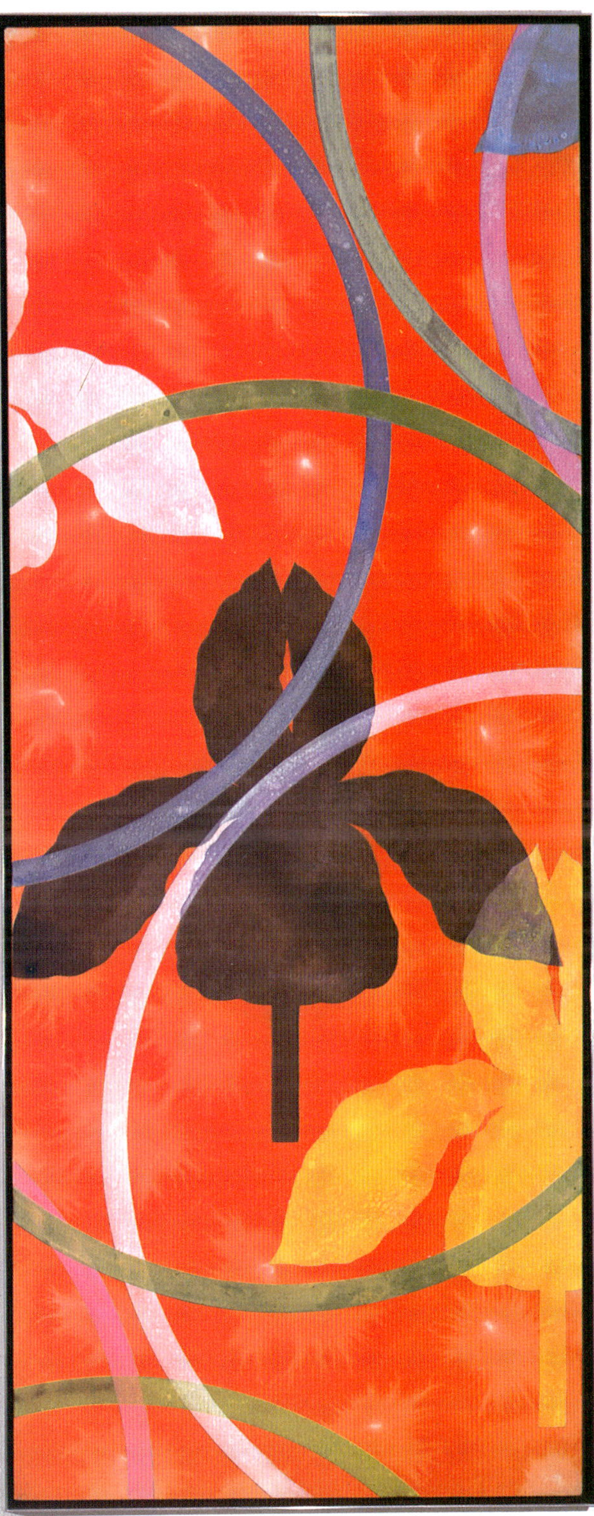

PLATE 25
CHINA POINT DRACULAS
1976

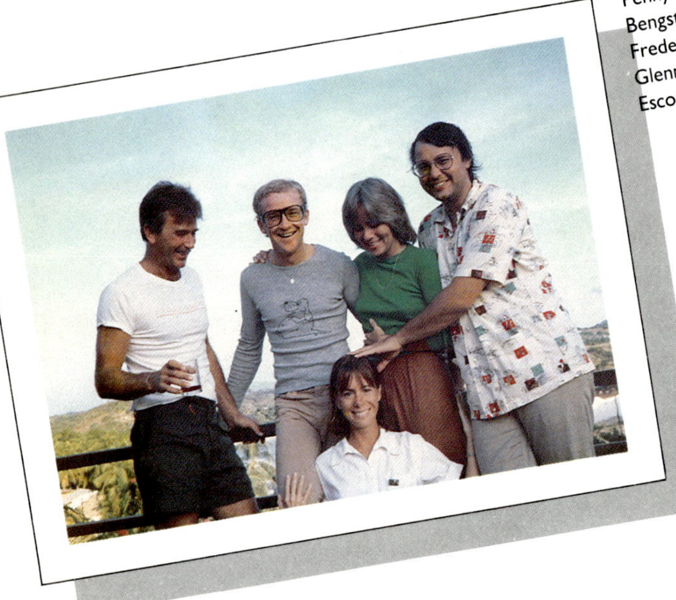

Penny Little (sitting), Billy Al Bengston, Nils Arne Nilsson, Fredericka Hunter, and Ian Glennie (left to right), Puerto Escondido, Mexico, 1976.

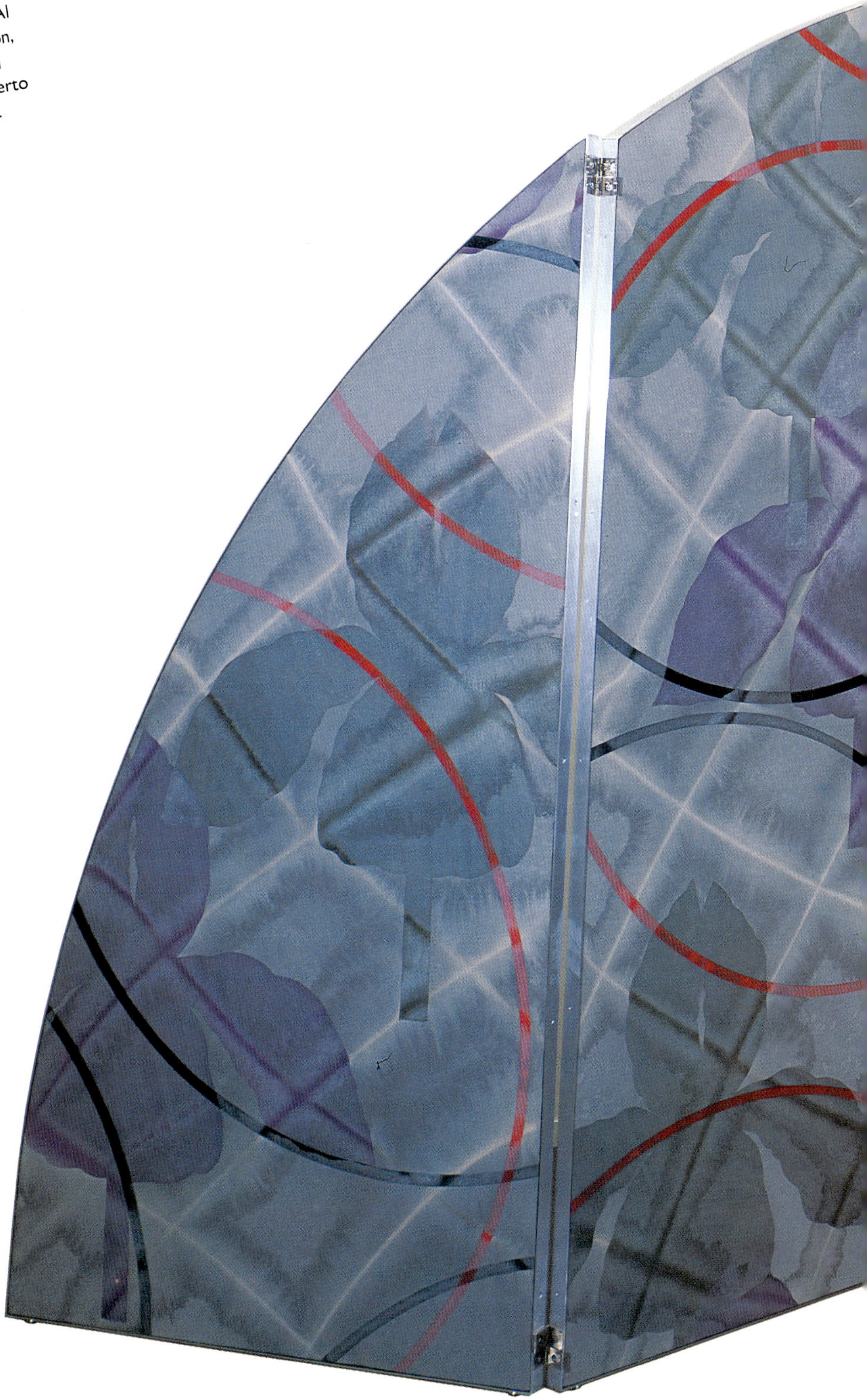

PLATE 26
EAGLE REEF DRACULAS
1976

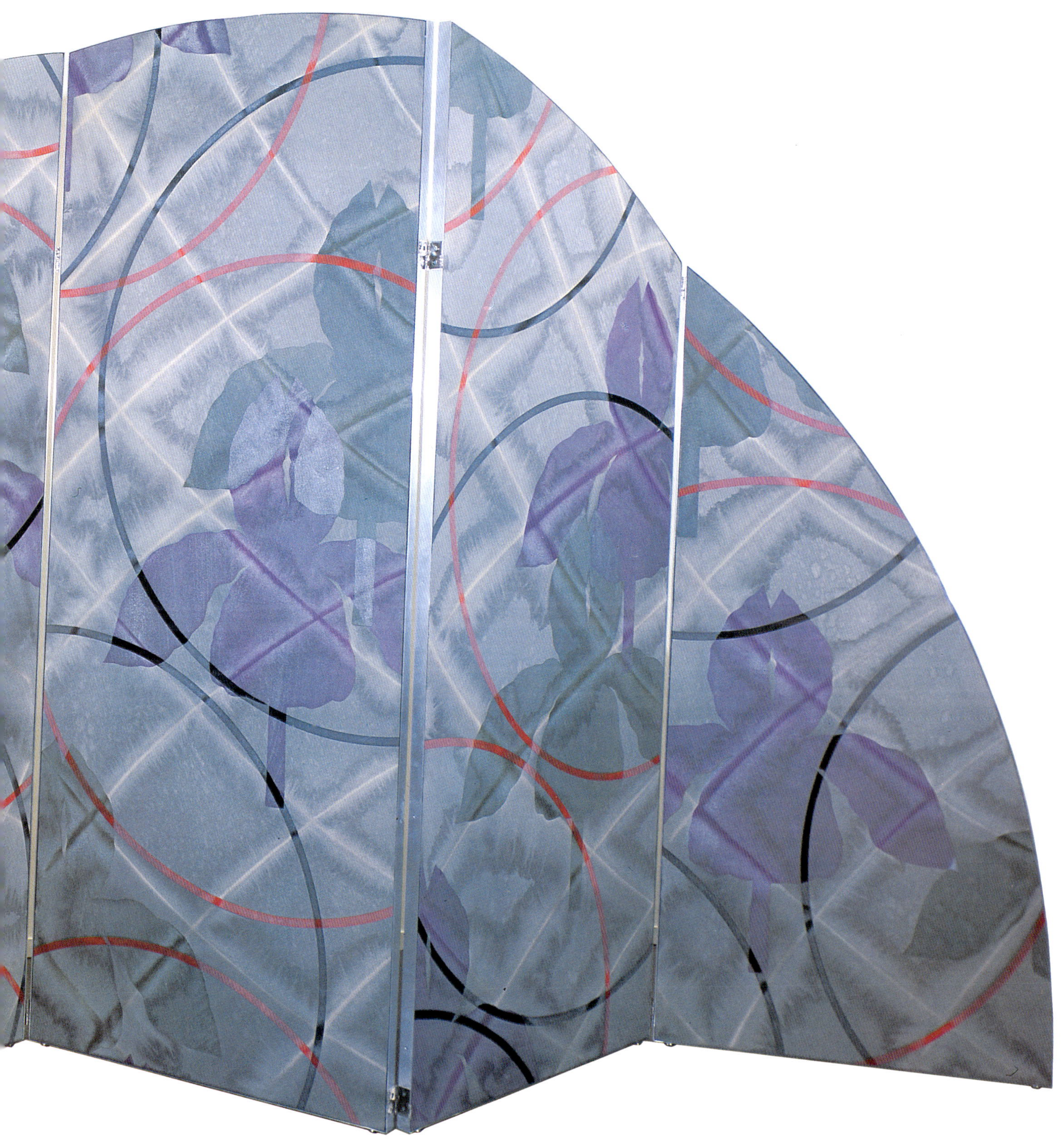

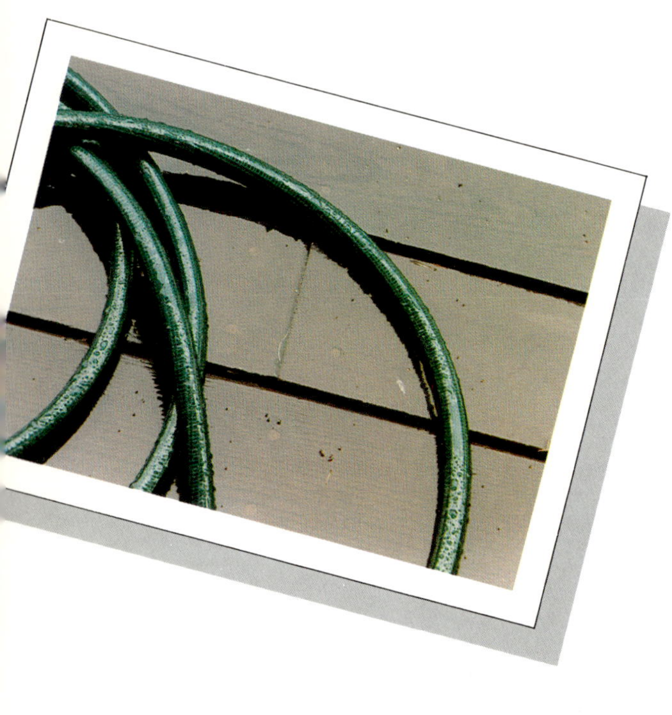

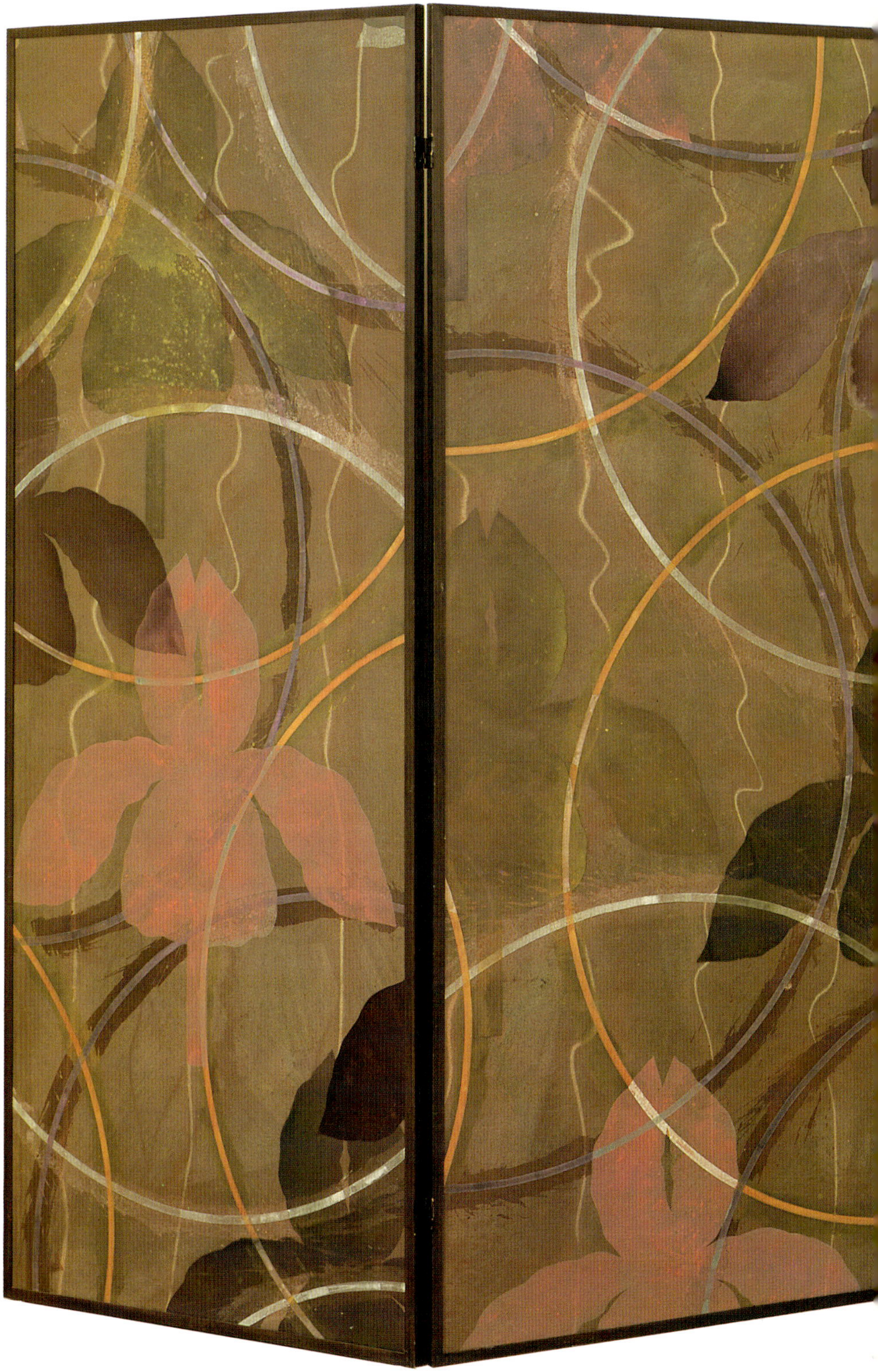

PLATE 27
IRON BOUND COVE DRACULAS
1976

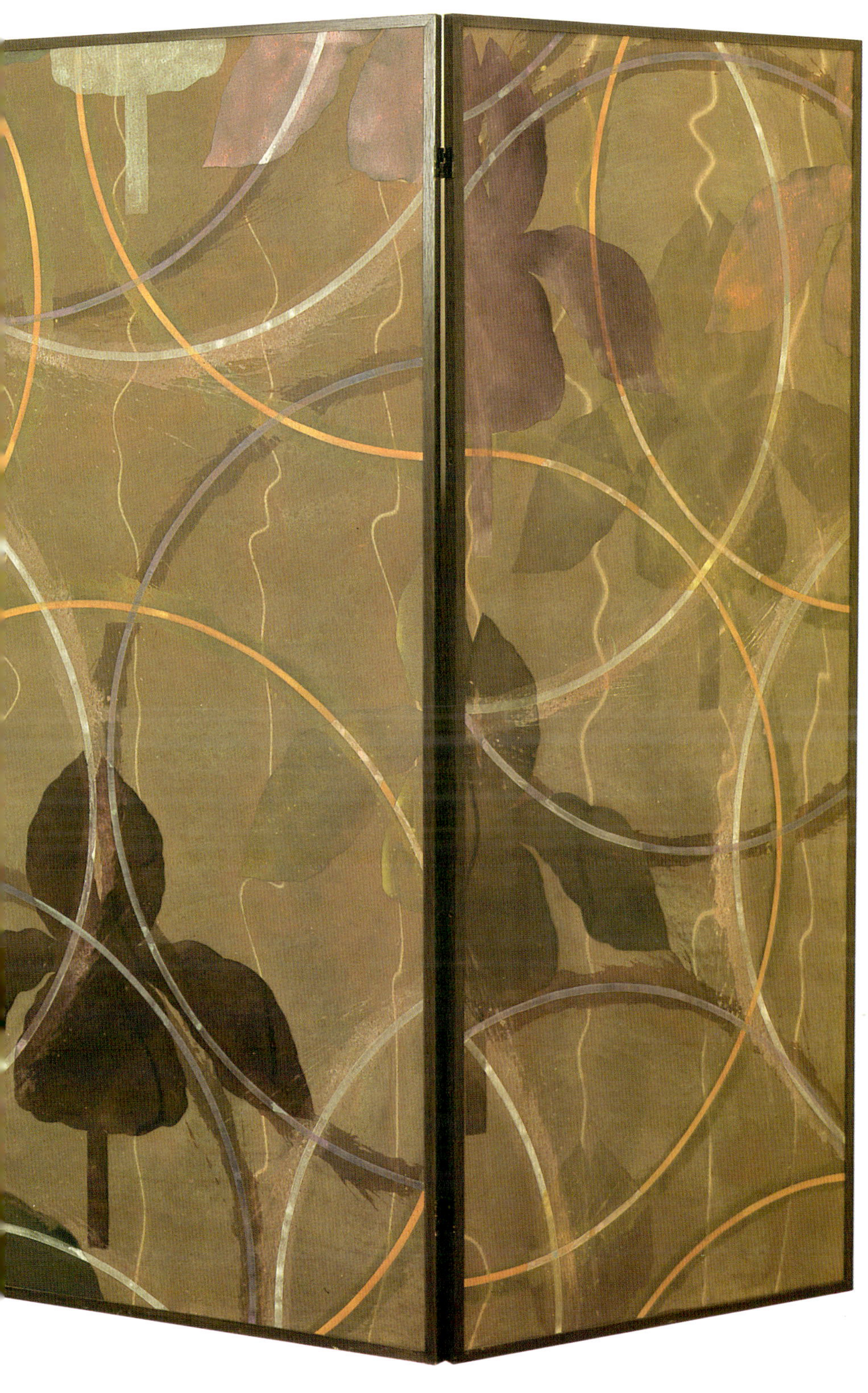

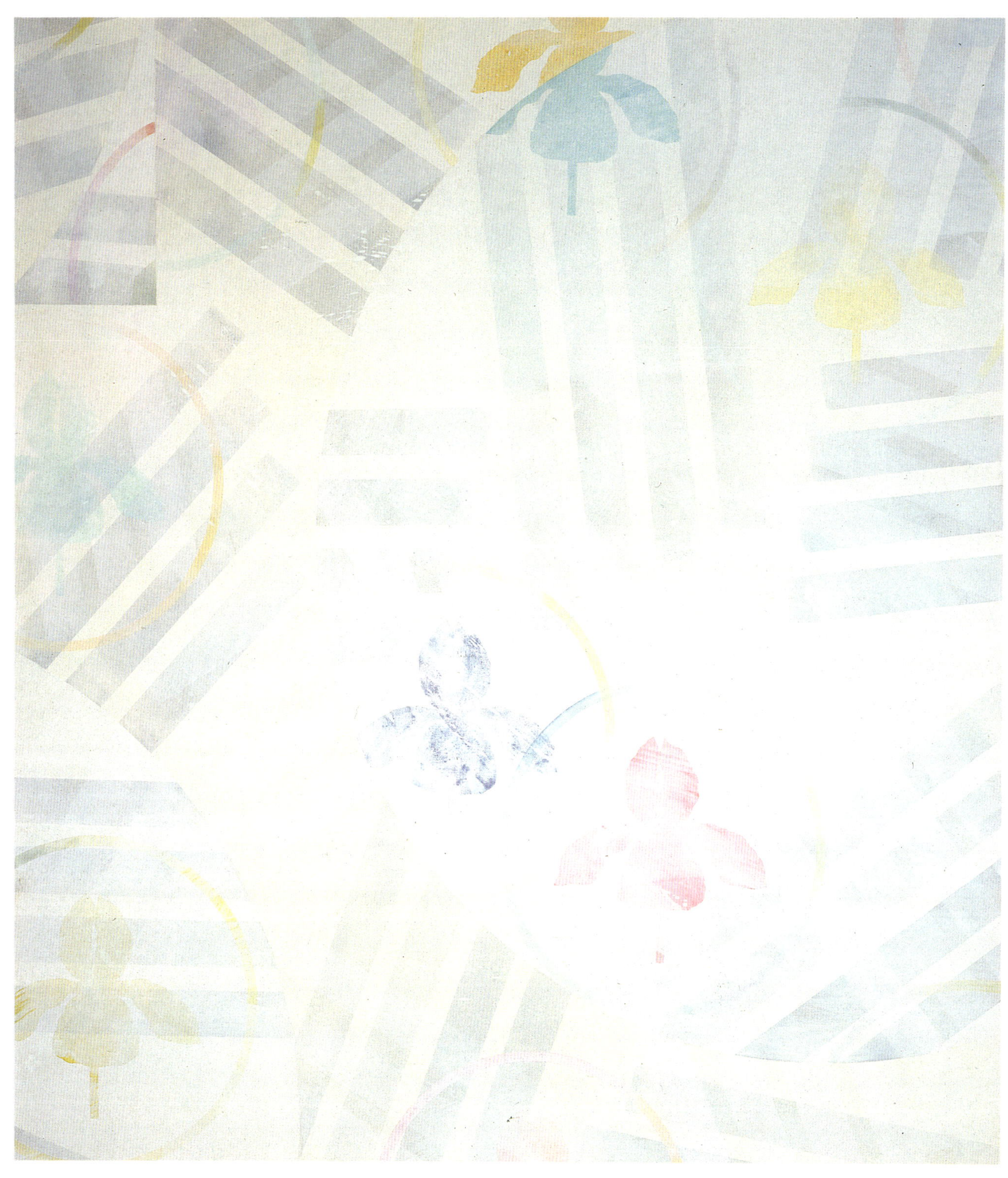

PLATE 28
ANTARAS DRACULAS
1977

PLATE 29
CAPELLA DRACULAS
1977

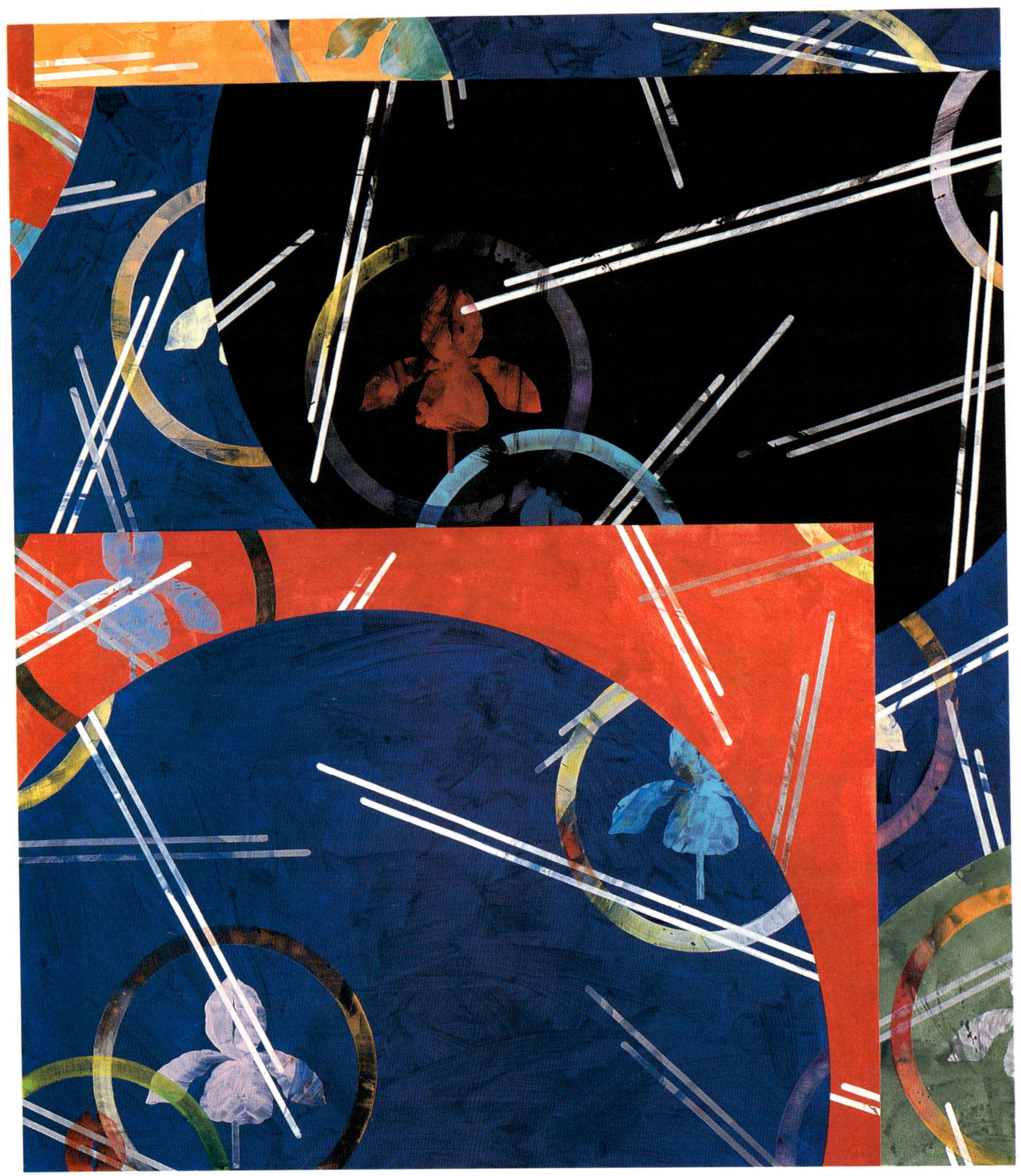

PLATE 30
CHOKLADKRANSAR DRACULAS
1977

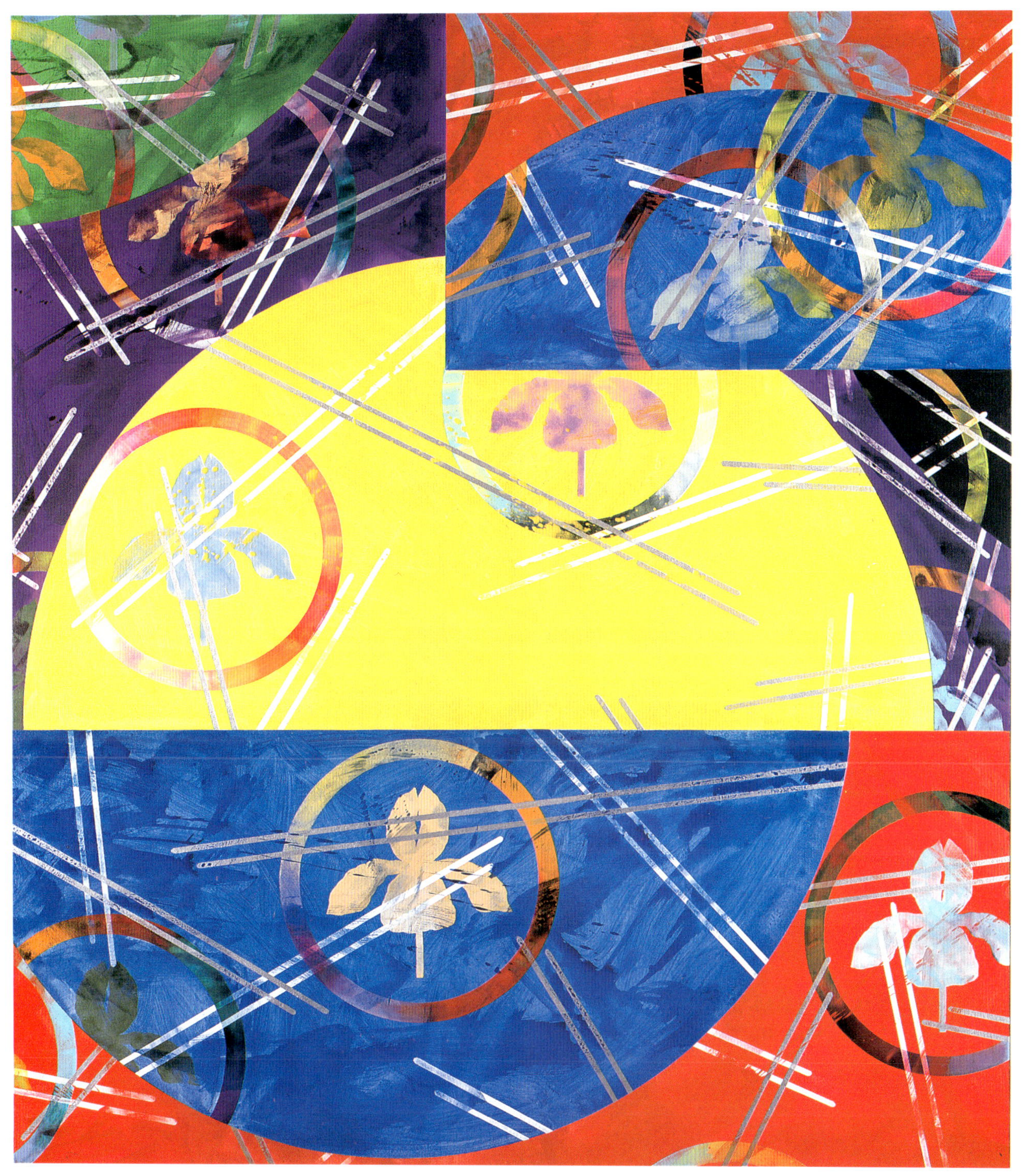

PLATE 31
TREVAPPLINGER DRACULAS
1978

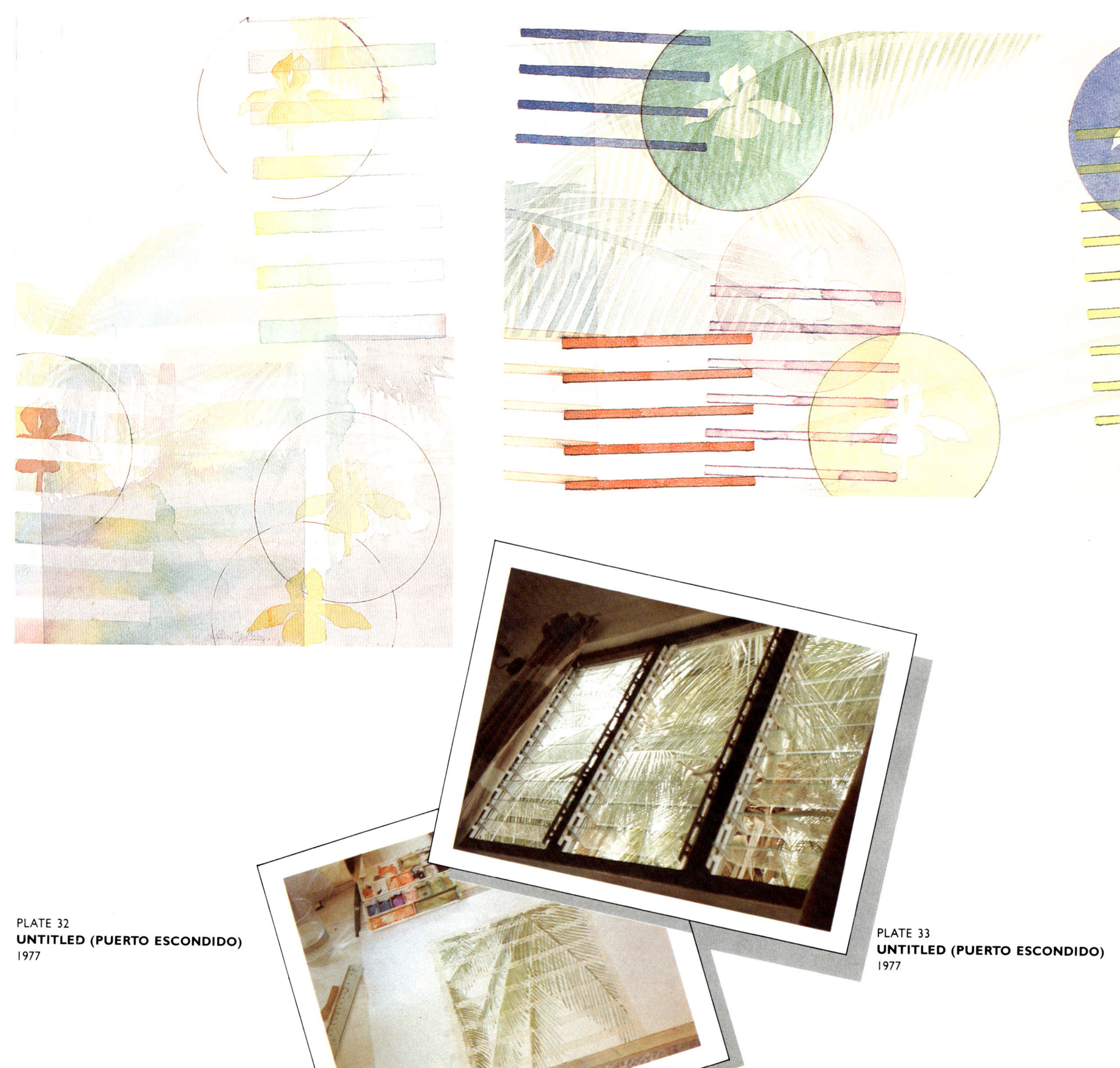

PLATE 32
UNTITLED (PUERTO ESCONDIDO)
1977

PLATE 33
UNTITLED (PUERTO ESCONDIDO)
1977

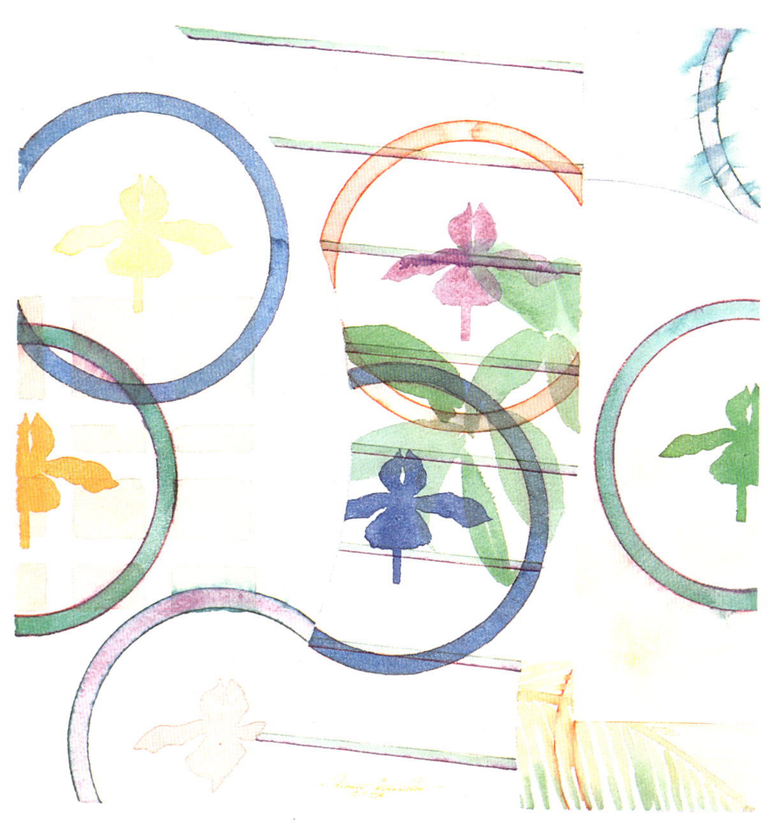

PLATE 34
UNTITLED (PUERTO ESCONDIDO)
1978

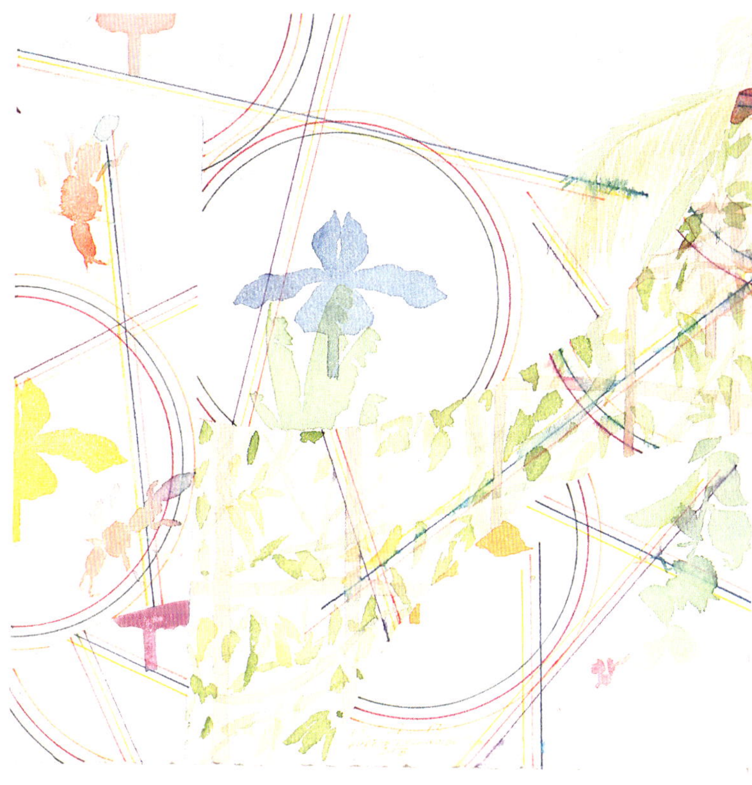

PLATE 35
UNTITLED (PUERTO ESCONDIDO)
1978

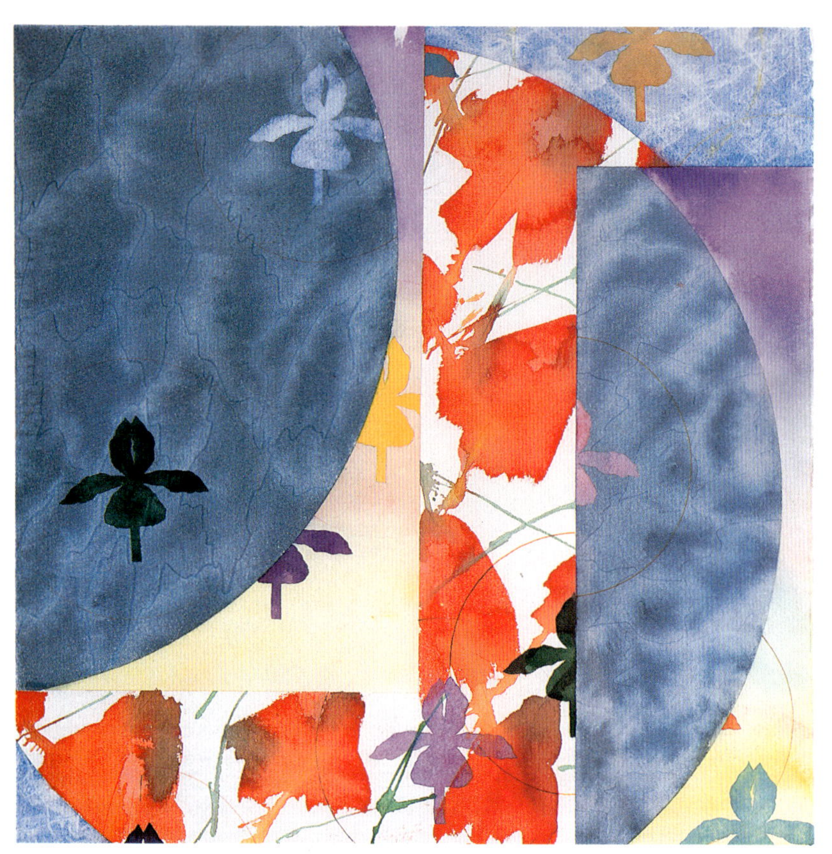

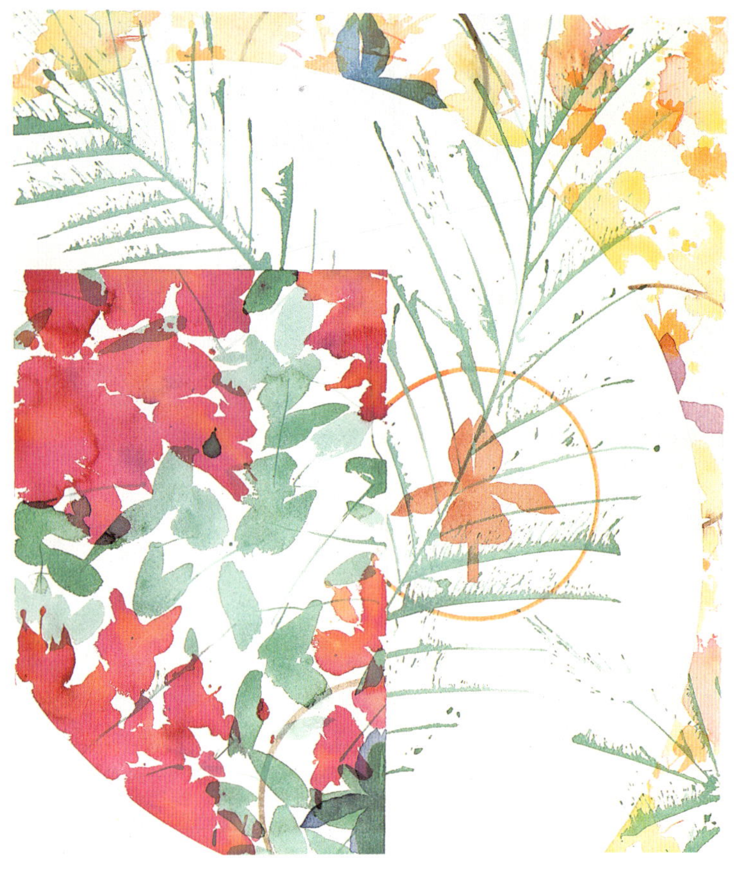

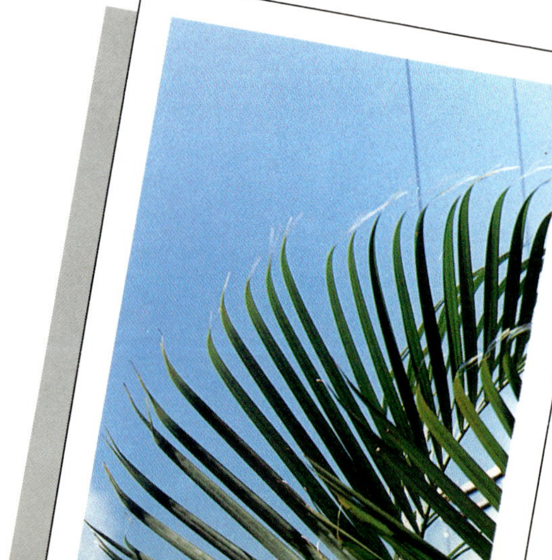

PLATE 36
UNTITLED (LAHAINA)
1978

PLATE 37
UNTITLED (LAHAINA)
1978

94

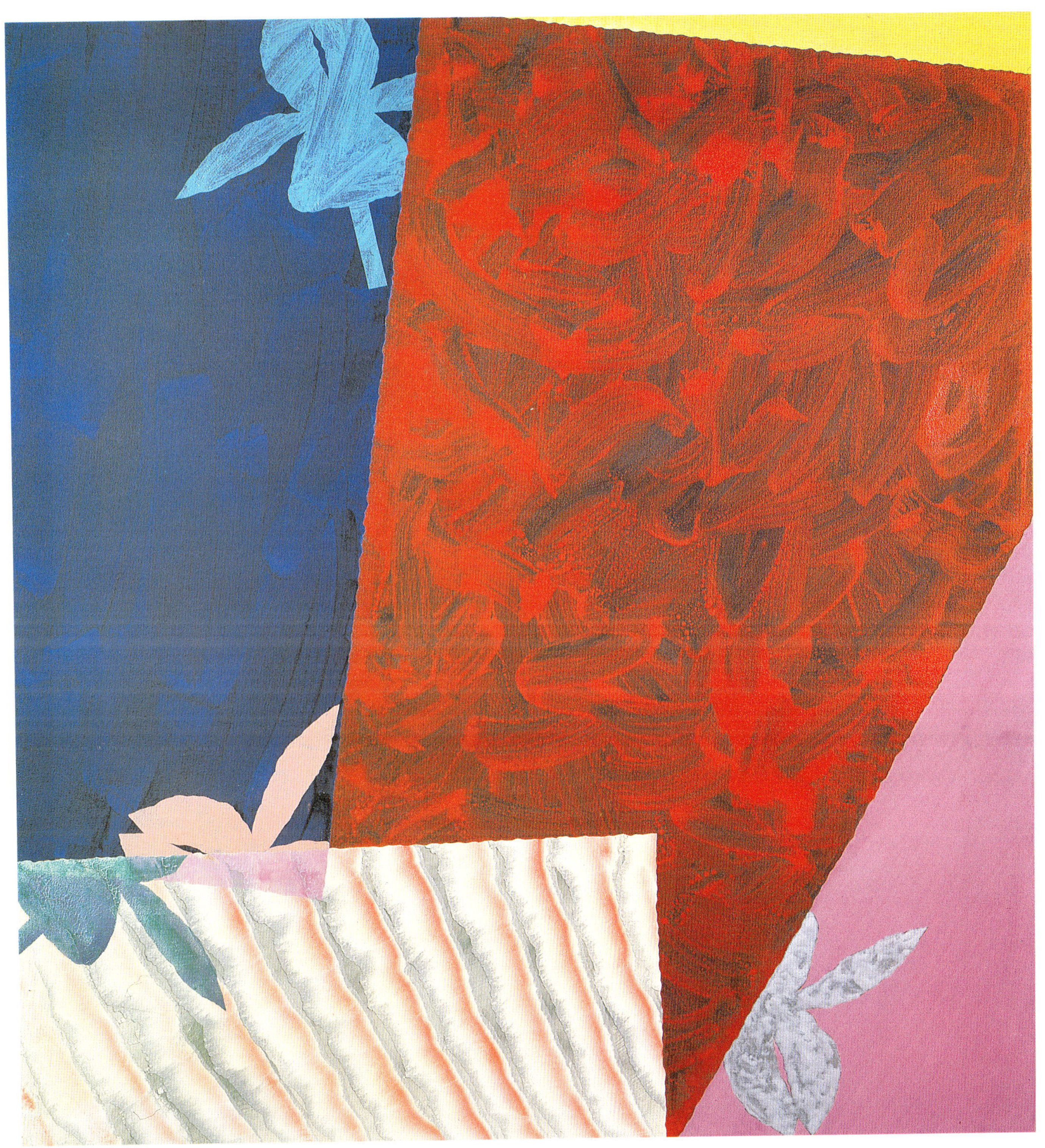

PLATE 38
ALOHA DRACULAS
1979

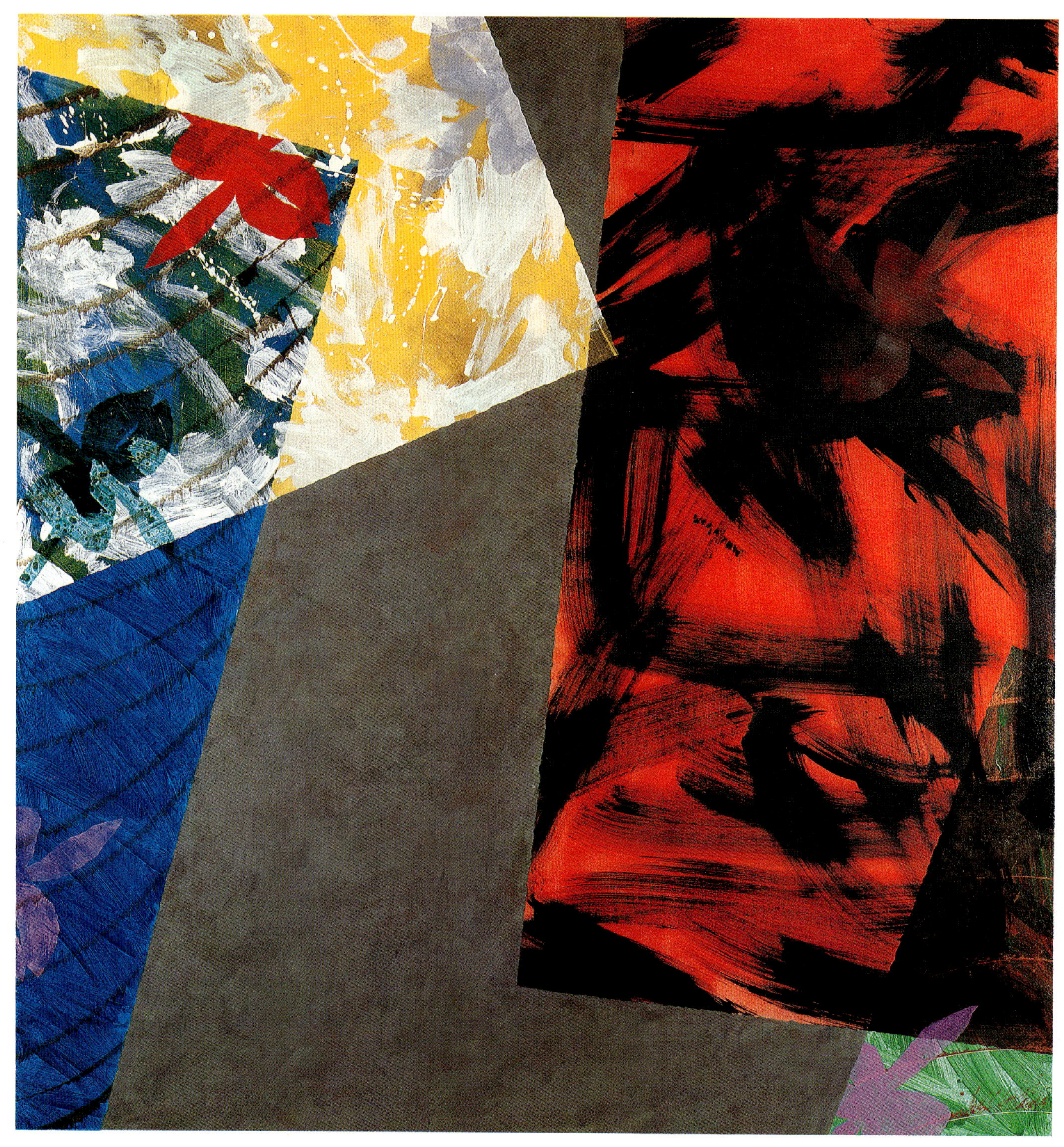

PLATE 39
NAKOOKOO DRACULAS
1979

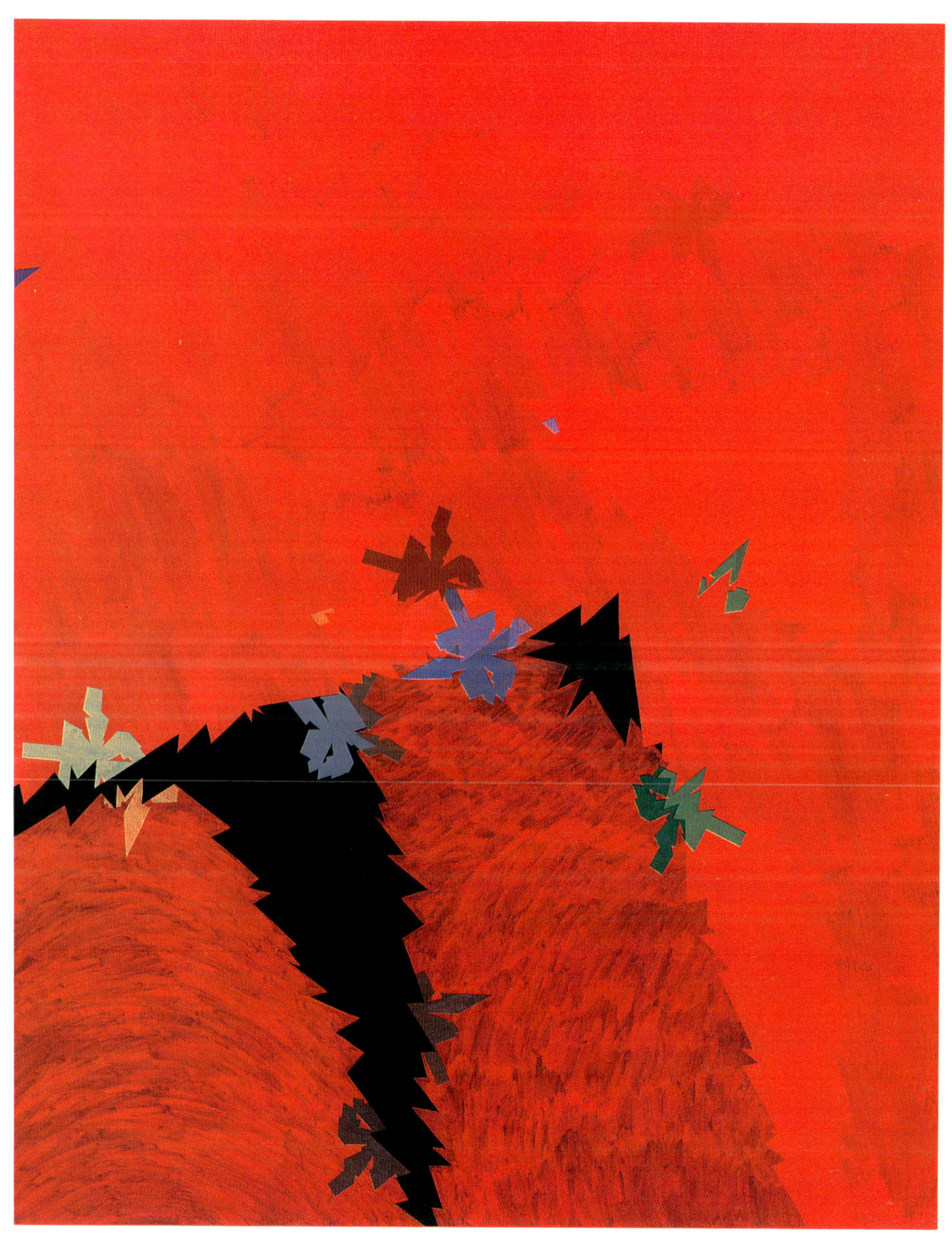

PLATE 40
EHUKAI DRACULAS
1981

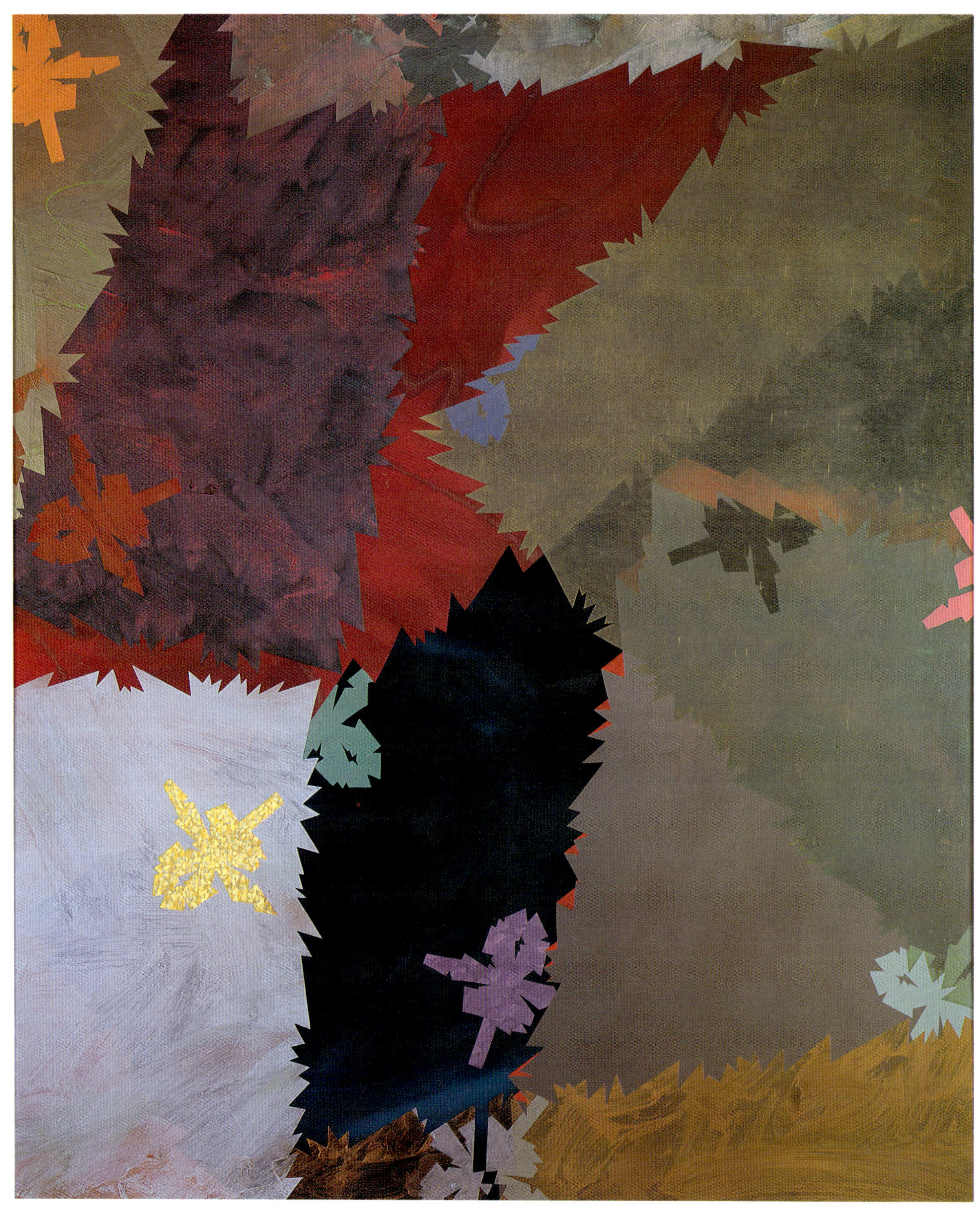

PLATE 41
KAONA DRACULAS
1981

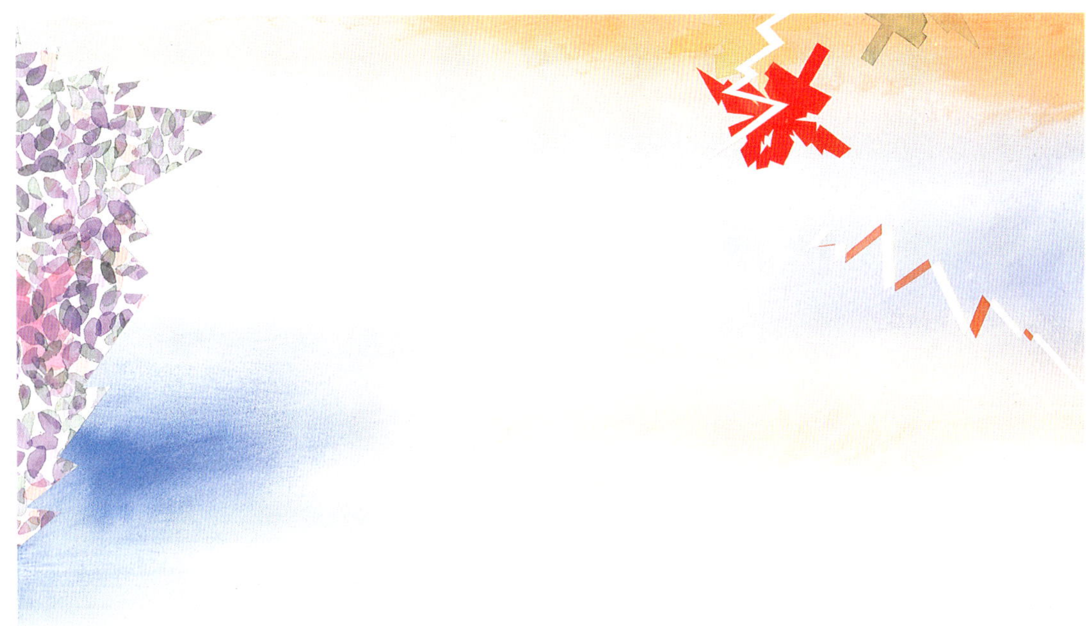
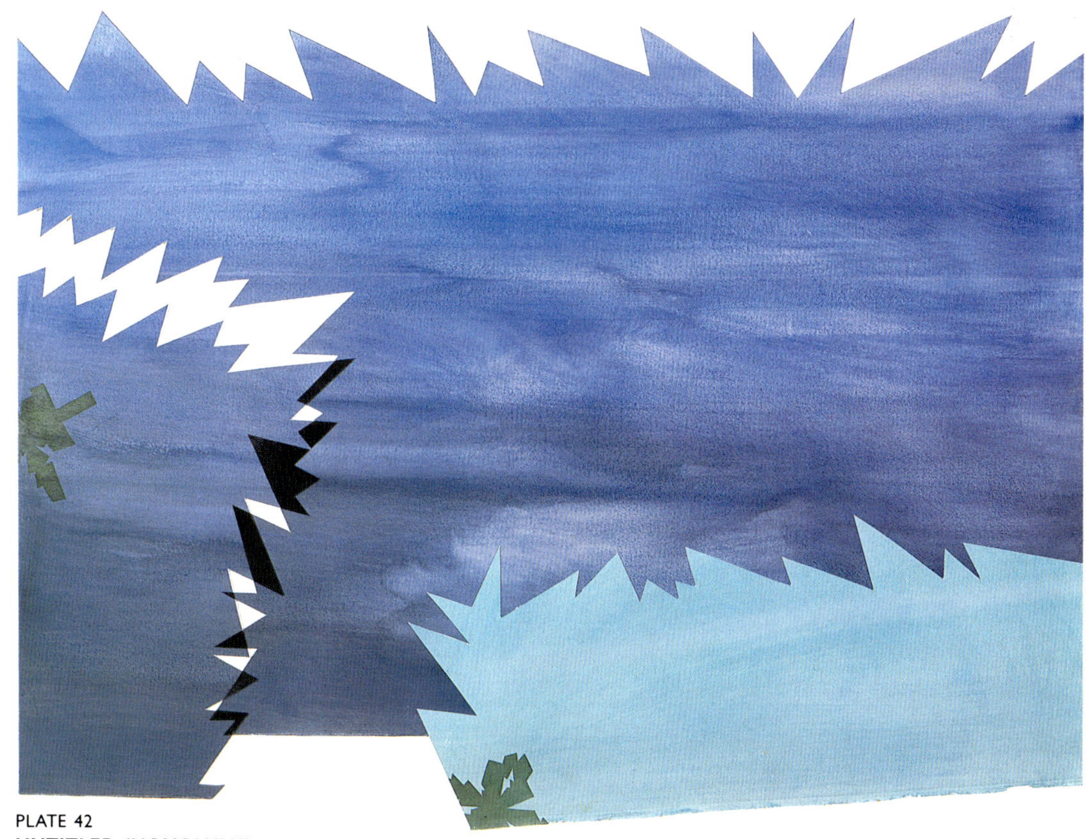

PLATE 42
UNTITLED (HONOLULU)
1981

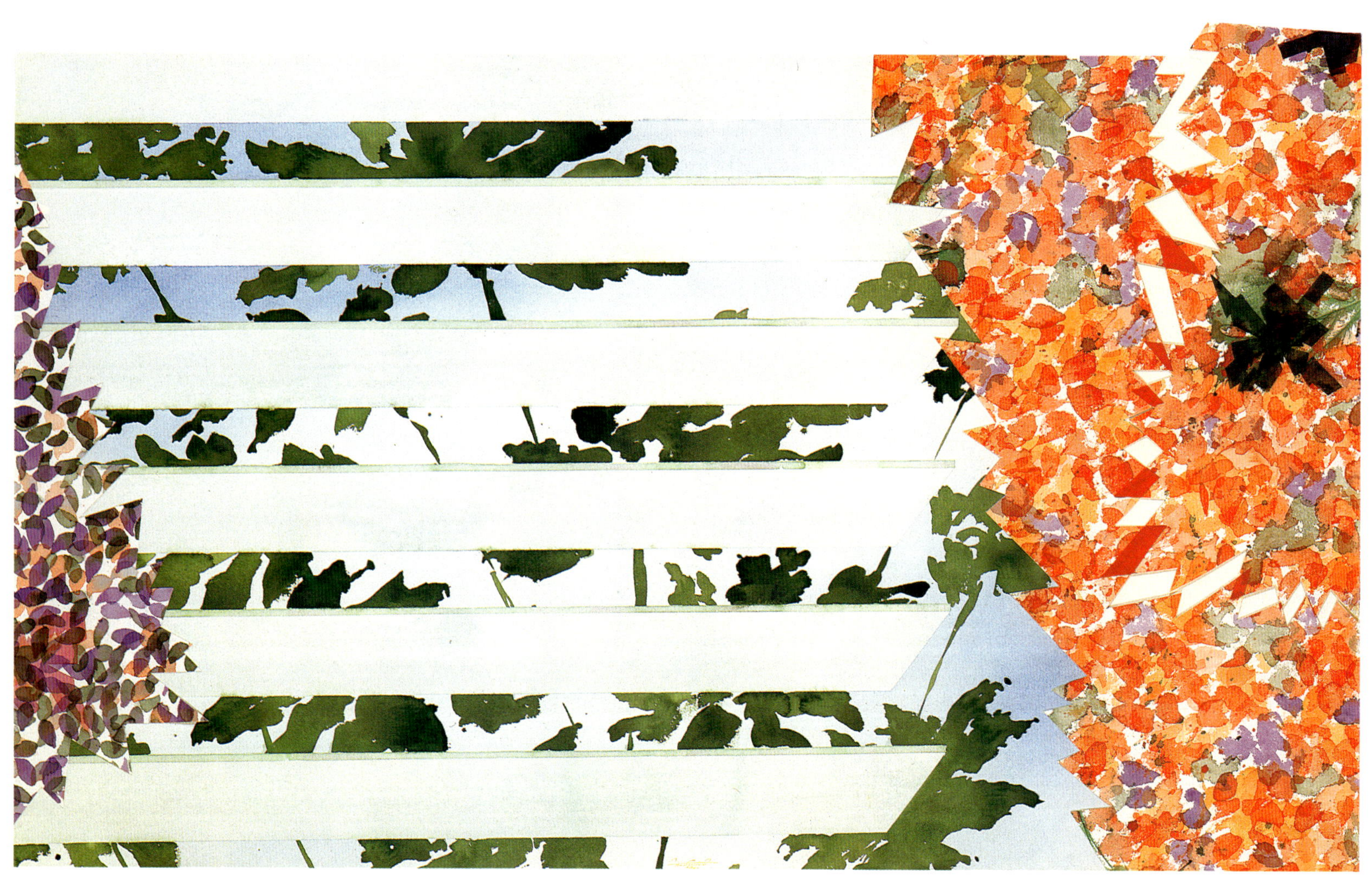

PLATE 43
UNTITLED (HONOLULU)
1981

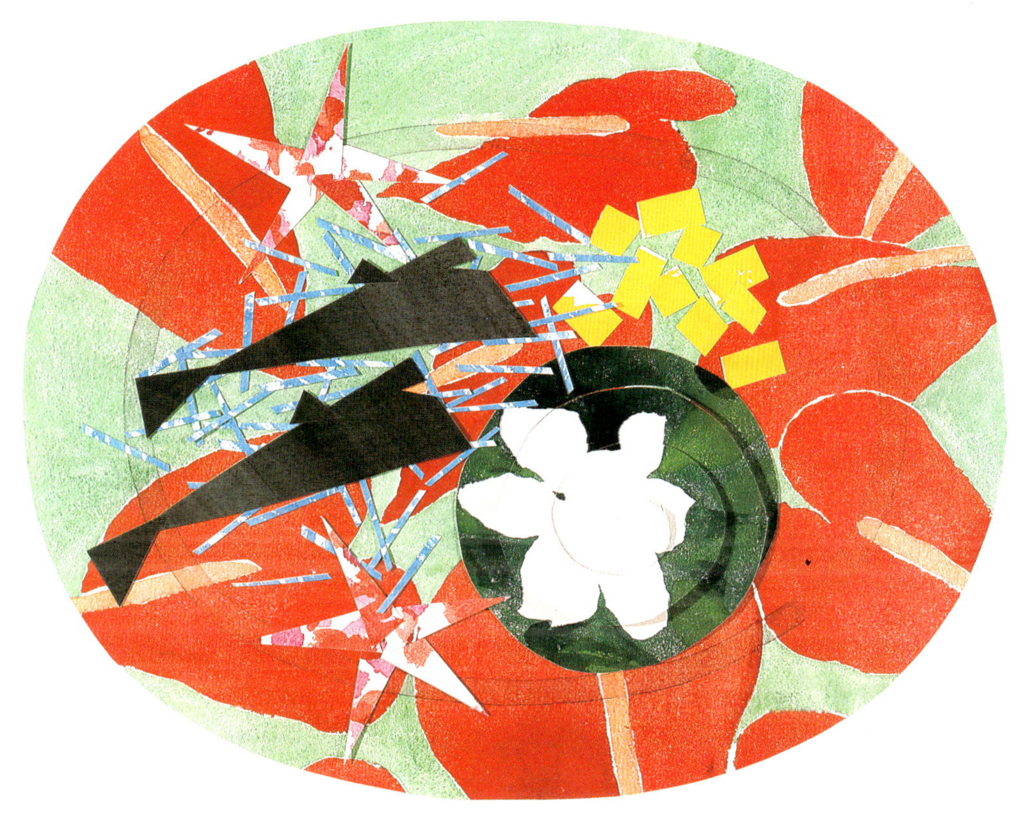

PLATE 44
PA'PEPA
1982

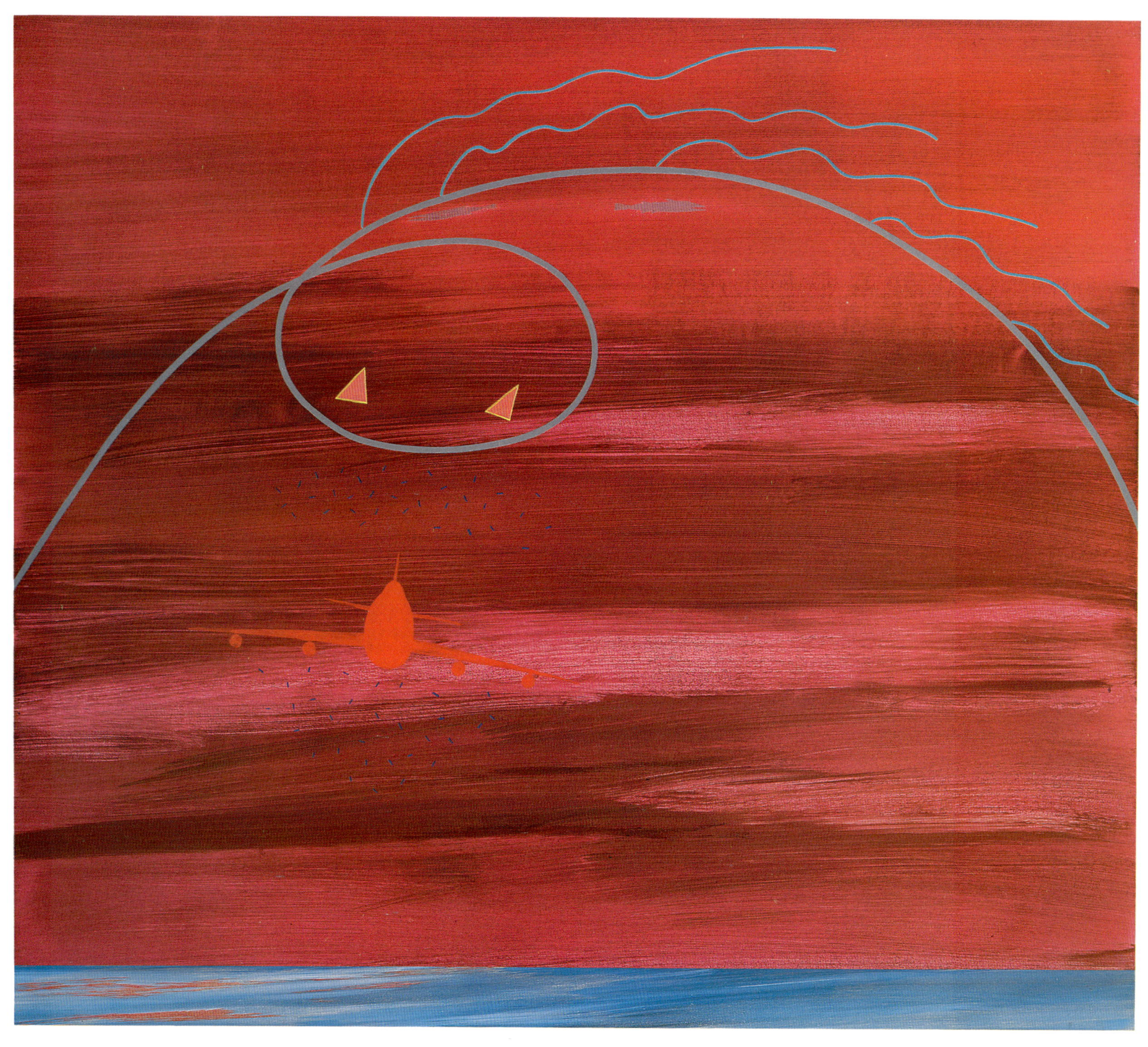

PLATE 45
KIPUKA
1982

102

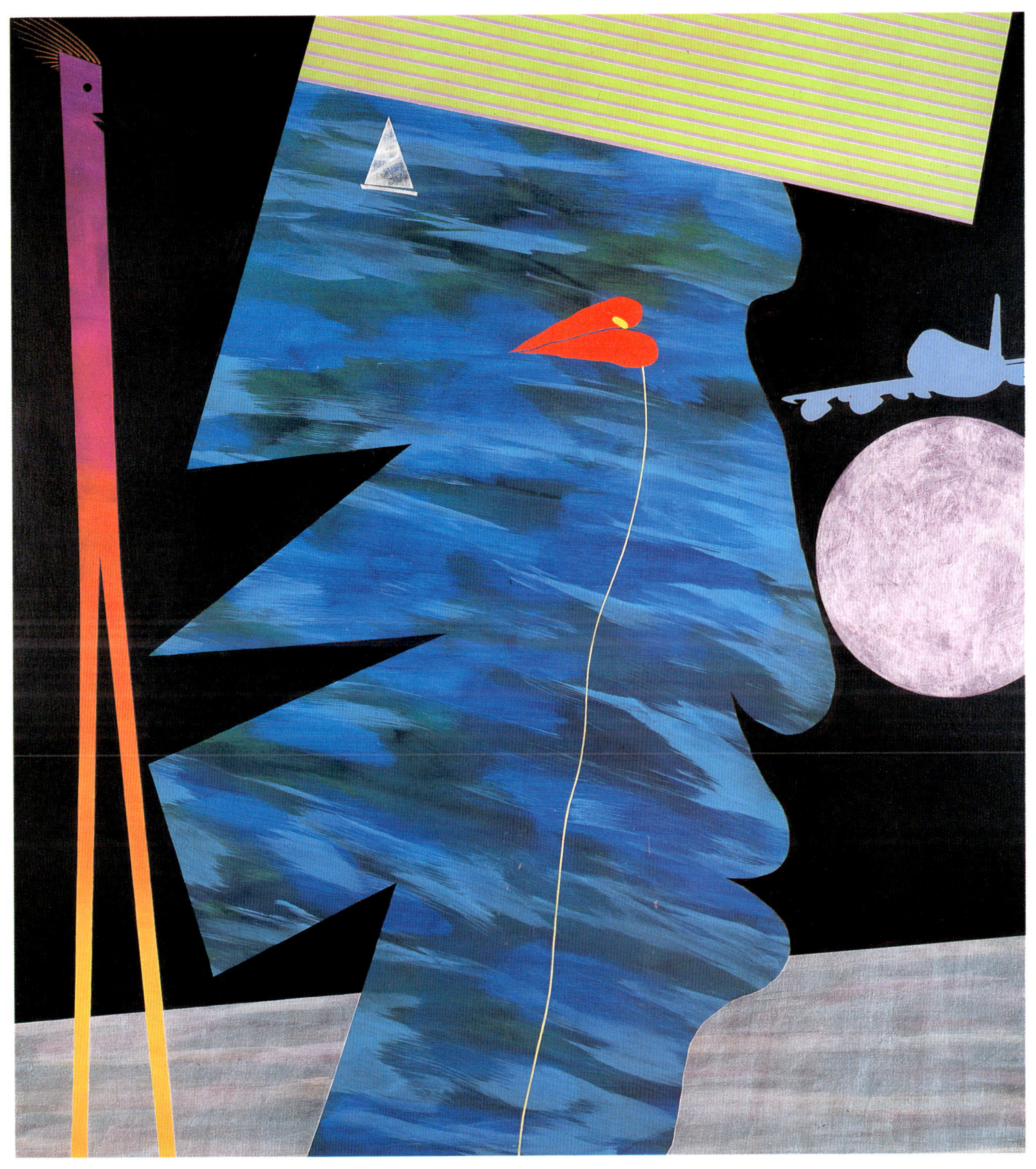

PLATE 46
IKE OLE IA PO
1983

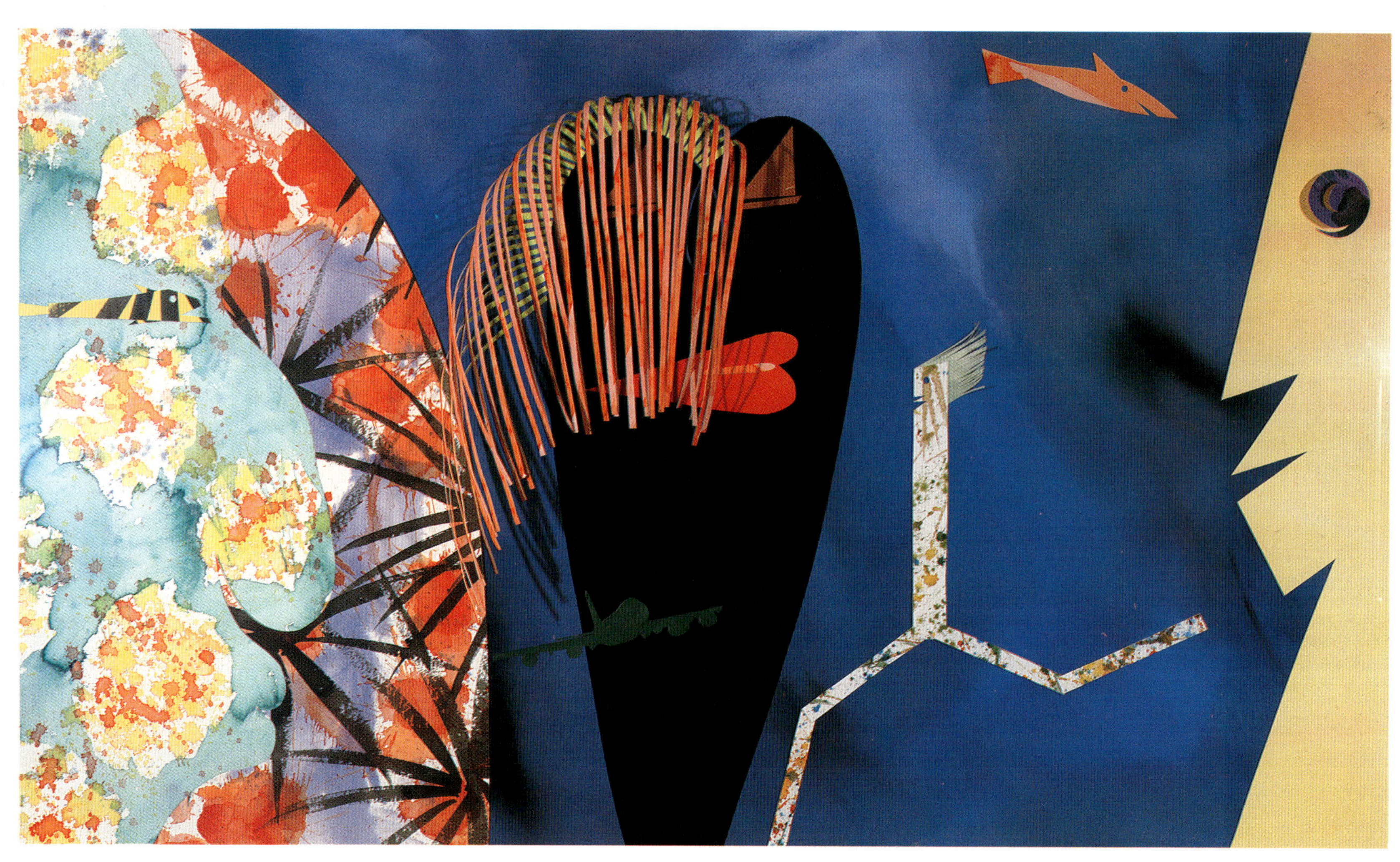

PLATE 47
KA'AO
1983

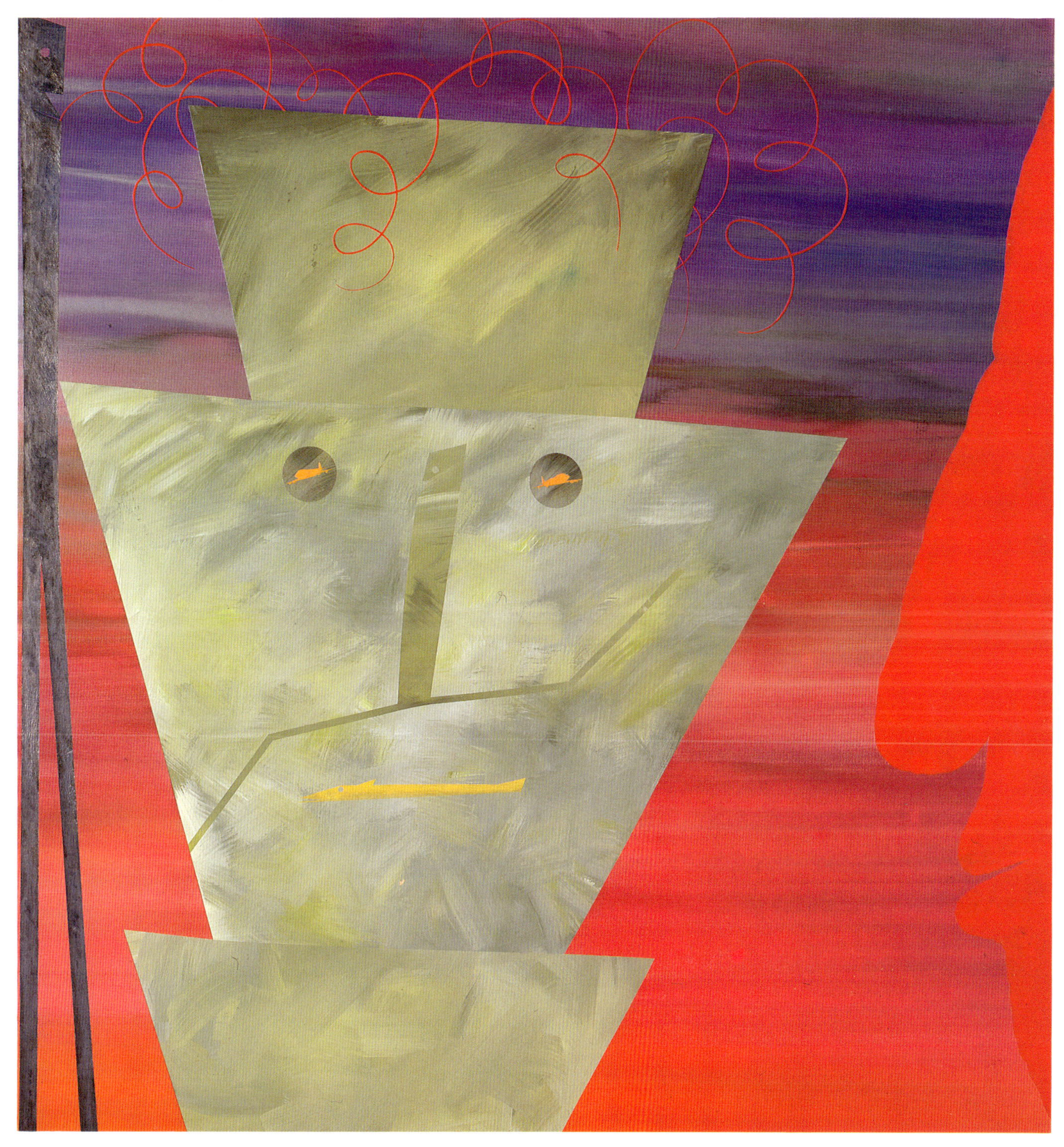

PLATE 48
NUI IPU POO
1983

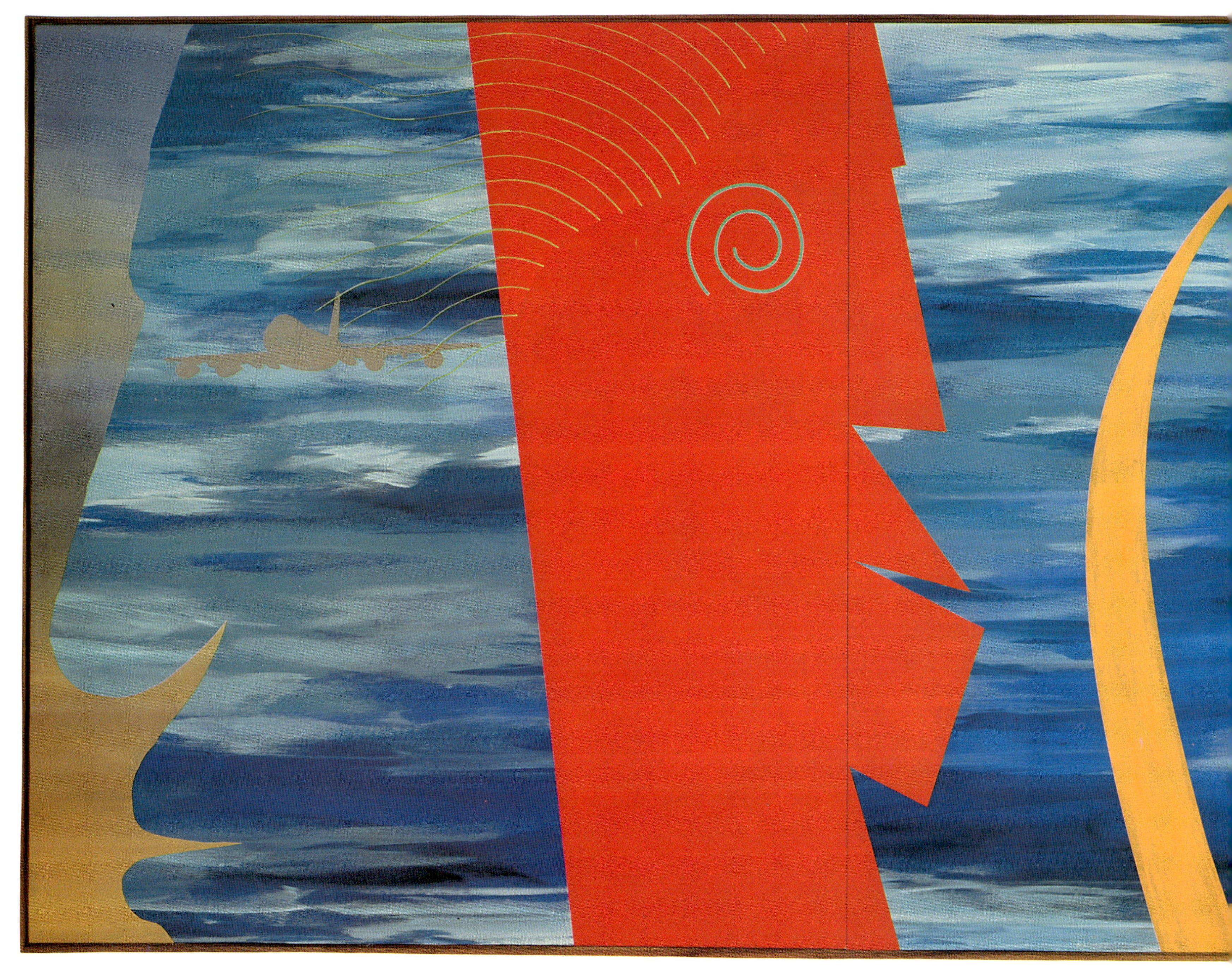

PLATE 49
KAUKOLU HANA PAEWAEWA
1983

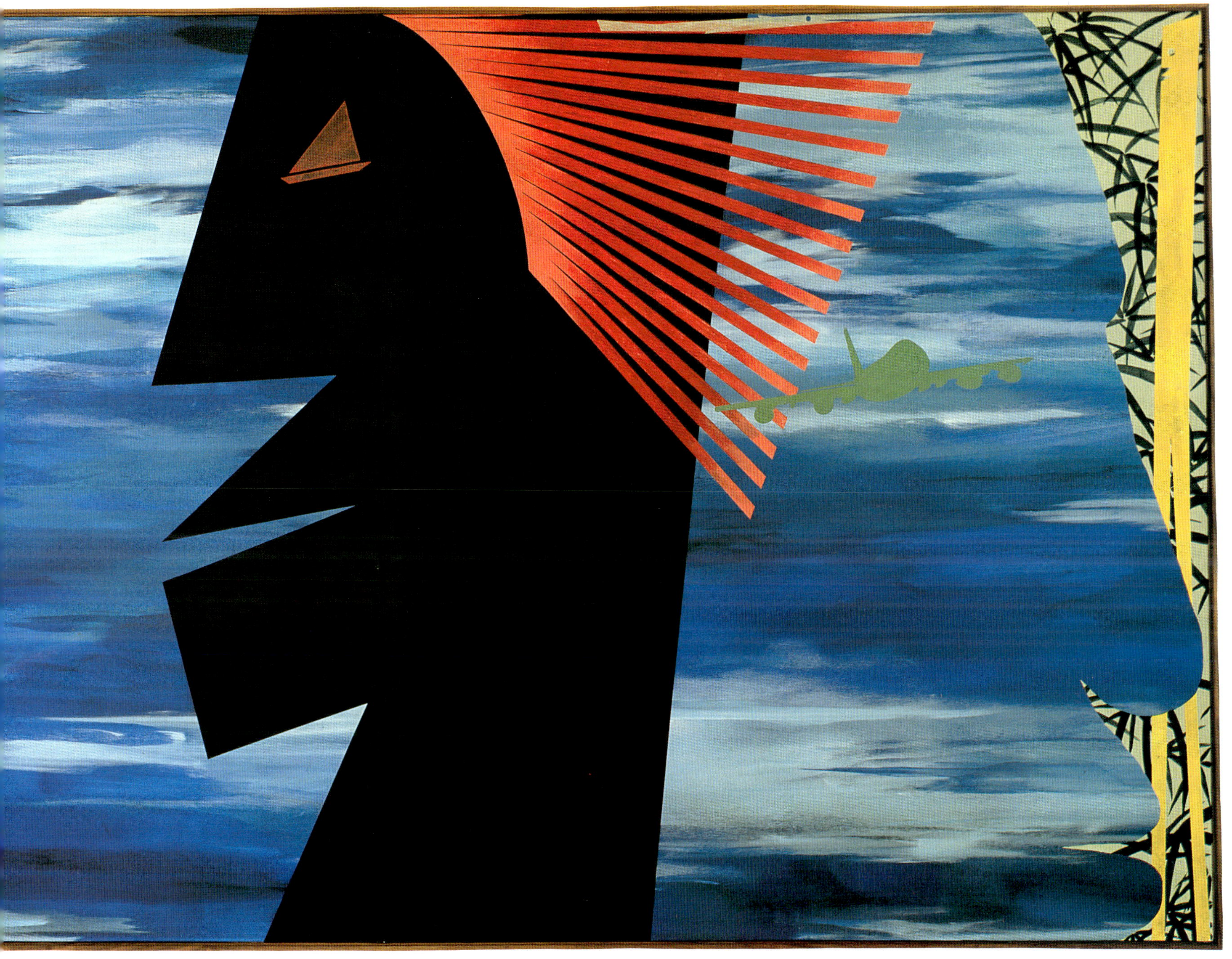

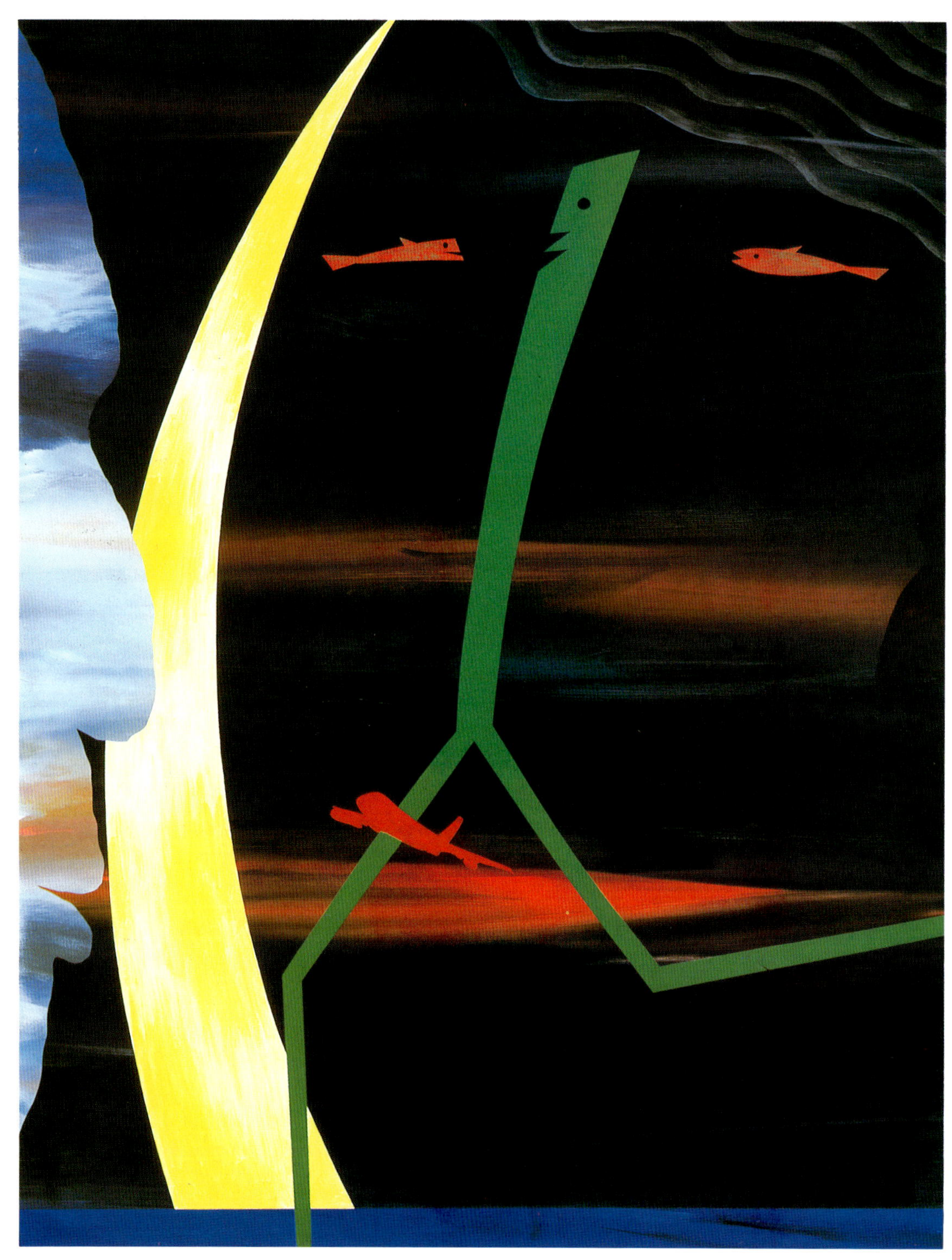

PLATE 50
POPOKI A OKOLE
1983

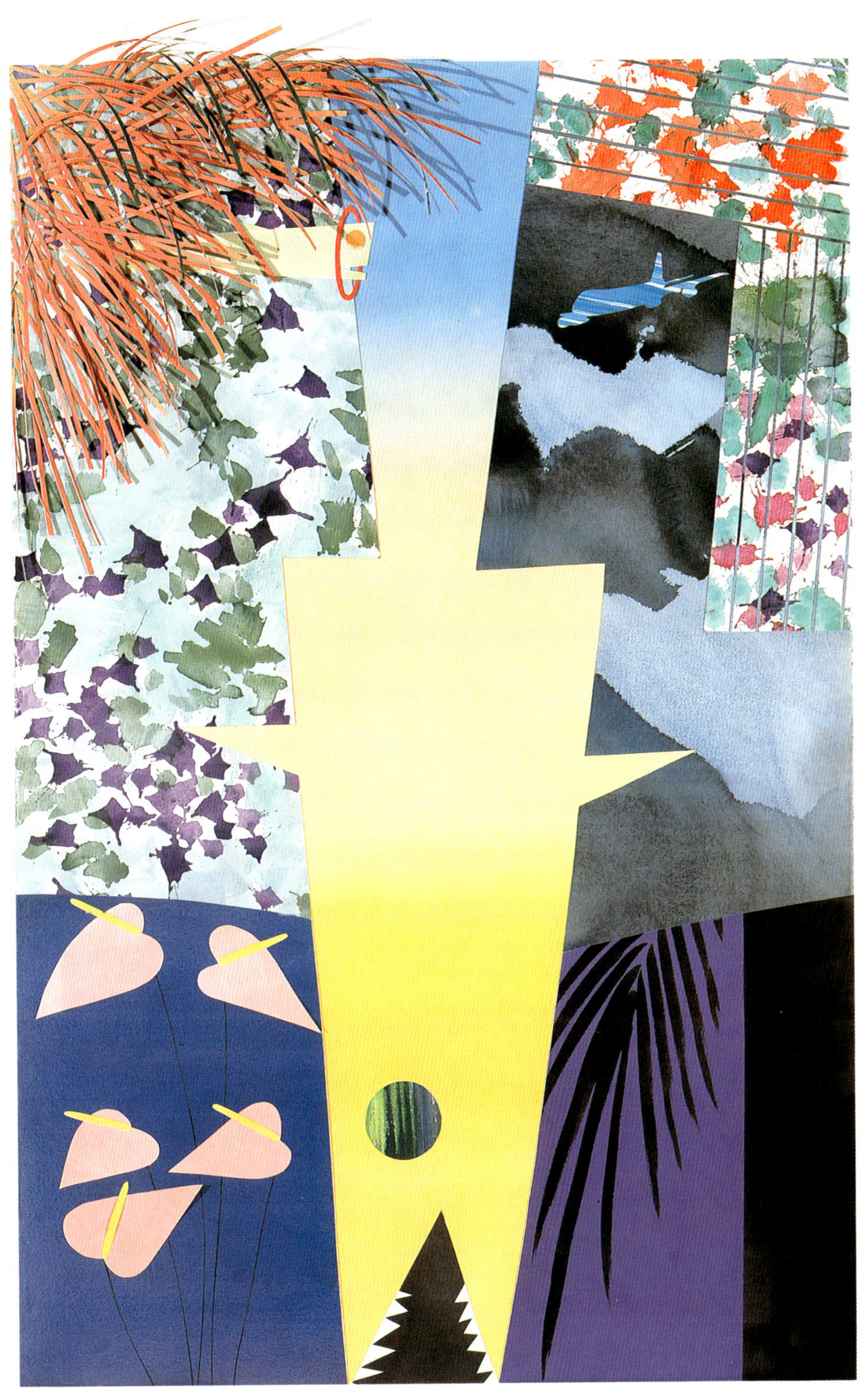

PLATE 51
KA'AO
1984

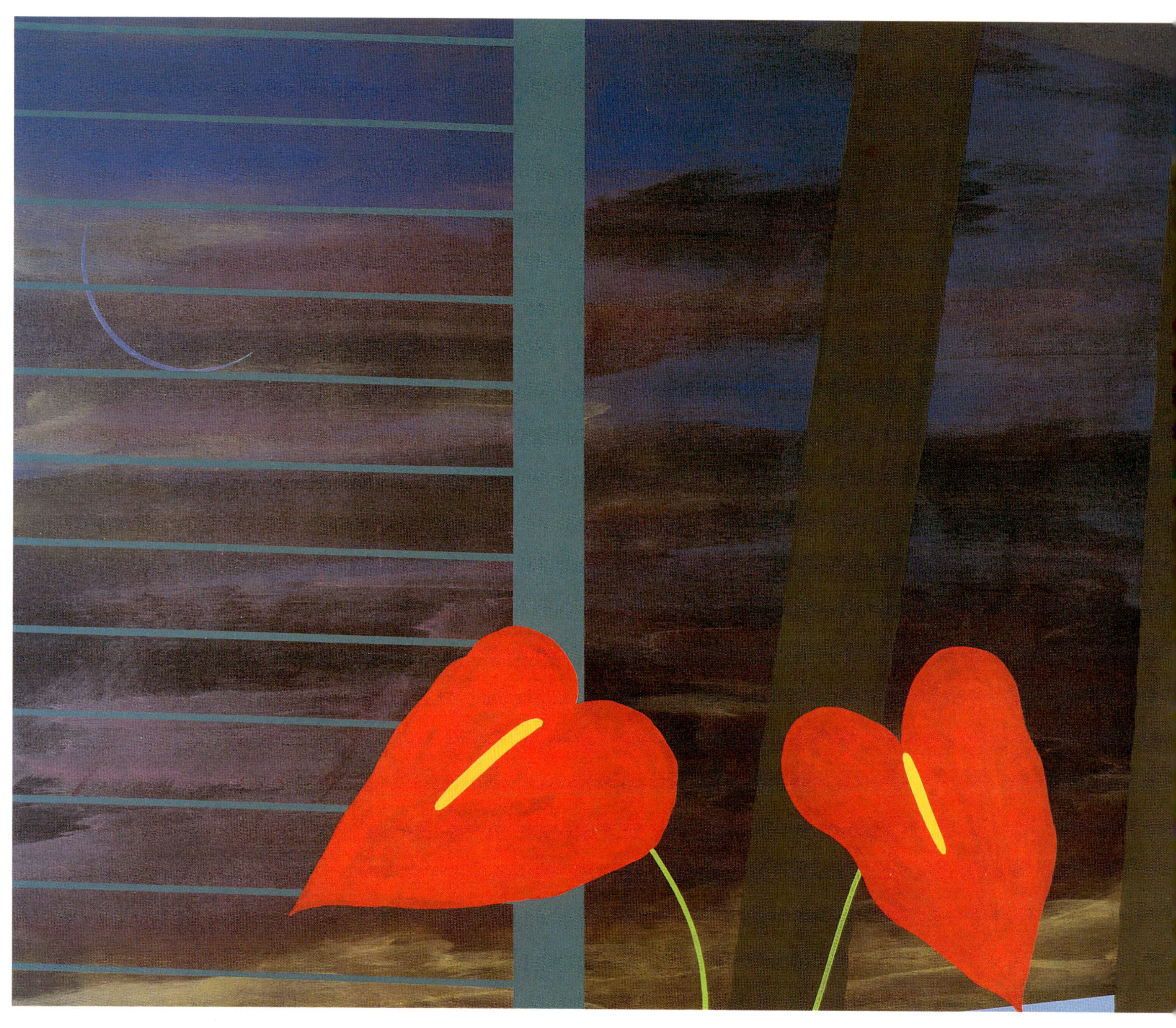

PLATE 52
OBAKE MADNESS
1984

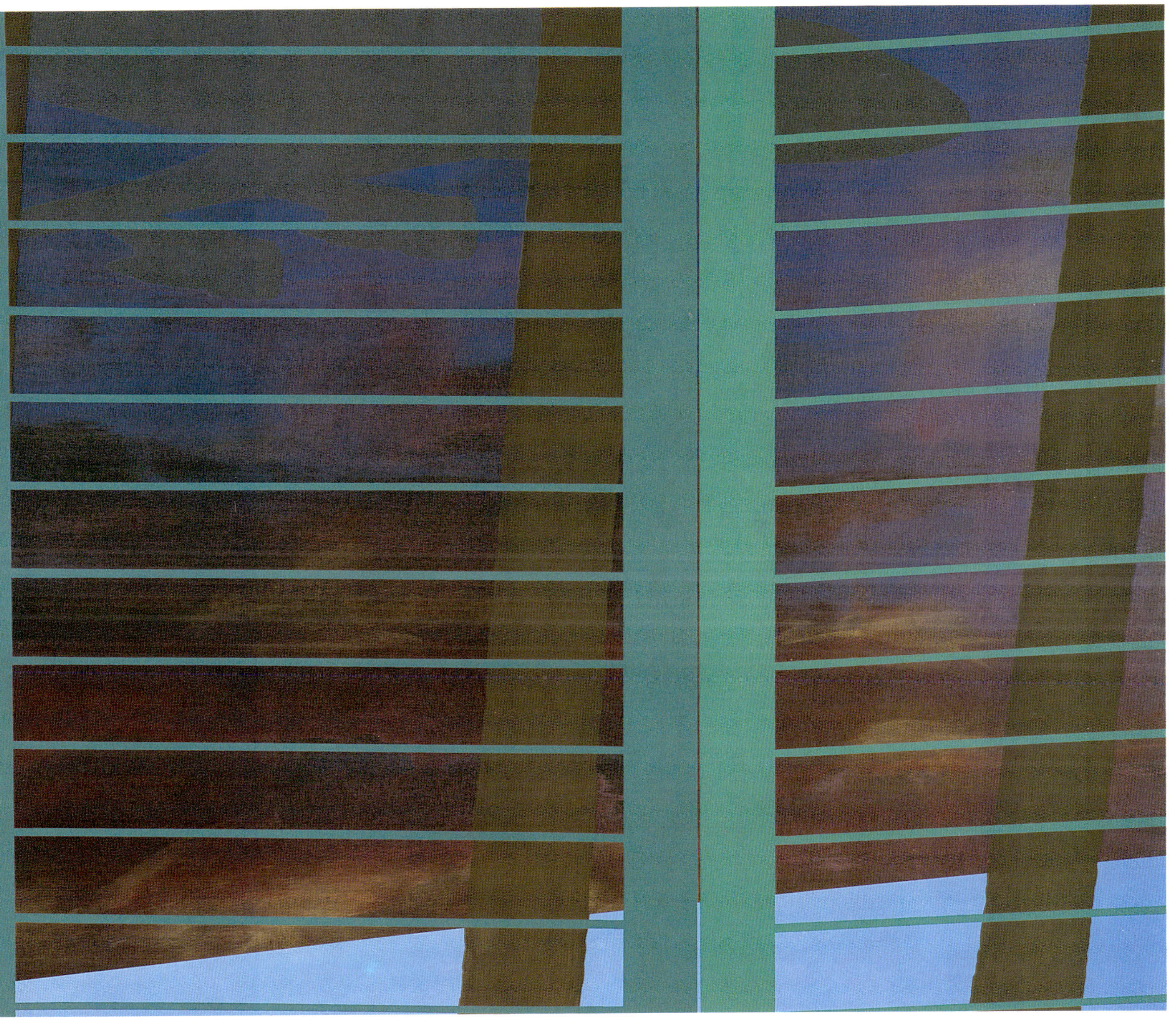

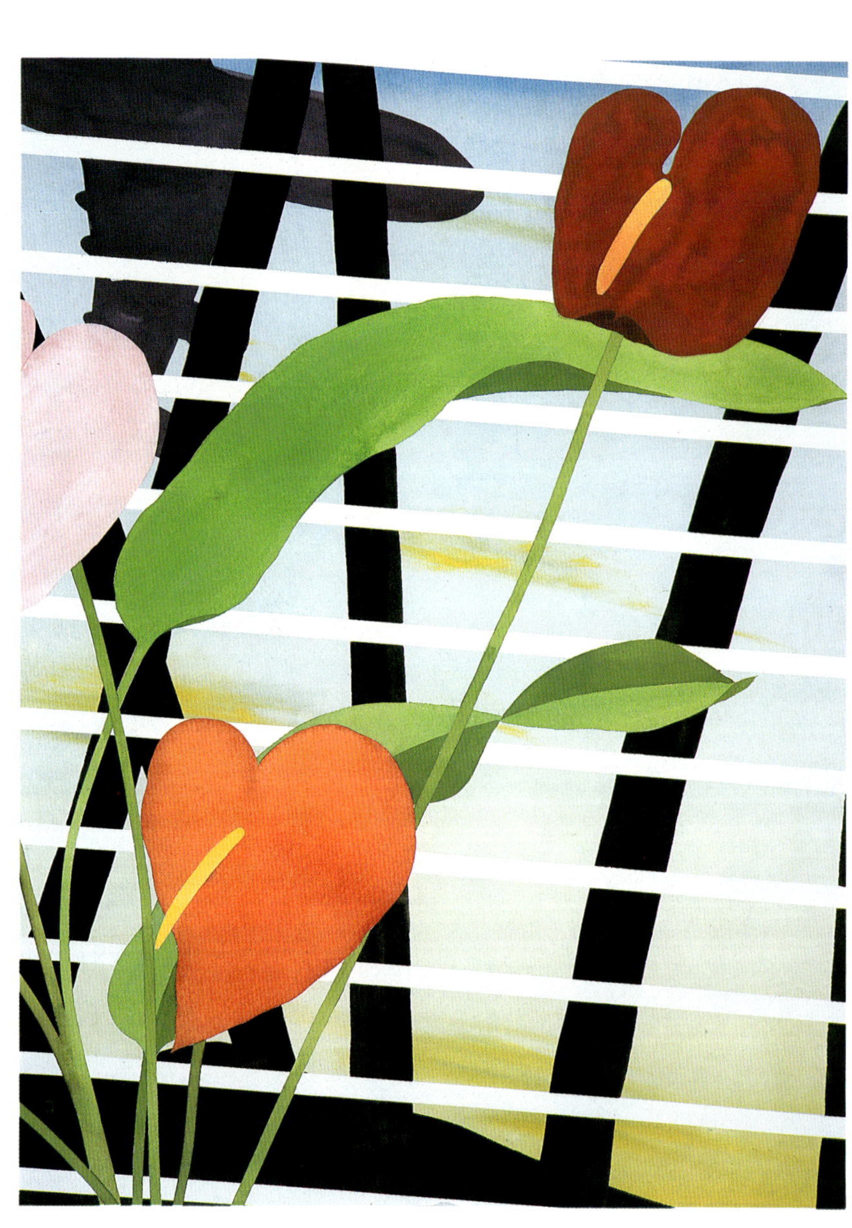

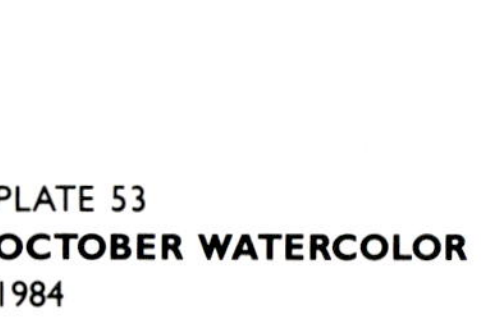

PLATE 53
OCTOBER WATERCOLOR
1984

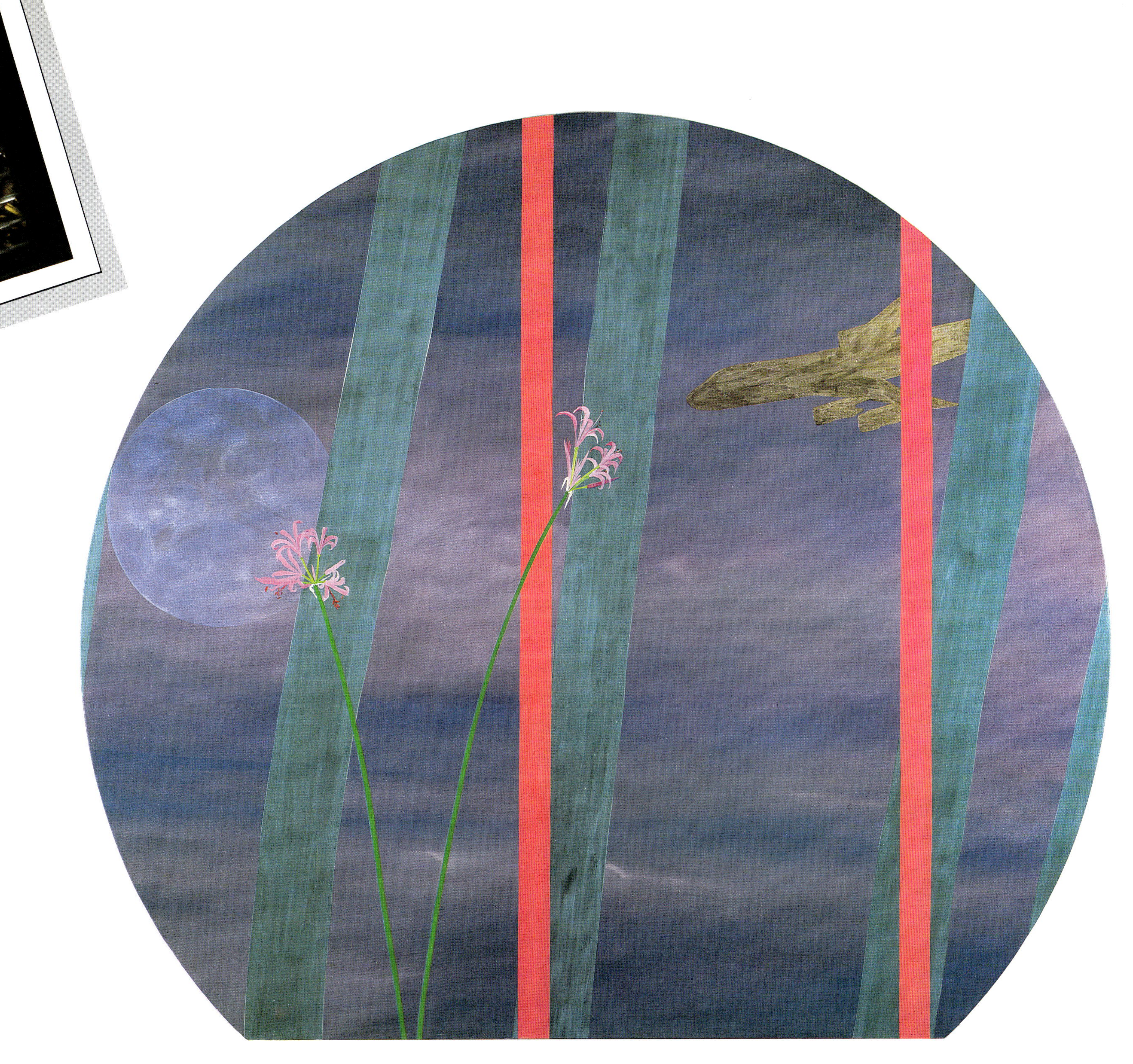

PLATE 54
HONG KONG
1985

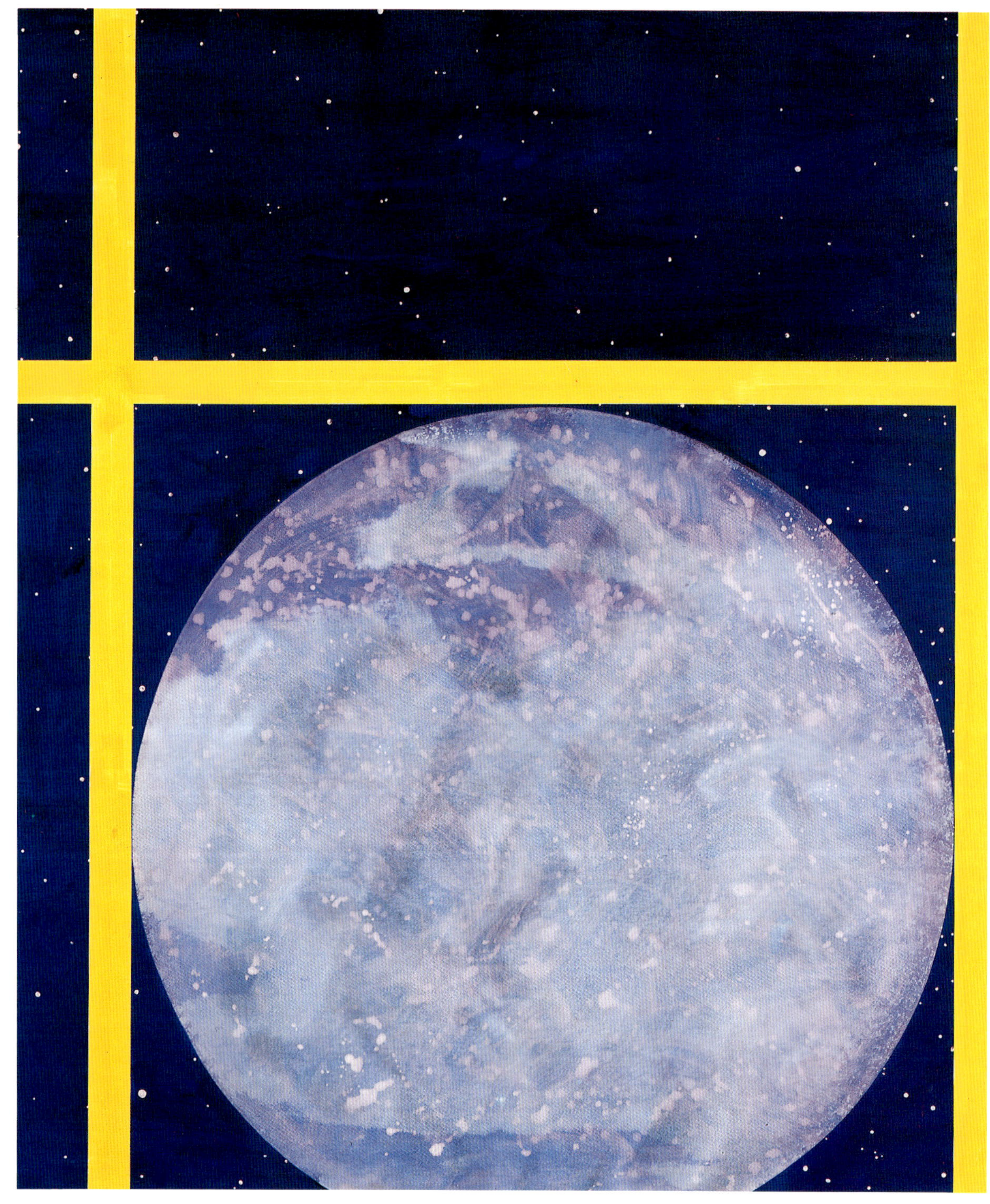

PLATE 55
FINLAND
1986

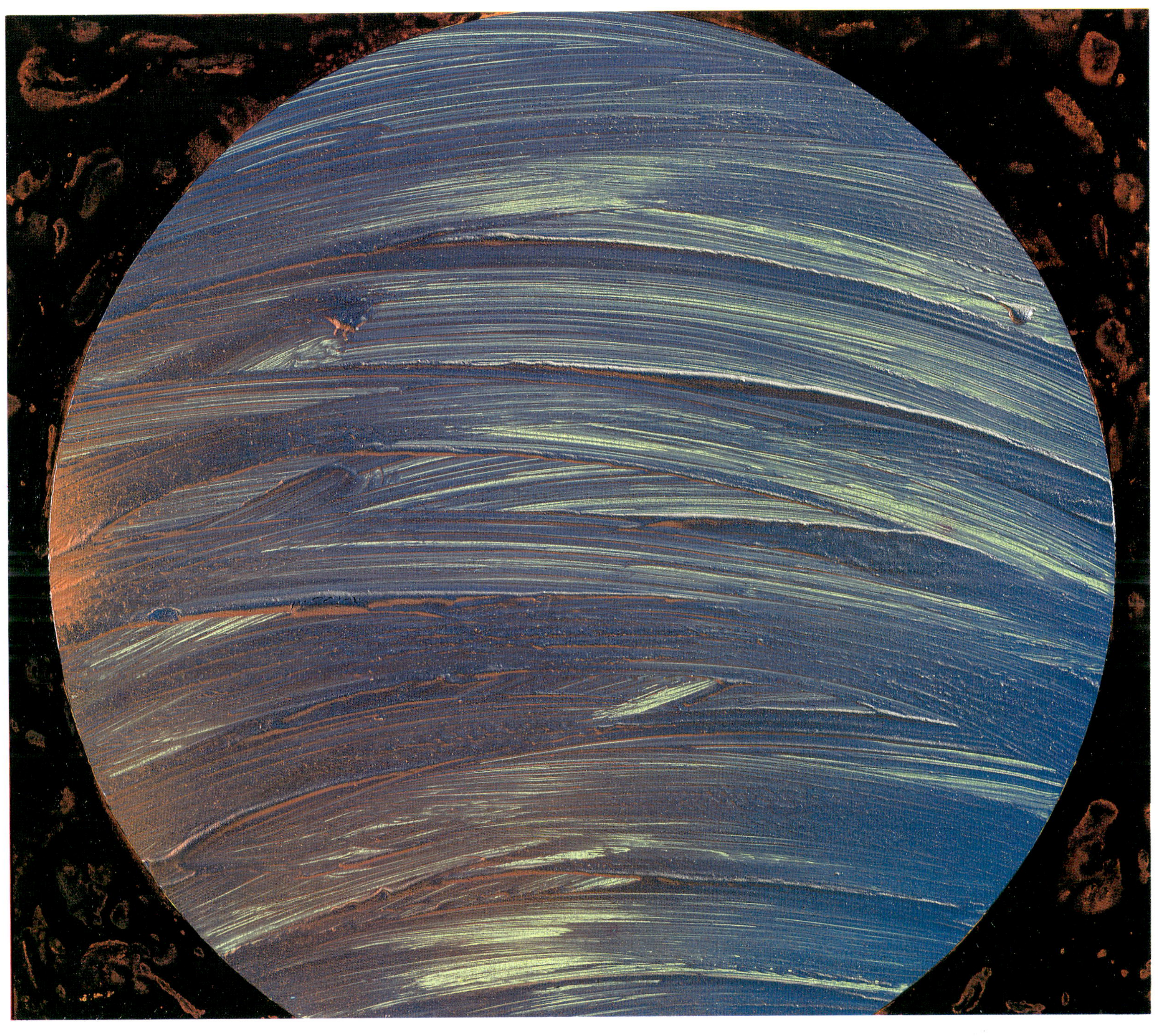

PLATE 56
MAKATO
1987

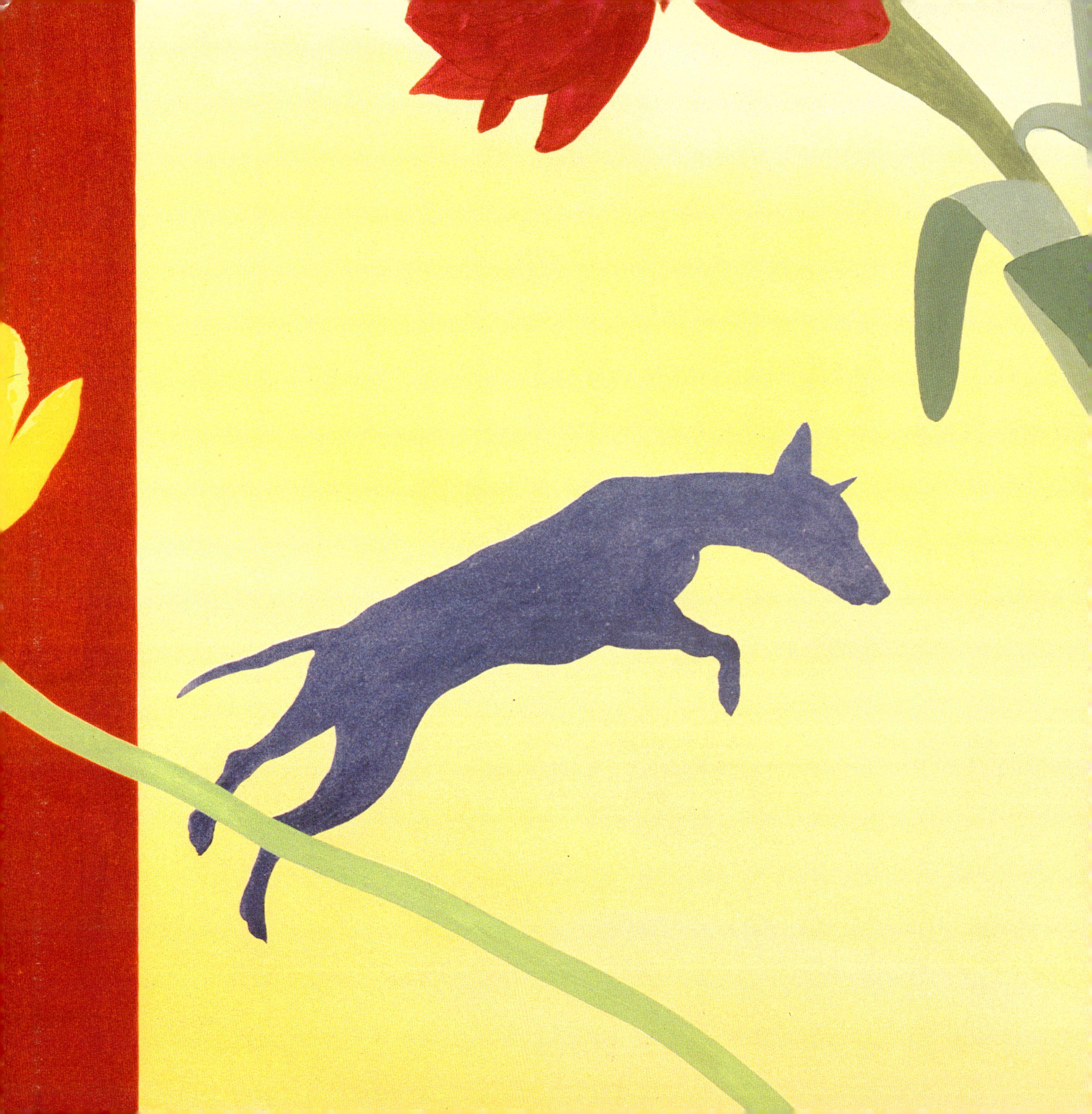

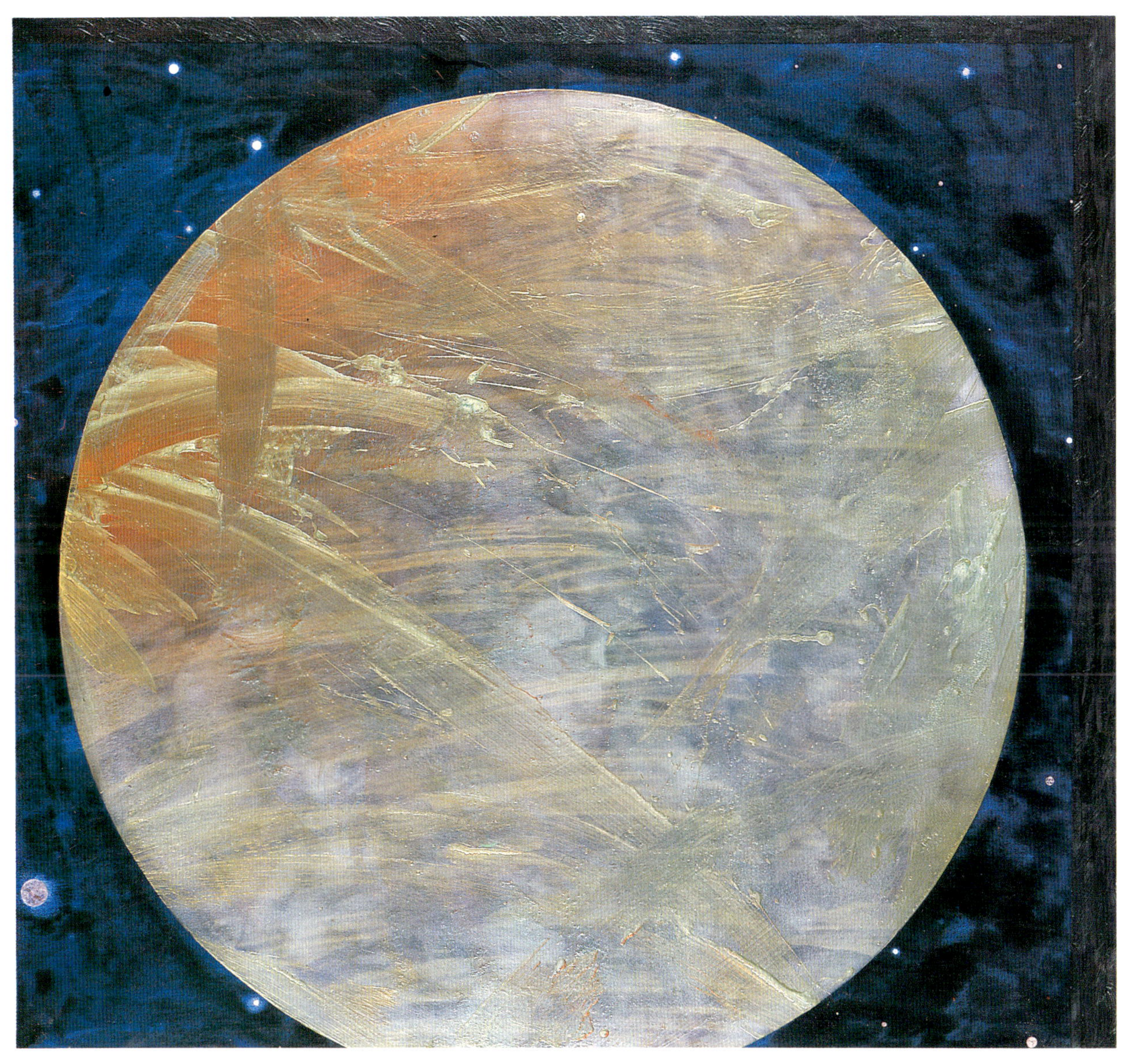

PLATE 58
AGRA
1987

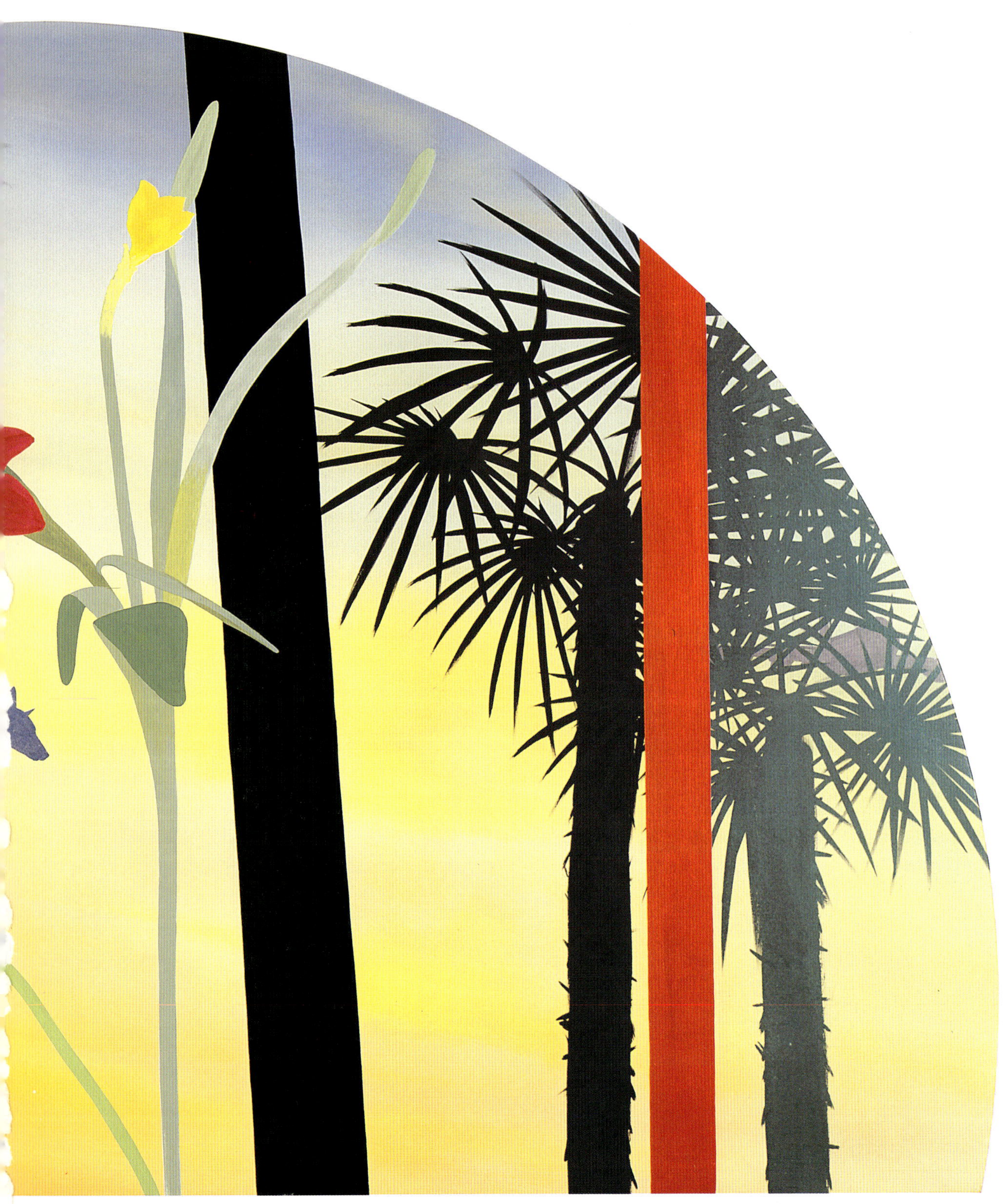

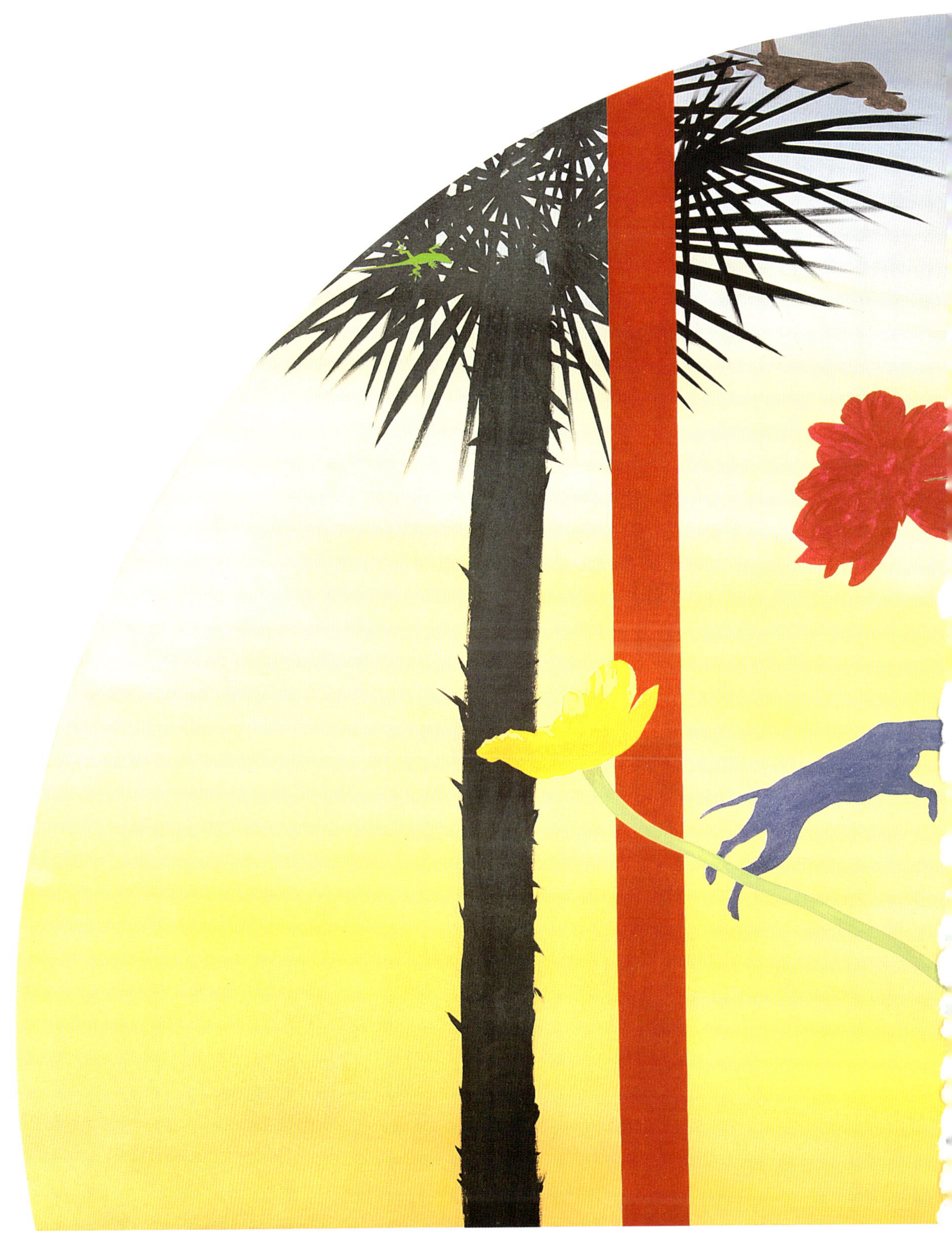

PLATE 57
MOSES
1986

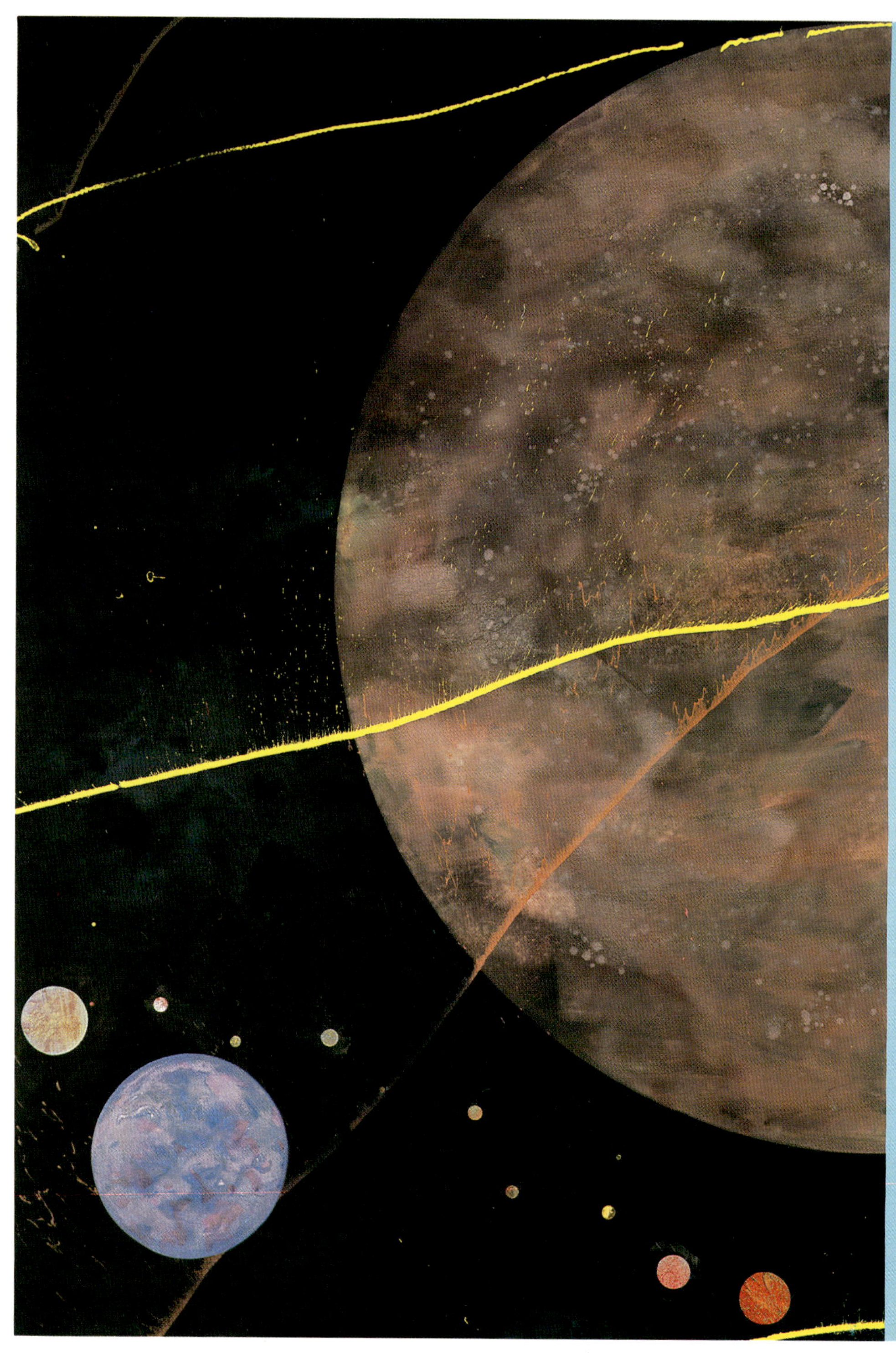

PLATE 59
ALTOONA
1987

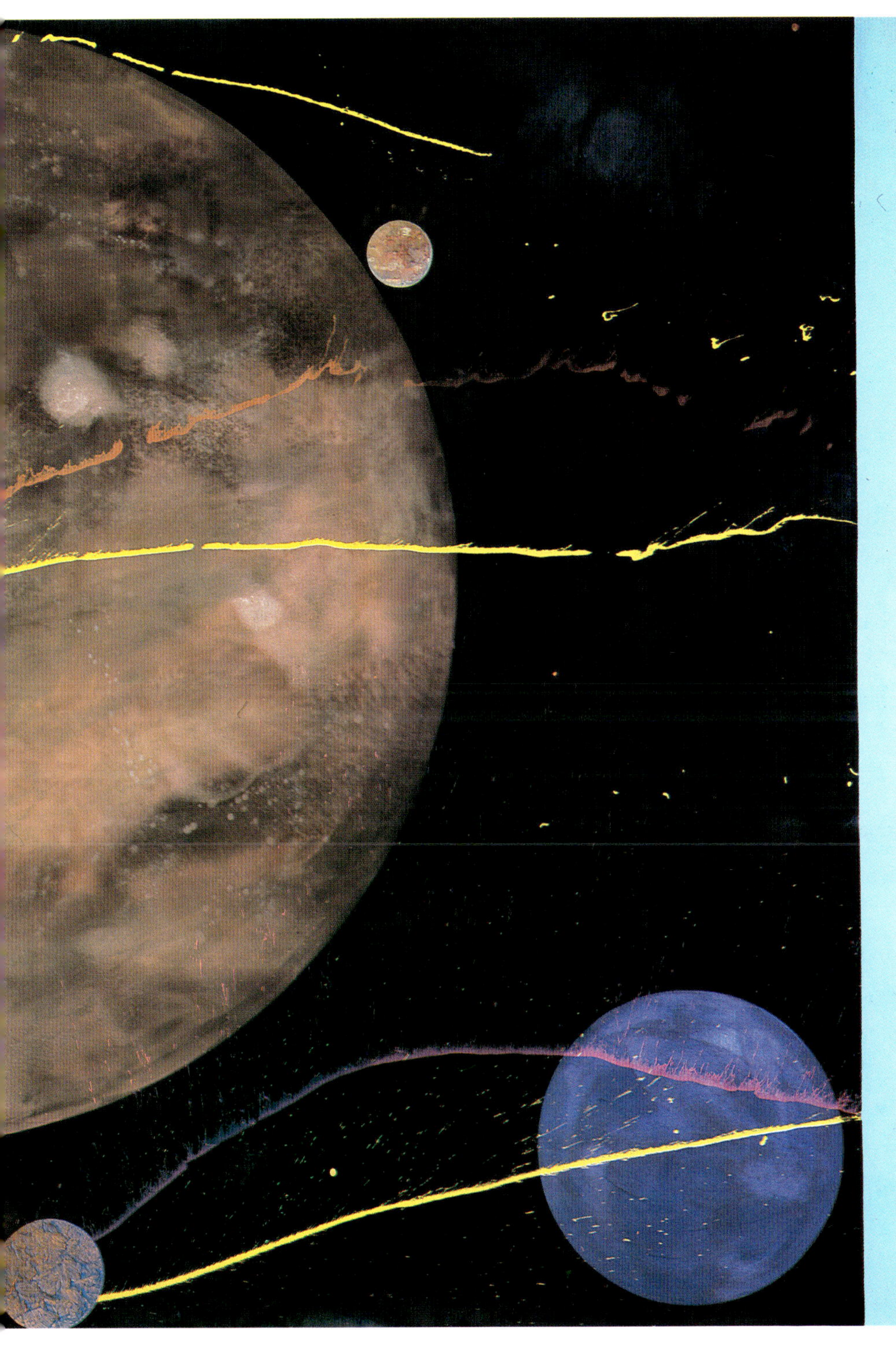

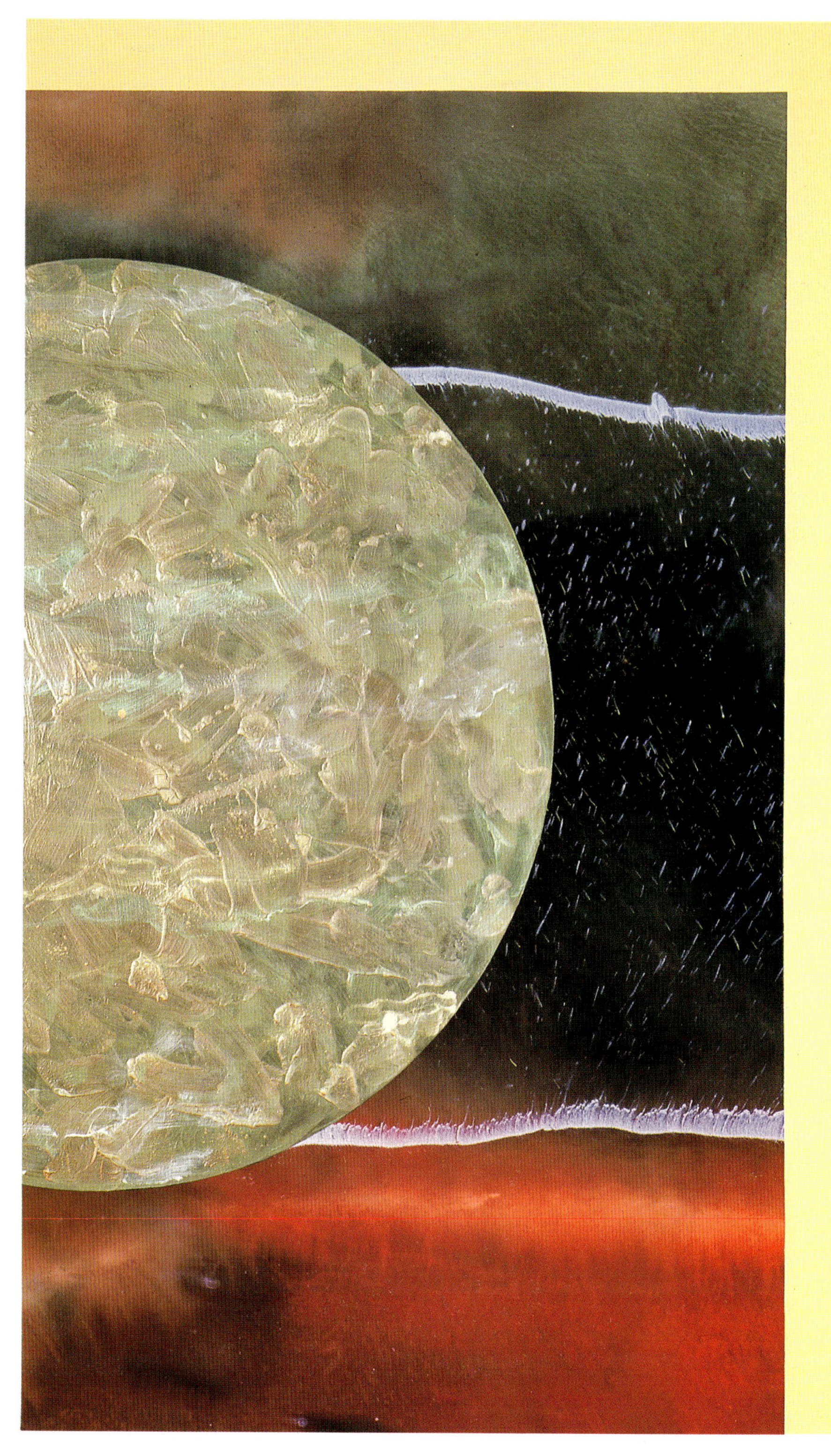

PLATE 60
PORTOLA
1987

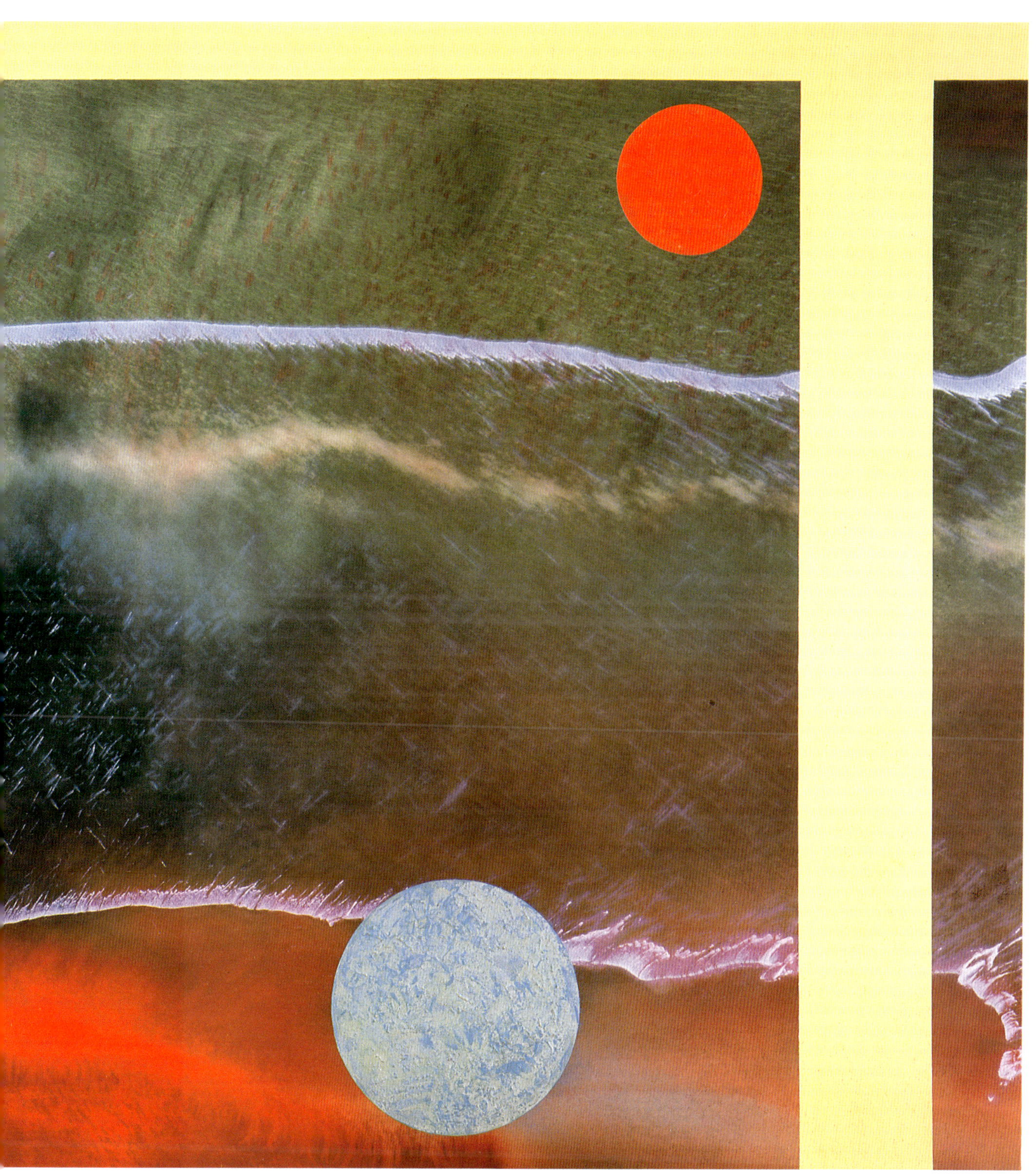

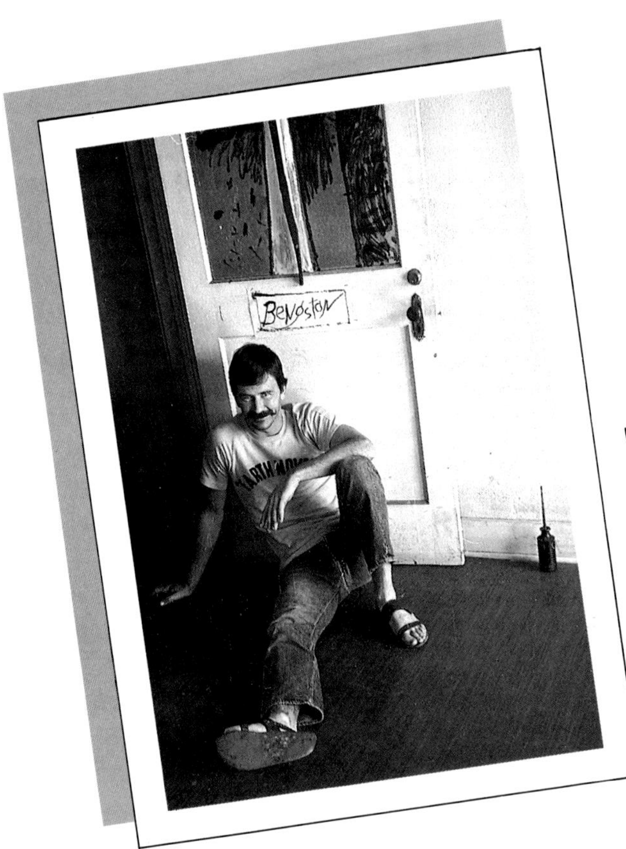

Billy Al Bengston,
Los Angeles studio, 1957.

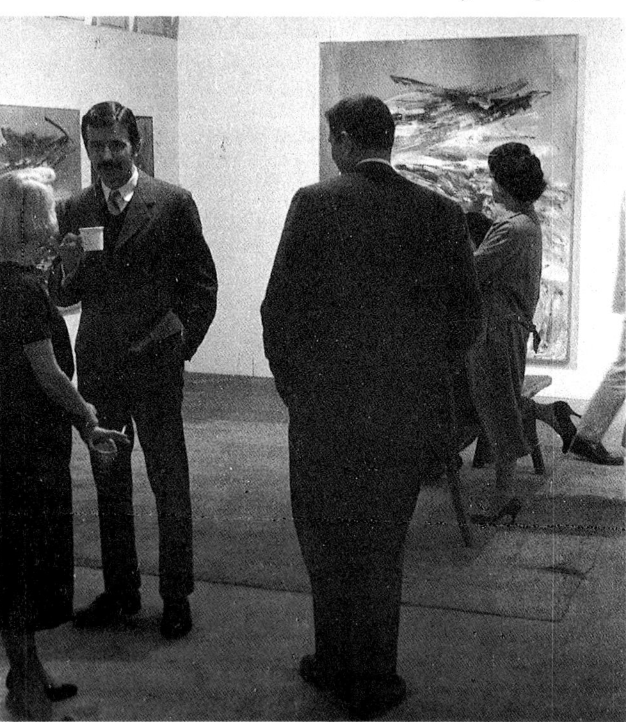

Billy Al Bengston at opening of first one-man
exhibition at Ferus Gallery, Los Angeles, 1958.

Chronology

1934 Born 7 June in Dodge City, Kansas.

1948 Family moves to Los Angeles.

1949–52 Attends Manual Arts High School, Los Angeles. Develops interest in gymnastics and art, particularly ceramics. Becomes an avid surfer.

1952 Briefly attends Los Angeles Junior College (now Los Angeles City College).

1953 Works as beach attendant at Doheny State Beach, California, where he befriends fellow surfer, and later artist, Kenneth ("Whitewater") Price.

1953–55 Reenrolls in Los Angeles Junior College. Studies ceramics with Bernard Kester and competes in gymnastics.

1955–56 Attends California College of Arts and Crafts, Oakland. Studies painting with Richard Diebenkorn, drawing with Sabro Hasegawa, and printmaking with Nathan Oliveira.

1956 Participates in first gallery exhibition, a group drawing show at the 6 Gallery, San Francisco, one of the city's early avant-garde cooperative galleries.

1956–57 Attends Los Angeles County Art Institute (now the Otis Art Institute of Parsons School of Design). Studies ceramics with Peter Voulkos.

Shifts attention from ceramics to painting.

1957 Establishes association with the Ferus Gallery, one of Los Angeles's first contemporary art galleries, founded by Edward Kienholz and Walter Hopps. Participates in opening group exhibition, *Objects on the New Landscape Demanding of the Eye*, which features abstract expressionist work by northern and southern California artists.

1958 First solo gallery exhibition, *Paintings Done in 1957 and 1958 by Bengston*, Ferus Gallery, Los Angeles. Exhibits at Ferus regularly until gallery closes in 1966.

Travels for six months through Europe.
While abroad creates numerous small
abstract collages. En route to Europe
visits New York City to see art.

1959–60   Completes numerous drawings and
paintings with single centralized image,
most often a valentine. Dracula (iris
image) also appears in work for the first
time in 1960.

1960   Moves studio permanently to Venice,
California, near beach. Shares studio
with Kenneth Price until 1962.

Begins to race motorcycles
competitively.

Travels to Europe with Robert Irwin for
one month.

Begins painting centralized image of
sergeant stripes on Masonite, using
industrial spray-painting technique.

1961   Completes series of oil paintings based
on motorcyle imagery, which is subsequently featured in an exhibition at
Ferus Gallery.

Instructor, Chouinard Art Institute, Los
Angeles.

1962   First solo exhibition, *Billy Al Bengston*, in
New York at Martha Jackson Gallery.
Exhibits paintings of sergeant stripes for
the first time.

Moves to present studio on Mildred
Avenue in Venice.

1962–63   Instructor in painting and drawing,
University of California, Los Angeles.

1965   Included in *VIII São Paulo Bienal*, Brazil.

Begins painting on dented aluminum.

1967   One of three artists to receive first
grants from the National Foundation for
the Arts (now the National Endowment
for the Arts).

Guest artist, University of Oklahoma,
Norman.

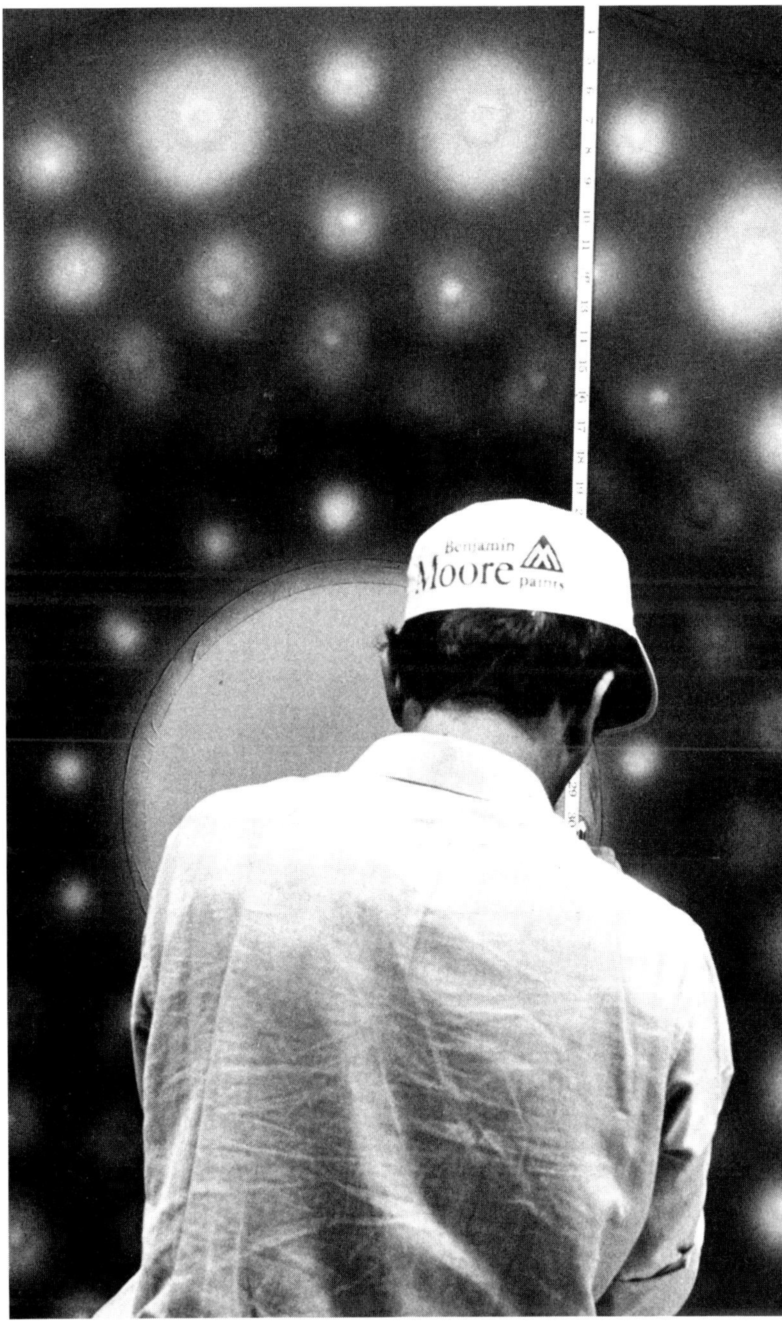

Billy Al Bengston,
Los Angeles studio, 1962.
Photo: Marvin Silver.

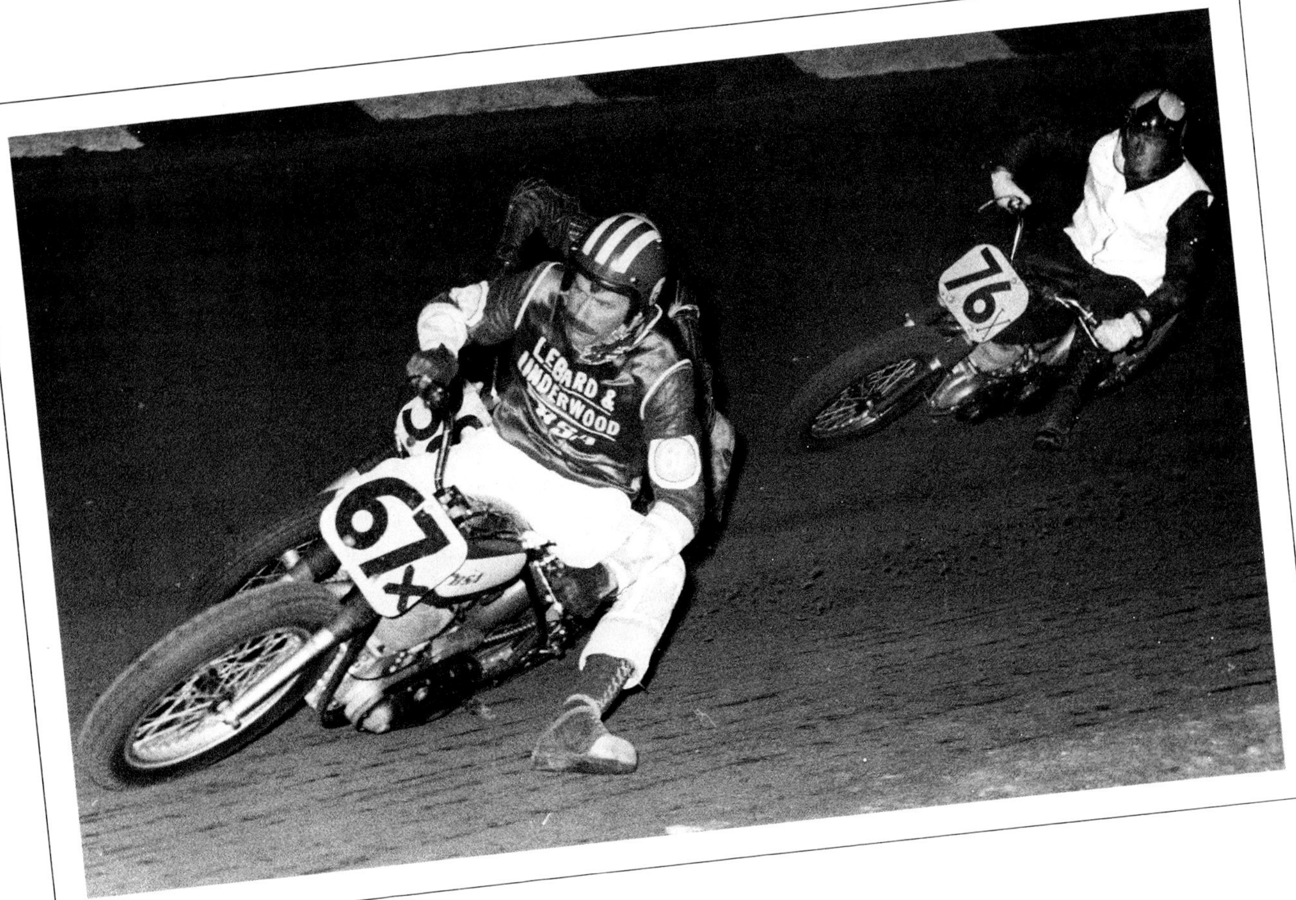

Billy Al Bengston,
Ascot Park night racing,
Los Angeles, 1967.
Photo: Walt Mahoney.

1968 First solo museum exhibition, *Billy Al Bengston*, opens at the Los Angeles County Museum of Art. Exhibition travels to Corcoran Gallery, Dupont Center, Washington D.C., and Vancouver Art Gallery.

Receives fellowship at Tamarind Lithography Workshop, Los Angeles; reintroduces the dracula motif into his work.

Collaborates with Edward Ruscha in publishing *Business Cards*, a small book illustrating the artists' designs for one another's business cards.

1969 Summer. Guest instructor, University of Colorado, Boulder.

1970 First solo exhibition in Europe, *Billy Al Bengston*, at Galeries Neuendorf, Hamburg and Cologne. Begins frequent travels to Baja California, Mexico. Begins scuba diving.

1971 Incorporates dracula as exclusive motif in work. Begins gallery association with Fredericka Hunter, at Contract Graphics, Houston, later to become the Texas Gallery.

Discovers Puerto Escondido, a remote and primitive bay town on the west coast of Mexico, to which he returns frequently.

1972 Travels to Europe for three months and has solo exhibition at Felicity Samuel Gallery, London. Begins to work regularly in watercolor.

1973 Meets James Corcoran, with whom he establishes gallery affiliation, first at Corcoran and Corcoran Gallery, Coral Gables, Florida, and then at James Corcoran Gallery, Los Angeles.

Guest instructor in ceramics, University of California, Irvine.

1974 — Travels to Hawaii for first time, visiting all of the islands.

Continues travel to Mexico and Baja peninsula, most often staying at Puerto Vallarta, Puerto Meija, and Puerto Escondido, where he completes numerous watercolors and begins to run regularly on beach.

1975 — Receives John Simon Guggenheim Memorial Foundation Fellowship for painting.

Invited by Everson Museum of Art, Syracuse, New York, to produce work in clay for 1976 ceramics exhibition featuring artists generally associated with other media. Produces set of dinnerware with dracula motif at Syracuse China Corporation.

Begins to swim regularly; continues wide-ranging travels.

1975–76 — Produces first suspended paintings and folding screens.

1976–77 — Travels to Puerto Meija and Puerto Escondido, Mexico, to work on watercolors. In 1977 commissions Zapotec Indian weaver Alberto Vasquez to weave blankets and textiles incorporating dracula imagery.

1978 — Visits Maui. Works on watercolors, swims, and trains for New York City marathon. Also competes in Maui Rough Water Channel Swim.

1978–82 — Creates decorative elements for cabinets, swimming pool, and balustrade in Carol and Roy Doumani residence, Venice, California, designed by artist Robert Graham.

1979 — Establishes second studio in Honolulu in which he very frequently works.

Travels to Japan with Charles Arnoldi and James Corcoran.

Makes first monotypes at Experimental Printmaking Workshop, San Francisco.

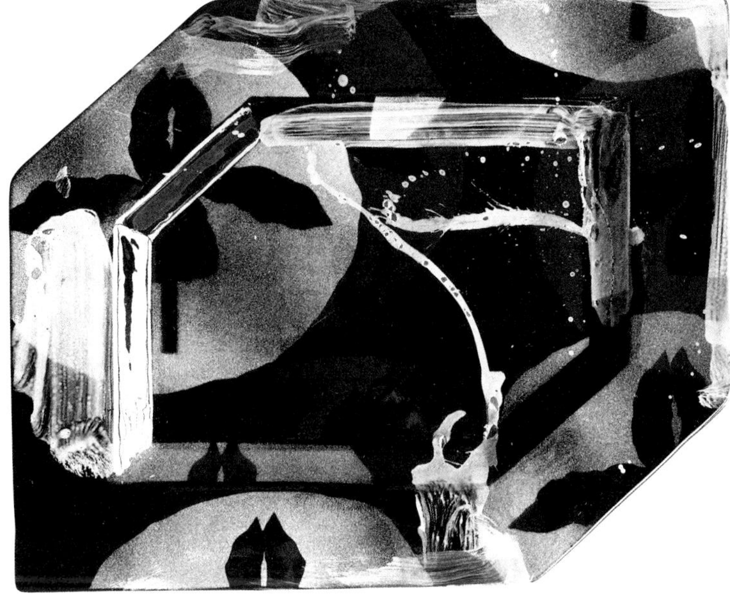

Billy Al Bengston, dinner plate from *Syracuse China*, 1975–76, flintware, 10½ × 12½″ (26.7 × 31.8 cm.).

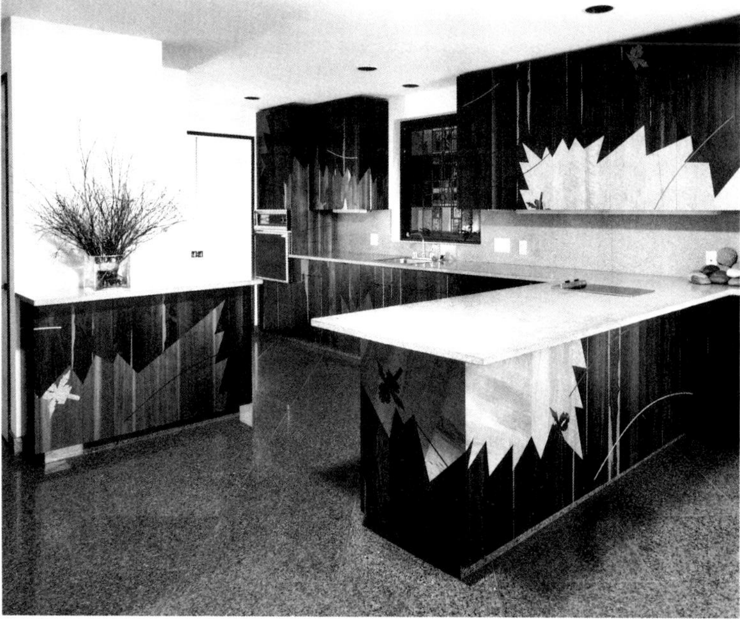

Cabinets designed by Billy Al Bengston for residence of Carol and Roy Doumani, Venice, California, 1978–82.

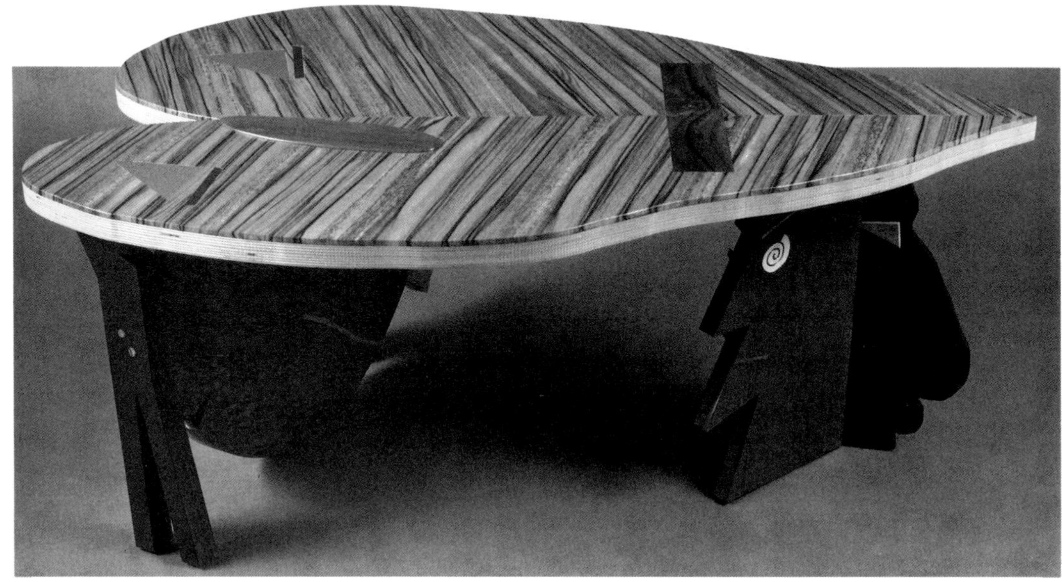

Billy Al Bengston, *Pilli Pua Variation*, 1983, various hardwoods, 18⅛ × 47¼ × 30″ (46.1 × 120.0 × 76.2 cm.).

1981 Major survey exhibition of watercolors, *Billy Al Bengston: Watercolors 1974–1980*, The Corcoran Gallery of Art, Washington, D.C.

Receives commission from California Arts Council, Art in Public Buildings Program. Completes suspended painting for State Office Building, Long Beach.

Establishes affiliation with Thomas Babeor Gallery, La Jolla, California.

1982 Hawaiian imagery—kahuna heads, sunsets, flowers, fish—begins to dominate work.

Begins collaboration with woodworkers Greg Erickson and Benno Spingler, designing furniture—primarily small tables—which incorporates Hawaiian imagery.

Invited by Tamarind Lithography Workshop, Albuquerque, New Mexico, to produce prints.

1984 With Charles Arnoldi, builds second studio complex in Venice.

1986 Begins painting large-scale canvases in which motif of moon dominates work.

Included in opening exhibition of The Museum of Contemporary Art, Los Angeles, *Individuals: A Selected History of Contemporary Art 1945–1986*.

1987 Represented in major survey exhibition of pop art, *Made in U.S.A.*, organized by University Art Museum, Berkeley, and circulated nationally.

Invited to work at Tamarind Lithography Workshop, Albuquerque, to produce prints.

Checklist of the Exhibition

In the listing of dimensions, height precedes width. The first measurements listed are in inches; centimeter measurements follow in parentheses. For works on paper, measurements indicate sheet size unless otherwise noted. To help identify untitled works, parenthetical descriptions are provided.

1. **Grace**, 1959 (Plate 1)
   oil on canvas
   49¾ × 42½" (126.4 × 108.0)
   Collection Betty Asher

2. **Count Dracula II**, 1960 (Plate 2)
   oil on canvas
   48 × 48" (121.9 × 121.9)
   Collection Newport Harbor Art Museum, Newport Beach, California; purchased by the Acquisition Committee with a matching grant from the National Endowment for the Arts

3. **Mr. Britt**, 1960 (Plate 3)
   lacquer and oil on Masonite
   48 × 48" (121.9 × 121.9)
   Collection Joan and Jack Quinn

4. **Stainless Bob Steel**, 1960 (Plate 4)
   enamel on Masonite
   48 × 48" (121.9 × 121.9)
   Collection Albright-Knox Art Gallery, Buffalo, New York; gift of Mr. and Mrs. David K. Anderson to The Martha Jackson Collection, 1978

5. **BSA**, 1961 (Plate 5)
   oil on canvas
   36 × 34" (91.4 × 86.4)
   Collection Newport Harbor Art Museum, Newport Beach, California; gift of Dr. and Mrs. Merle S. Glick [For exhibition in Houston, Oakland, and Los Angeles only.]

6. **Buster**, 1962 (Plate 6)
   lacquer and oil on Masonite
   60 × 60" (152.4 × 152.4)
   Collection La Jolla Museum of Contemporary Art, California

7. **Boris**, 1963 (Plate 7)
   oil, polymer, and lacquer on Masonite
   62½ × 48½" (158.8 × 123.2)
   Collection Joan and Jack Quinn

8. **Tubesteak**, 1965 (Plate 8)
   lacquer on Formica
   37 × 28" (94.0 × 71.1)
   Courtesy the artist; James Corcoran Gallery, Los Angeles; Texas Gallery, Houston; Thomas Babeor Gallery, La Jolla, California

9. **Holy Smoke**, 1966 (Plate 9)
   lacquer and polyurethane on aluminum
   48 × 48" (121.9 × 121.9)
   Collection Laura Lee Stearns

10. **Hatari**, 1968 (Plate 10)
    polyester resin and lacquer on aluminum
    87 × 77" (221.0 × 195.6)
    Collection Los Angeles County Museum of Art; gift of the Kleiner Foundation

11. **Paradise Canyon**, 1969 (Plate 11)
    lacquer and polyurethane on aluminum
    48 × 44" (121.9 × 111.8)
    Collection Laura-Lee Woods

12. **Blood Alley**, 1970 (Plate 12)
    lacquer and polyester resin on aluminum
    23 × 22" (58.4 × 55.9)
    Collection Charles and Katie Arnoldi

13. **El Cortez Dracula**, 1971 (Plate 13)
    acrylic on canvas
    72 × 72" (182.9 × 182.9)
    Collection Laila and Thurston Twigg-Smith

14. **Bahia San Luis Gonzaga Dracula**, 1972 (Plate 14)
    acrylic on canvas
    114 × 114" (289.6 × 289.6)
    Courtesy the artist; James Corcoran Gallery, Los Angeles; Texas Gallery, Houston; Thomas Babeor Gallery, La Jolla, California

15. **Flor de Acapulco Dracula**, 1972
    acrylic on canvas
    48 × 48" (121.9 × 121.9)
    Courtesy the artist; James Corcoran Gallery, Los Angeles; Texas Gallery, Houston; Thomas Babeor Gallery, La Jolla, California

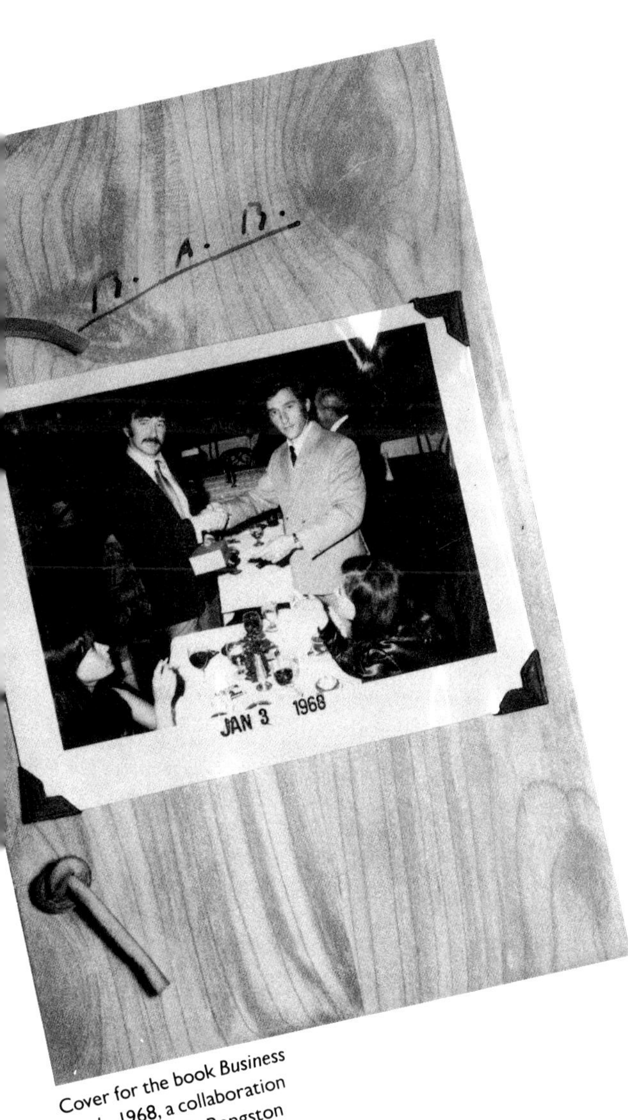

Cover for the book *Business Cards*, 1968, a collaboration between Billy Al Bengston and Edward Ruscha documenting the artists' designs of one another's business cards.

16. **Jermyn Dracula**, 1972 (PLATE 15)
acrylic on canvas
48 × 48" (121.9 × 121.9)
Collection Robert and Honey Dootson

17. **Untitled (London)**, 1972 (PLATE 16)
watercolor on paper
8½ × 8½" (21.6 × 21.6)
Collection Edwin Janss

18. **Untitled (London)**, 1972
watercolor on paper
8½ × 8½" (21.6 × 21.6)
Collection Edwin Janss

19. **Untitled (Venice)**, 1972
watercolor on paper
13 × 13" (33.0 × 33.0)
Collection Mr. and Mrs. John Wilson Kelsey

20. **Untitled (Venice)**, 1972 (PLATE 17)
watercolor on paper
25¾ × 26" (65.4 × 66.0)
Collection Fredericka Hunter

21. **Untitled (Venice)**, 1973 (PLATE 18)
watercolor on paper
25 × 25" (63.5 × 63.5)
Collection The Capital Group, Inc., Los Angeles

22. **El Limona Draculas**, 1974 (PLATE 19)
acrylic on canvas
three-panel screen; each panel 70 × 40"
(177.8 × 101.6)
Collection Mr. and Mrs. Fayez Sarofim

23. **Garropa de Astillero Draculas**, 1974 (PLATE 21)
acrylic on canvas
120 × 192" (304.8 × 487.7)
Courtesy the artist; James Corcoran Gallery, Los
Angeles; Texas Gallery, Houston; Thomas Babeor
Gallery, La Jolla, California

24. **Honolulu Dracula**, 1974 (PLATE 20)
acrylic on canvas
60 × 60" (152.4 × 152.4)
Courtesy the artist; James Corcoran Gallery, Los
Angeles; Texas Gallery, Houston; Thomas Babeor
Gallery, La Jolla, California

25. **Playa Estrella Dracula**, 1974
acrylic on canvas
60 × 60" (152.4 × 152.4)
Courtesy the artist; James Corcoran Gallery, Los
Angeles; Texas Gallery, Houston; Thomas Babeor
Gallery, La Jolla, California

26. **Untitled (Venice)**, 1974 (PLATE 22)
watercolor on paper
three sheets; each sheet 22½ × 30½" (57.2 × 77.5)
Collection Fan and Peter Morris
(For exhibition in Houston only.)

27. **Alaria Valida Draculas**, 1975 (PLATES 23 AND 24)
acrylic on muslin
186 × 42" (472.4 × 106.7)
Courtesy the artist; James Corcoran Gallery, Los
Angeles; Texas Gallery, Houston; Thomas Babeor
Gallery, La Jolla, California

28. **Bossea Draculas**, 1975 (PLATES 23 AND 24)
acrylic on muslin
five panels; each panel 41 × 19" (104.1 × 48.3)
Courtesy the artist; James Corcoran Gallery, Los
Angeles; Texas Gallery, Houston; Thomas Babeor
Gallery, La Jolla, California

29. **Delesseria Decipiens Draculas**, 1975 (PLATES 23
AND 24)
acrylic on muslin
187 × 43" (475.0 × 109.2)
Courtesy the artist; James Corcoran Gallery, Los
Angeles; Texas Gallery, Houston; Thomas Babeor
Gallery, La Jolla, California

30. **Hymenena Flabelligra Draculas**, 1975 (PLATES 23
AND 24)
acrylic on canvas
128 × 94" (325.1 × 238.8)
Courtesy the artist; James Corcoran Gallery, Los
Angeles; Texas Gallery, Houston; Thomas Babeor
Gallery, La Jolla, California

31. **Iridophycus Draculas**, 1975 (PLATES 23 AND 24)
acrylic on canvas
188 × 35" (477.5 × 88.9)
Courtesy the artist; James Corcoran Gallery, Los
Angeles; Texas Gallery, Houston; Thomas Babeor
Gallery, La Jolla, California

32. **China Point Draculas**, 1976 (PLATE 25)
acrylic on canvas
four panels; each panel 80 × 32" (203.2 × 81.3)
Collection Don and Aimee McCrory

33. **Eagle Reef Draculas**, 1976 (PLATE 26)
acrylic on canvas
five-panel screen; overall 78 × 160" (198.1 × 406.4)
Collection Torrey Enterprise, La Jolla, California

34. **Iron Bound Cove Draculas**, 1976 (PLATE 27)
acrylic on canvas
four-panel screen; each panel 80 × 32" (203.2 × 81.3)
Collection Mr. and Mrs. E. Rudge Allen

35. **Untitled (Puerto Meija)**, 1976
watercolor on paper
four sheets; each sheet 14⅛ × 10¼" (35.9 × 26.0)
Courtesy the artist; James Corcoran Gallery, Los
Angeles; Texas Gallery, Houston; Thomas Babeor
Gallery, La Jolla, California

36. **Antaras Draculas**, 1977 (PLATE 28)
acrylic on canvas
76¼ × 68" (193.7 × 172.7)
Collection William F. Stern

37. **Capella Draculas**, 1977 (PLATE 29)
acrylic on canvas
60 × 56¼" (152.4 × 142.9)
Collection Virginia Sherwin

38. **Chokladkransar Draculas**, 1977 (PLATE 30)
acrylic on canvas
90 × 80" (228.6 × 203.2)
Collection Iris and Allen Mink

39. **Untitled (Puerto Escondido)**, 1977 (PLATE 32)
watercolor on paper
14⅛ × 10¼" (35.9 × 26.0)
Collection Norman Lear

40. **Untitled (Puerto Escondido)**, 1977 (PLATE 33)
watercolor on paper
10¼ × 14⅛" (26.0 × 35.9)
Collection Samantha Eggar

41. **Brysselkex Draculas**, 1978
acrylic on canvas
44 × 44″ (111.8 × 111.8)
Collection Dr. and Mrs. Michael D. Dake

42. **Trevapplinger Draculas**, 1978 (Plate 31)
acrylic on canvas
90 × 80″ (228.6 × 203.2)
Collection Dona S. and Dwight M. Kendall

43. **Untitled (Lahaina)**, 1978 (Plate 36)
watercolor on paper
16 × 16¼″ (40.6 × 41.3)
Collection Dr. and Mrs. William C. Janss, Jr.

44. **Untitled (Lahaina)**, 1978
watercolor on paper
29¾ × 22¾″ (75.6 × 57.8)
Collection John and Susie Kalil

45. **Untitled (Lahaina)**, 1978 (Plate 37)
watercolor on paper
20¼ × 17¼″ (51.4 × 43.8)
Collection Mr. and Mrs. Nathan M. Avery

46. **Untitled (Puerto Escondido)**, 1978 (Plate 34)
watercolor on paper
9⅞ × 10″ (25.1 × 25.4)
Collection Mary Ralph Lowe

47. **Untitled (Puerto Escondido)**, 1978
watercolor on paper
10⅛ × 9⅞″ (25.7 × 25.1)
Collection Mary Ralph Lowe

48. **Untitled (Puerto Escondido)**, 1978 (Plate 35)
watercolor on paper
8⅛ × 8⅛″ (20.7 × 20.7)
Collection Mr. and Mrs. Theodore S. Hochstim

49. **Aloha Draculas**, 1979 (Plate 38)
acrylic on canvas
60¼ × 56″ (153.0 × 142.2)
The Menil Collection, Houston

50. **Nakookoo Draculas**, 1979 (Plate 39)
acrylic on canvas
80 × 76″ (203.2 × 193.0)
Collection Sondra and Marvin Smalley

51. **Untitled (Honolulu)**, 1979
watercolor on paper
22¾ × 29¾″ (57.8 × 75.6)
Collection Mr. and Mrs. Philip C. Keevil

52. **Ehukai Draculas**, 1981 (Plate 40)
acrylic on canvas
76 × 60″ (193.0 × 152.4)
Courtesy the artist; James Corcoran Gallery, Los
Angeles; Texas Gallery, Houston; Thomas Babeor
Gallery, La Jolla, California

53. **Kaona Draculas**, 1981 (Plate 41)
acrylic on canvas
96 × 80″ (243.8 × 203.2)
Courtesy James Corcoran Gallery, Los Angeles

54. **Untitled (Honolulu)**, 1981 (Plate 42)
watercolor collage
56 × 42¼″ (142.2 × 107.3)
Private collection

55. **Untitled (Honolulu)**, 1981 (Plate 43)
watercolor collage
30¼ × 50″ (76.8 × 127.0)
Collection Helen Runnells

56. **Kahuna**, 1982
watercolor collage
41½ × 29¼″ (105.4 × 74.3)
Courtesy the artist; James Corcoran Gallery, Los
Angeles; Texas Gallery, Houston; Thomas Babeor
Gallery, La Jolla, California

57. **Kipuka**, 1982 (Plate 45)
acrylic on canvas
42 × 48″ (106.7 × 121.9)
Collection Leopold and Pamela Wyler

58. **Pa'Pepa**, 1982 (Plate 44)
watercolor collage
17 × 22″ (43.2 × 55.9)
Collection Carl and Elaine Smith

59. **Ike Ole Ia Po**, 1983 (Plate 46)
acrylic on canvas
72 × 66″ (182.9 × 167.6)
Courtesy the artist; James Corcoran Gallery, Los
Angeles; Texas Gallery, Houston; Thomas Babeor
Gallery, La Jolla, California

60. **Ka'ao**, 1983 (Plate 47)
watercolor collage
29¾ × 50″ (75.6 × 127.0)
Collection Jean Edmonson

61. **Ka'ao**, 1983
watercolor collage
29 × 67″ (73.7 × 170.2)
Robert H. Cowgill Collection

62. **Kaukolu Hana Paewaewa**, 1983 (Plate 49)
acrylic on canvas
72 × 198″ (182.9 × 502.9)
Collection Laila and Thurston Twigg-Smith
(For exhibition in Honolulu only.)

63. **Nui Ipu Poo**, 1983 (Plate 48)
acrylic on canvas
80 × 76″ (203.2 × 193.0)
Collection The Oakland Museum; Timken Fund
Purchase

64. **Popoki A Okole**, 1983 (Plate 50)
acrylic on canvas
56½ × 44″ (143.5 × 111.8)
Collection Mr. and Mrs. Roy S. O'Connor

65. **Ka'ao**, 1984 (Plate 51)
watercolor collage
59½ × 39″ (151.1 × 99.1)
Courtesy the artist; James Corcoran Gallery, Los
Angeles; Texas Gallery, Houston; Thomas Babeor
Gallery, La Jolla, California

66. **Kipu Ahiahi**, 1984
acrylic on canvas
60 × 144½″ (152.4 × 367.0)
Frederick R. Weisman Collection
˙(For exhibition in Houston, Oakland, and Los Angeles
only.)

67. **Obake Madness**, 1984 (PLATE 52)
acrylic on canvas
48 × 120″ (121.9 × 304.8)
Courtesy the artist; James Corcoran Gallery, Los
Angeles; Texas Gallery, Houston; Thomas Babeor
Gallery, La Jolla, California

68. **October Watercolor**, 1984 (PLATE 53)
watercolor on paper
40 × 30″ (101.6 × 76.2)
Courtesy the artist; James Corcoran Gallery, Los
Angeles; Texas Gallery, Houston; Thomas Babeor
Gallery, La Jolla, California

69. **Hong Kong**, 1985 (PLATE 54)
acrylic on canvas
89 × 108″ (226.1 × 274.3)
Courtesy the artist; James Corcoran Gallery, Los
Angeles; Texas Gallery, Houston; Thomas Babeor
Gallery, La Jolla, California

70. **Finland**, 1986 (PLATE 55)
acrylic on canvas
84 × 72″ (213.4 × 182.9)
Courtesy the artist; James Corcoran Gallery, Los
Angeles; Texas Gallery, Houston; Thomas Babeor
Gallery, La Jolla, California

71. **May Watercolor**, 1986
watercolor on paper
30 × 23″ (76.2 × 58.4)
Courtesy the artist; James Corcoran Gallery, Los
Angeles; Texas Gallery, Houston; Thomas Babeor
Gallery, La Jolla, California

72. **Moses**, 1986 (PLATE 57)
acrylic on canvas
88 × 145″ (223.5 × 368.3)
Courtesy the artist; James Corcoran Gallery, Los
Angeles; Texas Gallery, Houston; Thomas Babeor
Gallery, La Jolla, California

73. **Agra**, 1987 (PLATE 58)
acrylic on canvas
44 × 48″ (111.8 × 121.9)
Courtesy the artist; James Corcoran Gallery, Los
Angeles; Texas Gallery, Houston; Thomas Babeor
Gallery, La Jolla, California

74. **Altoona**, 1987 (PLATE 59)
acrylic on canvas
116 × 172″ (294.6 × 436.9)
Courtesy the artist; James Corcoran Gallery, Los
Angeles; Texas Gallery, Houston; Thomas Babeor
Gallery, La Jolla, California

75. **Makato**, 1987 (PLATE 56)
acrylic on canvas
36 × 42″ (91.4 × 106.7)
Collection Joan and Jack Quinn

76. **Portola**, 1987 (PLATE 60)
acrylic on canvas
86 × 136″ (218.4 × 345.4)
Collection Dr. and Mrs. William C. Janss, Jr.

Exhibition of work by Billy Al Bengston, John Berggruen Gallery, San Francisco, 1974.

Robert Graham, Billy Al Bengston, and Jack Quinn (left to right) at Bengston's 50th birthday party, 1984. Photo: Ann Kresl.

Installation of painting by Billy Al Bengston, Everson Museum of Art, Syracuse, New York, 1976.

Selected One-Person Exhibitions

Compiled by Barbara Bowman

*An * indicates that we were unable to locate documentation for the exhibition. A catalog is defined as any publication that includes a checklist of the exhibition.*

1958 Ferus Gallery, Los Angeles. *Paintings Done in 1957 and 1958 by Bengston*. 3–29 March 1958.

1960 Ferus Gallery, Los Angeles. *Bengston*. 15 February–12 March 1960.

1961 Ferus Gallery, Los Angeles. *An Exhibition of Recent Work by Billy Al Bengston*. 13 November–2 December 1961.

1962 Martha Jackson Gallery, New York. *Billy Al Bengston*. 1–26 May 1962.

Ferus Gallery, Los Angeles. *Billy Al Bengston*. 12 November–9 December 1962.

1968 San Francisco Museum of Art (now San Francisco Museum of Modern Art). *Motel Dracula*. 1 September–2 October 1968.

Los Angeles County Museum of Art. *Billy Al Bengston*. 26 November 1968–12 January 1969. Catalog published, essay by James Monte. Traveled to: Corcoran Gallery-Dupont Center, Washington, D.C., 4 March–6 April 1969; Vancouver Art Gallery, British Columbia, 27 May–22 June 1969.

1969 Pasadena Art Museum (now Norton Simon Museum), California. *Motel Dracula*. 12 March–20 April 1969.

Utah Museum of Fine Arts, Salt Lake City. *Art Works by Billy Al Bengston*. 9 November–7 December 1969.

1970 Santa Barbara Museum of Art, California. *Billy Al Bengston: Selected Paintings*. 3 February–15 March 1970.

Mizuno Gallery, Los Angeles. 1–31 March 1970.

* Galerie Neuendorf, Hamburg, West Germany. 15 April–15 May 1970.

Galerie Neuendorf, Cologne, West Germany. *Billy Al Bengston*. 11 September–10 October 1970.

1971 Margo Leavin Gallery, Los Angeles. *Exposition Especial: Billy Al Bengston*. April 1971.

La Jolla Museum of Art (now La Jolla Museum of Contemporary Art), California. *Prints and Multiple Dentos by Billy Al Bengston*. 22 September–3 November 1971.

Contract Graphics (now Texas Gallery), Houston. *Billy Al Bengston: Prints and Aluminum Drawings*. 12 October–12 November 1971.

* Galerie Neuendorf, Cologne, West Germany. November 1971.

1972 Felicity Samuel Gallery, London. *Billy Al Bengston*. 9 October–3 November 1972.

* Galerie Neuendorf, Hamburg, West Germany. October 1972.

1973 Corcoran and Corcoran Gallery, Coral Gables, Florida. *Billy Al Bengston: Recent Paintings and Dentos*. 4–28 January 1973.

Nicholas Wilder Gallery, Los Angeles. *All New Paintings by Billy Al Bengston*. 20 January–10 February 1973.

Pollock Galleries, Meadows School of the Arts, Southern Methodist University, Dallas. *Recent Works by Billy Al Bengston*. 3 February–4 March 1973.

Contemporary Arts Museum, Houston. *Billy Al Bengston*. 23 February–15 April 1973.

Nicholas Wilder Gallery, Los Angeles. *Recent Watercolors of Billy Al Bengston*. 26 June–28 July 1973.

Texas Gallery, Houston. 6 October–6 November 1973.

1974 John Berggruen Gallery, San Francisco. *Billy Al Bengston: Paintings and Watercolors*. 21 February–23 March 1974.

The Jared Sable Gallery, Toronto. *Billy Al Bengston*. 1–15 June 1974.

Texas Gallery, Houston. *Billy Al Bengston: New Paintings and Watercolors*. 20 August–7 September 1974.

Nicholas Wilder Gallery, Los Angeles. *Billy Al Bengston: New Paintings*. 15 October–3 November 1974.

1975 Pyramid Galleries Ltd., Washington, D.C. *Billy Al Bengston*. 14 January–10 February 1975.

Seder/Creigh Gallery, Coronado, California. *Billy Al Bengston: Paintings and Watercolors*. 15 February–22 March 1975.

La Tortue Galerie (now Tortue Gallery), Santa Monica, California. *Billy Al Bengston: Paintings, Sculptures, and Multiples of the '60's*. 24 May–5 July 1975.

Dootson-Calderhead Gallery, Seattle, Washington. 11 September–11 October 1975.

1976 Texas Gallery, Houston. *Billy Al Bengston: New Paintings and Watercolors*. 26 January–21 February 1976.

Dobrick Gallery, Chicago. *Watercolors by Billy Al Bengston*. 10 September–8 October 1976.

Portland Center for the Visual Arts, Oregon. 5 November–11 December 1976.

1977 Gallery of Visual Arts, University of Montana, Missoula. *Billy Al Bengston: Recent Paintings*. 2–18 March 1977.

James Corcoran Gallery, Los Angeles. *Billy Al Bengston: Puerto Escondido, Watercolor Suite 1977*. 17 May–18 June 1977.

   Catalog published.

Texas Gallery, Houston. *Billy Al Bengston: New Screen Paintings*. 19 June–21 July 1977.

1978 James Corcoran Gallery, Los Angeles. *Billy Al Bengston: New Paintings*. 13 January–11 February 1978

Security Pacific Bank (now Gallery at the Plaza, Security Pacific National Bank), Los Angeles. *Billy Al Bengston: Paintings of the Seventies*. 27 February–16 April 1978.

   Catalog published, essay by Fredericka Hunter.

John Berggruen Gallery, San Francisco. *Billy Al Bengston: Paintings and Watercolors*. 8 March–8 April 1978.

Sarah Campbell Blaffer Gallery, University of Houston, Texas. *Recent Works by Billy Al Bengston*. 17 June–23 July 1978.

Texas Gallery, Houston. *Billy Al Bengston: Watercolors and Paintings*. 31 October–18 November 1978.

James Corcoran Gallery, Los Angeles. 8 December 1978–1 January 1979.

1979 * Conejo Valley Art Museum, Thousand Oaks, California. *Billy Al Bengston: 20 Years on Paper*. 21 January–4 March 1979.

Thomas Segal Gallery, Boston. *Billy Al Bengston*. 31 March–25 April 1979.

Acquavella Contemporary Art, Inc., New York. *Billy Al Bengston: Paintings*. 14 September–20 October 1979.

Cantor/Lemberg Gallery, Birmingham, Michigan. *Billy Al Bengston: Current Acrylic and Watercolor Paintings*. 16 October–10 November 1979.

Mizuno Gallery, Los Angeles. 14 November–15 December 1979.

Texas Gallery, Houston. *Billy Al Bengston: New Paintings and Watercolors*. 26 November–29 December 1979.

1980 James Corcoran Gallery, Los Angeles. *Billy Al Bengston: Current Watercolors*. 18 March–10 April 1980.

Malibu Art & Design, California. *Billy Al Bengston Watercolors*. 4 May–8 June 1980.

Honolulu Academy of Arts, Hawaii. *Watercolors by Billy Al Bengston*. 12 July–24 August 1980.

1981 The Corcoran Gallery of Art, Washington, D.C. *Billy Al Bengston: Watercolors 1974-1980*. 31 January–29 March 1981.

   Catalog published, essay by Jane Livingston.

Acquavella Contemporary Art, Inc., New York. *Billy Al Bengston: Paintings*. 5–31 March 1981.

San Diego State University, California. *A Decade of Billy Al Bengston: The Seventies*. 25 April–23 May 1981.

   Catalog published, essay by Jeff Perrone.

Thomas Babeor Gallery, La Jolla, California. *Billy Al Bengston*. 25 April–3 June 1981.

James Corcoran Gallery, Los Angeles. *Billy Al Bengston: Paintings*. 1–30 May 1981.

Texas Gallery, Houston. *Billy Al Bengston: Hawaiian Watercolors*. 10 November–4 December 1981.

1982 Linda Farris Gallery, Seattle, Washington. *Billy Al Bengston: Honolulu Watercolors*. 4–28 February 1982.

James Corcoran Gallery, Los Angeles. *Billy Al Bengston: New Paintings*. 1–31 May 1982.

Thomas Babeor Gallery, La Jolla, California. *Billy Al Bengston: New Watercolor Collages*. 9 September–9 October 1982.

1983 James Corcoran Gallery, Los Angeles. *Billy Al Bengston: New Paintings*. 1–31 May 1983.

John Berggruen Gallery, San Francisco. *Billy Al Bengston: Recent Work*. 14 July–13 August 1983.

Thomas Babeor Gallery, La Jolla, California. *Billy Al Bengston: Paintings, Watercolors, Furniture, Prints*. 4 September–8 October 1983.

Acquavella Contemporary Art, Inc., New York. *Billy Al Bengston*. 1 December 1983–14 January 1984.

1984 Smith Andersen Gallery, Palo Alto, California. *Billy Al Bengston*. 28 March–28 April 1984.

James Corcoran Gallery, Los Angeles. *Billy Al Bengston: Acrylic and Watercolor Paintings*. 1–31 May 1984.

Douglas Drake Gallery, Kansas City, Kansas. *Billy Al Bengston: Watercolor Collages*. 6–28 July 1984.

Thomas Babeor Gallery, La Jolla, California. *Billy Al Bengston*. 7 September–5 October 1984.

Texas Gallery, Houston. *Billy Al Bengston: Watercolor Collages*. 14 November–22 December 1984.

1985 James Corcoran Gallery, Los Angeles. 1–30 May 1985.

Thomas Babeor Gallery, La Jolla, California. *Billy Al Bengston: 5th Annual Exhibition*. 6 September–5 October 1985.

Texas Gallery, Houston. *Billy Al Bengston: New Paintings and Watercolors*. 10 December 1985–4 January 1986.

1986 Thomas Babeor Gallery, La Jolla, California. *Sixth Annual Billy Al Bengston Exhibition: New Paintings*. 5 September–11 October 1986.

Smith Andersen Gallery, Palo Alto, California. *Billy Al Bengston: New Paintings*. 23 October–26 November 1986.

1987 James Corcoran Gallery, Santa Monica, California. 1–31 May 1987.

Thomas Babeor Gallery, La Jolla, California. *Seventh Annual Billy Al Bengston Exhibition*. 11 September–10 October 1987.

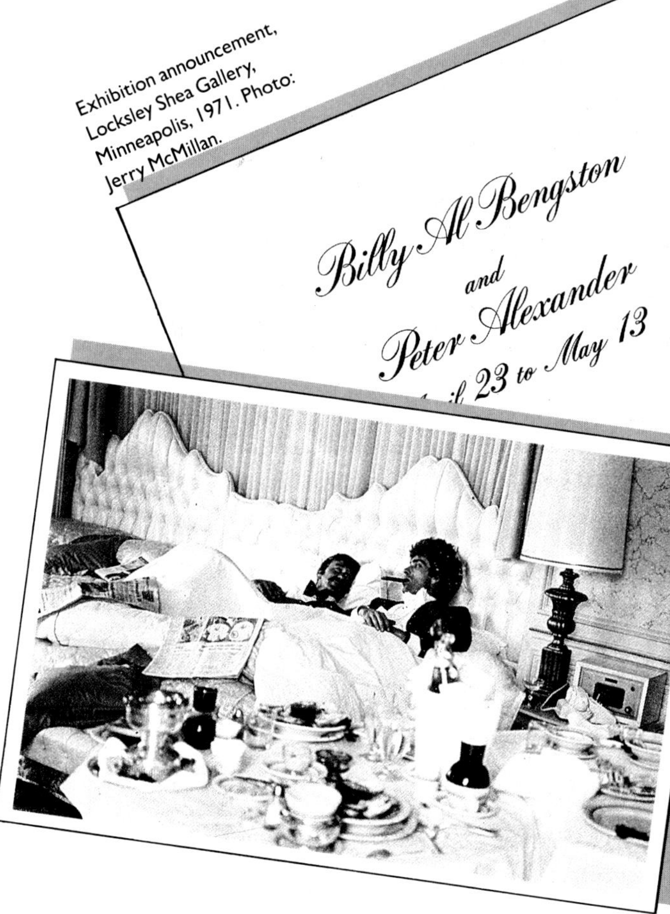

Exhibition announcement, Locksley Shea Gallery, Minneapolis, 1971. Photo: Jerry McMillan.

1956 Richmond Art Center, California. *Fifth Annual Exhibition: Watercolor, Print, Decorative Arts.* 2–30 April 1956.
Catalog published.
6 Gallery, San Francisco. *Drawings.* 4–30 July 1956.

1957 * Exodus Gallery, San Pedro, California. *First Annual Los Angeles Area Drawing Exhibition.* 1957.
Ferus Gallery, Los Angeles. *Objects on the New Landscape Demanding of the Eye.* 15 March–11 April 1957.
Los Angeles County Museum (now Los Angeles County Museum of Art). *1957 Annual Exhibition: Artists of Los Angeles and Vicinity.* 22 May–30 June 1957.
Catalog published.

1958 Ferus Gallery, Los Angeles. Group Exhibit. 9–31 May 1958.

1959 Bolles Gallery, San Francisco. *California Group Exhibition.* 9 January–12 February 1959.
Ferus Gallery, Los Angeles. *Collage Constructions: B.A. Bengston/Edw. Kienholz.* 17 February–14 March 1959.
Los Angeles County Museum (now Los Angeles County Museum of Art). *Artists of Los Angeles and Vicinity: 1959 Annual Exhibition.* 4 August–6 September 1959.
Catalog published.

1960 UCLA Art Galleries (now Wight Art Gallery), University of California, Los Angeles. *Fifty Paintings by Thirty-Seven Painters of the Los Angeles Area.* 20 March–10 April 1960.
Catalog published, preface by Frederick S. Wight, introduction by Henry T. Hopkins.
Ferus Gallery, Los Angeles. Group Exhibit. 20 June–16 July 1960.

1961 Ferus Gallery, Los Angeles. Group Exhibit. 3–29 April 1961.
Pasadena Art Museum (now Norton Simon Museum), California. *Pacific Profile of Young West Coast Painters.* 11 June–26 July 1961.
Catalog published, essay by Constance Perkins.

1962 UCLA Art Galleries (now Wight Art Gallery), University of California, Los Angeles. *The Gifford and Joann Phillips Collection.* 4 November–9 December 1962.
Catalog published, essay by Frederick S. Wight.

Whitney Museum of American Art, New York. *Fifty California Artists.* 23 October–2 December 1962 (organized by San Francisco Museum of Art with assistance from Los Angeles County Museum of Art).
Catalog published, essay by Lloyd Goodrich.
Traveled to: Walker Art Center, Minneapolis, 17 February–17 March 1963; Albright-Knox Art Gallery, Buffalo, 10 April–8 May 1963; Des Moines Art Center, Iowa, 24 May–23 June 1963.
Fine Arts Gallery of San Diego (now San Diego Museum of Art), California. *Pacific Coast Invitational.* 1–25 November 1962 (organized by The Santa Barbara Museum of Art).
Catalog published.
Traveled nationally, 30 November 1962–23 June 1963.

1963 The Art Institute of Chicago. *66th Annual American Exhibition.* 11 January–10 February 1963.
Catalog published, foreword by A. James Speyer.
Musée cantonal des beaux-arts, Lausanne, Switzerland. *Miroir et Mémoire du Premier Salon International de Galeries Pilotes Lausanne.* 20 June–6 October 1963.
Catalog published, essays by René Berger, Anne-Marie Karlen, Marie-Madeleine Brumagne, Jacques Monnier, and Jean-Pierre Clavel.
Los Angeles County Museum of Art. *Six More.* 24 July–25 August 1963.
Catalog published, essay by Lawrence Alloway.
Oakland Art Museum (now The Oakland Museum). *Pop Art USA.* 7–29 September 1963.
Catalog published, foreword by Paul Mills, essay by John Coplans.
* Martha Jackson Gallery, New York. *Contemporary Americans.* 16 September–12 October 1963.
Pasadena Art Museum (now Norton Simon Museum), California. *Hard-Edge and Emblem: New Work—England and America.* 12 November–26 December 1963.

1964 UCLA Art Galleries (now Wight Art Gallery), University of California, Los Angeles. *From the Sterling Holloway Collection.* 20 September–25 October 1964.
Catalog published, essay by Henri Dorra.
Ferus Gallery, Los Angeles. *The Studs: Moses, Irwin, Price and Bengston.* December 1964.

1965 Milwaukee Art Center, Wisconsin. *Pop Art and the American Tradition.* 9 April–9 May 1965.
Catalog published, essay by Tracy Atkinson.

Museu de Arte Moderna de São Paulo, Brazil. *VIII São Paulo Bienal: United States of America.* 4 September–28 November 1965 (organized by Pasadena Art Museum, California).
Catalog published, preface and introduction by Walter Hopps.
Traveled to: National Collection of Fine Arts (now National Museum of American Art), Smithsonian Institution, Washington, D.C., 27 January–6 March 1966.

1966 Seattle Art Museum Pavilion, Washington. *Ten from Los Angeles.* 15 July–5 September 1966.
Catalog published, introduction by John Coplans.
Art Gallery, University of California, Irvine. *Abstract Expressionist Ceramics.* 28 October–27 November 1966.
Catalog published, essay by John Coplans.

1967 Lytton Center of the Visual Arts, Los Angeles. *Artists' Artists.* 1967.
The Santa Barbara Museum of Art, California. *Three Young Collections.* 15 January–26 February 1967.
Catalog published, introduction by Thomas W. Leavitt.
Portland Art Museum, Oregon. *Ninety-Four Works from the Collection of Sterling Holloway.* 24 January–12 February 1967.
Catalog published, statement by Sterling Holloway.
University of California, Irvine. *A Selection of Paintings and Sculptures from the Collections of Mr. and Mrs. Robert Rowan.* 2–21 May 1967.
Catalog published.
Traveled to: San Francisco Museum of Art (now San Francisco Museum of Modern Art), 2 June–2 July 1967.
Pasadena Art Museum (now Norton Simon Museum), California. *Selections from the Charles Cowles Collection.* 20 June–16 July 1967.
Traveled to: Stanford University Museum of Art, Stanford, California, 13 November 1967–21 January 1968.
The Museum of Modern Art, New York. *The 1960s: Painting and Sculpture from the Museum Collection.* 28 June–24 September 1967.
Catalog published.
The American Federation of Arts, New York. *From Synchromism Forward: A View of Abstract Art in America.*
Catalog published.

Traveled nationally, 12 November 1967–17 November 1968.

Whitney Museum of American Art, New York. *1967 Annual Exhibition of Contemporary Painting.* 13 December 1967–4 February 1968.
Catalog published.

1968 UCSD Art Gallery (now Mandeville Gallery), University of California, San Diego. *Contemporary Painting and Sculpture: New York—Los Angeles.* 13 February–10 March 1968.

Montgomery Gallery, Pomona College, Claremont, California. *Speed Sculpture.* 6–24 March 1968.

The Jewish Museum, New York. *Suites: Recent Prints.* 12 March–12 May 1968.
Catalog published.

*Janie C. Lee Gallery, Dallas. *Art from California.* 15 October–15 November 1968.

Art Gallery, California State College (now California State University), Fullerton. *Transparency/Reflection.* 18 October–17 November 1968.
Catalog published, essay by Kurt Von Meier.

Flint Institute of Arts, Michigan. *Made of Plastic.* 18 October–1 December 1968.
Catalog published, foreword by G. Stuart Hodge.

The American Federation of Arts, New York. *Some Younger American Painters and Sculptors.*
Traveled nationally and to British Columbia, 3 November 1968–12 October 1969.

Los Angeles County Museum of Art. *Late Fifties at the Ferus.* 12 November–17 December 1968.
Catalog published, essay by James Monte.

1969 The Museum of Modern Art, New York. *New Media: New Methods*
Traveled nationally and to Canada, 16 March 1969–16 August 1970.

Gallery Reese Palley, San Francisco. *Three Modern Masters: Billy Al Bengston, Edward Ruscha and Frank Lloyd Wright.* 24 March–19 April 1969.
Catalog published, essays by Carol Linsley.

The Jewish Museum, New York. *Superlimited: Books, Boxes and Things.* 16 April–29 June 1969.
Catalog published, introduction by Susan Tumarkin Goodman.

The Museum of Modern Art, New York. *Tamarind: Homage to Lithography.* 29 April–30 June 1969.
Catalog published, preface by William S. Lieberman, introduction by Virginia Allen.

Fine Arts Gallery of San Diego (now San Diego Museum of Art), California. *First National Invitational Print Exhibition.* 6 June–13 July 1969.

John Bolles Gallery, San Francisco. Group Exhibit. 31 July–31 August 1969.

The Denver Art Museum, Colorado. *American Report on the Sixties.* 25 October–7 December 1969.

Fort Worth Art Center Museum (now The Fort Worth Art Museum), Texas. *Contemporary American Drawings.* 28 October–30 November 1969.

Stedelijk Van Abbemuseum, Eindhoven, The Netherlands. *Kompas 4: Westkust USA.* 21 November 1969–4 January 1970.
Catalog published, foreword by Jean Leering, Eugen Thiemann, and Zdenek Felix; introduction by Jean Leering.

Pasadena Art Museum (now Norton Simon Museum), California. *West Coast 1945–1969.* 24 November 1969–18 January 1970.
Catalog published, introduction by John Coplans.

Galleria Milano, Milan, Italy. *Six West Coast Artists: Bengston, Goode, Graham, Moses, Price, Ruscha.* 10 December 1969–7 January 1970.

Whitney Museum of American Art, New York. *1969 Annual Exhibition: Contemporary American Painting.* 16 December 1969–1 February 1970.
Catalog published, foreword by John I. H. Baur.

1970 Institute of Contemporary Art, University of Pennsylvania, Philadelphia. *The Highway.* 14 January–25 February 1970.
Catalog published, essays by Denise Scott Brown, Robert Venturi, and John W. McCoubrey.
Traveled to: Institute for the Arts, Rice University, Houston, 12 March–18 May 1970; The Akron Art Institute, Ohio, 5 June–26 July 1970.

Janie C. Lee Gallery, Dallas. *Bengston/Price.* 14–30 March 1970.

The Contemporary Arts Foundation, Oklahoma City, Oklahoma. *Three California Friends: Joe Goode, Billy Al Bengston, Ed Ruscha.* 19 April–9 May 1970.

The Brooklyn Museum, New York. *Seventeenth National Print Exhibition.* 1 June–1 September 1970.
Catalog published, introduction by Jo Miller.

Artist Studio, Venice, California. Special exhibition. 7–13 September 1970.

Joslyn Art Museum, Omaha, Nebraska. *Looking West 1970.* 18 October–29 November 1970.
Catalog published, foreword by Richard N. Gregg, introduction by LeRoy Butler.

The Pace Gallery, New York. *A Decade of California Color, 1960-1970.* 7–25 November 1970.
Catalog published.

Mizuno Gallery, Los Angeles. *Tea-Tables and Tapestries* (Billy Al Bengston and Ed Moses). 24 November–20 December 1970.

Montgomery Gallery, Pomona College, Claremont, California. *Monoprints.* 5–27 December 1970.

The Oakland Museum, California. *More Than One.* 8 December 1970–3 January 1971.

1971 International Exhibitions Foundation, Washington, D.C. *Tamarind: A Renaissance of Lithography.*
Catalog published, introduction by E. Maurice Bloch.
Traveled: March 1971–72.

Minnesota Museum of Art, St. Paul. *Drawings USA/71.* 15 April–27 June 1971.
Catalog published.
Traveled nationally and to Canada, 28 August 1971–9 June 1973.

*Locksley Shea Gallery, Minneapolis. *Billy Al Bengston and Peter Alexander.* 23 April–13 May 1971.

The Santa Barbara Museum of Art, California. *Spray.* 24 April–30 May 1971.
Catalog published, essay by Paul C. Mills.

Newport Harbor Art Museum, Newport Beach, California. *Contemporary American Art from Orange County Collections.* 23 October–14 November 1971.
Catalog published, introduction by Thomas H. Garver.

1972 Kunstverein, Hamburg, West Germany. *1972 USA West Coast.* 1972.
Catalog published, essays by Helmut Heissenbüttel and Helene Winer.
Traveled to: Kunstverein, Hannover; Kölnischer Kunstverein, Cologne; Württembergisher Kunstverein, Stuttgart.

Fort Worth Art Center Museum (now The Fort Worth Art Museum), Texas. *Contemporary American Art: Los Angeles.* 12 January–6 February 1972.

Akron Art Institute, Ohio. *Four Artists* (Ruscha, Bengston, Alexander, Moses). 16 January–20 February 1972.
Catalog published.

Govett-Brewster Art Gallery, New Plymouth, New Zealand. *The State of California Painting.* 23 May–15 June 1972.
Catalog published, essay by Michael Walls.
Traveled in New Zealand, 7 August 1972–19 May 1973.

The Art Institute of Chicago. *Seventieth American Exhibition.* 24 June–20 August 1972.
Catalog published, introduction by A. James Speyer.

E. B. Crocker Art Gallery (now Crocker Art Museum), Sacramento, California. *West Coast '72: Painters & Sculptors.* 8 September–15 October 1972.
Catalog published, essay by Allan M. Gordon.

Albright-Knox Art Gallery, Buffalo, New York. *14 Artists Working in California.* 3 November–10 December 1972.

1973 The Corcoran Gallery of Art, Washington, D.C. *The Way of Color: Thirty-Third Biennial Exhibition of Contemporary American Painting.* 24 February–8 April 1973.
Catalog published, foreword by Roy Slade, introduction by Gene Baro.

Margo Leavin Gallery, Los Angeles. *Drawings.* 13 March–15 April 1973.

Pasadena Museum of Modern Art (now Norton Simon Museum), California. *The Betty and Monte Factor Family Collection.* 24 April–3 June 1973.
Catalog published.

Yale University Art Gallery, New Haven, Connecticut. *American Drawing 1970–1973.* 9 October–25 November 1973.
Catalog published, introduction by Christina Orr.

Willard Gallery, New York. *Contemporary Drawings.* 4–29 December 1973.

Edward Thorp Gallery, Santa Barbara, California. *Billy Al Bengston/Tom Holland: Works on Paper.* 4 December 1973–5 January 1974.

1974 The Santa Barbara Museum of Art, California. *15 Abstract Artists: Los Angeles.* 19 January–10 March 1974.
Catalog published, essay by Ronald A. Kuchta.

Krannert Art Museum, University of Illinois, Champaign. *Fifteenth Exhibition: Contemporary American Painting and Sculpture 1974.* 10 March–21 April 1974.
Catalog published, introduction by James R. Shipley and Allen S. Weller.

Lang Art Gallery, Scripps College, Claremont, California. *The Fred and Mary Marer Collection: 30th Annual Ceramics Exhibition.* 19 March–28 April 1974.
Catalog published, essays by Jim Melchert and Paul Soldner.

Whitney Museum of American Art, New York. *American Pop Art.* 6 April–16 June 1974.
Catalog published, essay by Lawrence Alloway.

Nicholas Wilder Gallery, Los Angeles. *Works on Paper.* 2–31 July 1974.

Lang Art Gallery, Scripps College, Claremont, California. *Painting: Color, Form and Surface.* 1–27 October 1974.
Catalog published, essay by Martha Alf.

1975 Willard Gallery, New York. *Drawings.* 4 January–8 February 1975.

Brooke Alexander, Inc., New York. *Hand Colored Prints.* 6 January–16 February 1975.
Catalog published, introduction by Carter Ratcliff.
Traveled nationally and to Canada, 3 March 1975–26 December 1976.

Los Angeles Institute of Contemporary Art. *Current Concerns: Part I.* 17 January–14 February 1975.
Catalog published in *Journal* (Los Angeles Institute of Contemporary Art), No. 4 (February 1975), pp. 54–65.

Texas Gallery, Houston. *Arnoldi, Benglis, Bengston, Wudl.* 1–25 February 1975.

The Art Galleries, University of California, Santa Barbara. *Four from the East/Four from the West.* 25 February–30 March 1975.
Catalog published, introduction by Phyllis Plous.

Los Angeles Institute of Contemporary Art. *Collage and Assemblage.* 29 March–23 May 1975.
Catalog published in *Journal* (Los Angeles Institute of Contemporary Art), No. 6 (June–July 1975), pp. 44–57.

Ruth S. Schaffner Gallery, Los Angeles. *60's and 70's: Trends of 6 California Artists.* 1 October–1 November 1975.

Tortue Gallery, Santa Monica, California. *Drawings: By Artists Who Live and Work in Santa Monica and Venice.* 18 October–29 November 1975.
1975), pp. 44–57.

Ruth S. Schaffner Gallery, Los Angeles. *60's and 70's: Trends of 6 California Artists.* 1 October–1 November 1975.

Tortue Gallery, Santa Monica, California. *Drawings: By Artists Who Live and Work in Santa Monica and Venice.* 18 October–29 November 1975.

1976 Everson Museum of Art, Syracuse, New York. *New Works in Clay: By Contemporary Painters and Sculptors.* 23 January–4 April 1976.
Catalog published, foreword by Ronald A. Kuchta, and introduction by Margie Hughto.

Fine Arts Gallery, California State University, Northridge. *Unclassified.* 9–29 February 1976.
Brochure published, introduction by Karen Carson.

Newport Harbor Art Museum, Newport Beach, California. *The Last Time I Saw Ferus, 1957–1966.* 7 March–17 April 1976.
Catalog published, essay by Betty Turnbull.

Akron Art Institute, Ohio. *Contemporary Images in Watercolor.* 14 March–25 April 1976.
Catalog published, essay by Robert Doty.
Traveled to: Indianapolis Museum of Art, Indiana, 29 June–8 August 1976; Memorial Art Gallery of the University of Rochester, New York, 1 October–14 November 1976.

James Corcoran Gallery, Los Angeles. *Billy Al Bengston and Ed Janss.* 27 April–23 May 1976.

San Francisco Museum of Modern Art. *Painting and Sculpture in California: The Modern Era.* 3 September–21 November 1976.
Catalog published, preface by Henry T. Hopkins, essays by Henry T. Hopkins and 16 contributors.
Traveled to: National Collection of Fine Arts (now the National Museum of American Art), Smithsonian Institution, Washington, D.C., 20 May–11 September 1977.

Georgia State University Art Gallery, Atlanta. *Ten Painters.* 4–29 October 1976.

Ruth S. Schaffner Gallery, Los Angeles. *Works on Paper.* 9 November–31 December 1976.

1977 Baxter Art Gallery, California Institute of Technology, Pasadena. *Watercolors and Related Media by Contemporary Californians.* 29 September–30 October 1977.
Catalog published, preface by Michael Smith.

Fine Arts Gallery, California State University, Los Angeles. *Miniature.* 3 October–10 November 1977.
Catalog published, essay by Sandy Ballatore.

1978 Margo Leavin Gallery, Los Angeles. *Three Generations: Studies in Collage.* 26 January–4 March 1978.

Janus Gallery (now Jan Turner Gallery), Venice, California. *Drawing Explorations: 1930–1978.* 17 November–23 December 1978.

The Art Museum and Galleries, California State University, Long Beach. *Selections from the Frederick Weisman Company Collection of California Art.* 20 November–17 December 1978.
Catalog published, introduction by Cecille Caterson, Lucinda H. Gedeon, and Joan Hemphill.
Traveled to: The Corcoran Gallery of Art, Washington, D.C., 15 September–4 November 1979; Albuquerque Museum, New Mexico, 14 July–12 October 1980; Fine Arts Gallery, California State University, Northridge, 9 February–6 March 1981.

Acquavella Contemporary Art, Inc., New York. *Post War American Masters*. 5 December 1978–12 January 1979.

1979 Whitney Museum of American Art, New York. *1979 Biennial Exhibition*. 6 February–8 April 1979.
Catalog published, preface by Tom Armstrong.

Montgomery Museum of Fine Arts, Alabama. *Art Inc.: American Paintings from Corporate Collections*. 7 March–6 May 1979.
Catalog published, essay by Mitchell Douglas Kahan.
Traveled to: The Corcoran Gallery of Art, Washington, D.C., 12 June–14 July 1979; Indianapolis Museum of Art, Indiana, 8 August–23 September 1979; San Diego Museum of Art, California, 17 November–30 December 1979.

Baxter Art Gallery, California Institute of Technology, Pasadena. *A Painting Installation*. 8 March–15 April 1979.
Catalog published, interview by Michael H. Smith with Donald Kaufman.

Georgia State University Art Gallery, Atlanta. *Billy Al Bengston/Alan Shields*. 9–27 April 1979.

Everson Museum of Art, Syracuse, New York. *A Century of Ceramics in the United States 1878–1978*. 5 May–23 September 1979.
Catalog published, foreword by Ronald A. Kuchta, preface by Margie Hughto, essay by Garth Clark.
Traveled to: Renwick Gallery of the National Collection of Fine Arts (now the National Museum of American Art), Smithsonian Institution, Washington, D.C., 9 November 1979–27 January 1980.

Institute of Contemporary Art, University of Pennsylvania, Philadelphia. *The Decorative Impulse*. 13 June–21 July 1979.
Catalog published, essay by Janet Kardon.
Traveled to: Mandeville Art Gallery, University of California at San Diego, La Jolla, 1 November–9 December 1979; Minneapolis College of Art and Design, Minnesota, 16 January–15 February 1980.

Texas Gallery, Houston. *From Allan to Zucker: Contemporary Works on Paper*. 17 August–28 September 1979.

Crocker Art Museum, Sacramento, California. *Aspects of Abstract: Recent West Coast Abstract Painting and Sculpture*. 27 October–24 November 1979.
Catalog published, essay by Roger D. Clisby.

1980 Lowe Art Museum, University of Miami, Coral Gables, Florida. *Fabrications*. 1 May–10 August 1980.
Traveled to: SVC Fine Arts Gallery, University of South Florida, Tampa, 15 September–23 November 1980.

Thomas Babeor Gallery, La Jolla, California. *Grand Opening Exhibition*. 17 May–10 July 1980.

Otis/Parsons Gallery, Los Angeles. *Furnishings by Artists*. 6 June–13 July 1980.
Catalog published, introduction by Hal Glicksman, essay by Howard Singerman.

Conejo Valley Art Museum, Thousand Oaks, California. *50's Abstract: A Summary of Los Angeles Painting from 1957 through 1960*. 28 September–9 November 1980.
Catalog published, essays by Vic Smith and Diana Zlotnick.

Tacoma Art Museum, Washington. *California Now*. 5–30 November 1980.

1981 Art Center College of Design, Pasadena, California. *Decade: Los Angeles Painting in the Seventies*. 17 February–14 March 1981.
Catalog published, introduction by Laurence Dreiband, essays by Walter Gabrielson, Michael Kurcfeld, and Peter Plagens.

Thomas Babeor Gallery, La Jolla, California. *Group Show*. 27 March–8 April 1981.

Los Angeles County Museum of Art. *Los Angeles Prints, 1883–1980*. 25 June–20 September 1981 (Part II).
Catalog published, essays by Ebria Feinblatt and Bruce Davis.

Los Angeles County Museum of Art. *Art in Los Angeles: Seventeen Artists in the Sixties*. 21 July–4 October 1981.
Catalog published, introduction by Maurice Tuchman, essays by Anne Bartlett Ayres, Susan C. Larsen, Christopher Knight, and Michele D. De Angelus.
Traveled to: San Antonio Museum of Art, Texas, 20 November 1981–31 January 1982.

Laguna Beach Museum of Art, California. *Southern California Artists: 1940–1980*. 24 July–13 September 1981.
Catalog published, introduction by Maudette Ball.

Judith Christian Gallery, New York. *Forty Famous Californians: Recent Unique Works on Paper*. 18 September–14 October 1981.

Fine Arts Gallery, California State University, Northridge. *Abstraction in Los Angeles 1950–1980: Selections from the Murray and Ruth Gribin Collection*.
27 September–23 October 1981.
Catalog published in *Journal* (Los Angeles Institute of Contemporary Art), No. 30 (September–October 1981). Introduction by Jean-Luc Bordeaux, essays by Melinda Wortz, William Hemmerdinger, and Jean-Luc Bordeaux.
Traveled to: Fine Arts Gallery, University of California, Irvine, 5 November–5 December 1981.

1982 Nagoya City Museum, Nagoya, Japan. *Exhibition of Contemporary Los Angeles Artists*. 16 February–14 March 1982.
Catalog published.
Traveled to: Los Angeles Municipal Art Gallery, 13 April–2 May 1982.

Montgomery Art Gallery, Pomona College, Claremont, California. *Contemporary Triptychs*. 27 February–9 April 1982.
Catalog published, essay by David S. Rubin.

Los Angeles County Museum of Art. *The Michael and Dorothy Blankfort Collection*. 1 April–13 June 1982.
Catalog published, foreword by Maurice Tuchman, essay by Michael Blankfort.

Thomas Babeor Gallery, La Jolla, California. *Recent Works*. 15 April–15 May 1982.

Garth Clark Gallery, Los Angeles. *Painters and Clay*. 5 June–10 July 1982.

Otis/Parsons Gallery, Los Angeles. *Dualism*. 18 June–17 July 1982.

Contemporary Arts Museum, Houston. *The Americans: The Collage*. 11 July–3 October 1982.
Catalog published, foreword and essay by Linda L. Cathcart.

Sun Valley Center Gallery, Idaho. *Three California Painters* (Billy Al Bengston, Margaret Nielsen, Wayne Thiebaud). 5–24 August 1982.

Garth Clark Gallery, Los Angeles. *Otis Clay: The Revolutionary Years 1954–1964*. 11 September–2 October 1982.

Texas Gallery, Houston. *Billy Al Bengston and Edward Ruscha: New Works on Paper*. 7 December 1982–15 January 1983.

1983 Arco Center for Visual Art, Los Angeles. *Los Angeles Pattern Painters*. 22 February–2 April 1983.
Catalog published, essay by Sandy Nelson-Ballatore.

Linda Farris Gallery, Seattle, Washington. *Billy Al Bengston, Laddie John Dill, Tom Holland, Edward Ruscha: New Works on Paper*. 23 March–17 April 1983.

Gallery Association of New York State, Hamilton.

Twentieth Century American Watercolor.
Catalog published, essay by Janice C. Oresman.
Traveled nationally, 5 April 1983–23 May 1984.

Monterey Peninsula Museum of Art, California.
California Contemporary: Recent Work of Twenty-Three Artists. 1–29 May 1983.
Catalog published, introduction by Henry T. Hopkins, essay by George DeGroat.

Thomas Babeor Gallery, La Jolla, California.
Selected Works. 22 July–3 September 1983.

The Oakland Museum, California. *On and Off the Wall: Shaped and Colored.* 8 October–24 December 1983.
Catalog published, preface by Christina Orr-Cahall, essay by Judith Bettelheim.
Traveled nationally, 20 January 1984–24 February 1985.

The Museum of Contemporary Art, Los Angeles.
The First Show: Painting and Sculpture from Eight Collections, 1940-1980. 18 November 1983–19 February 1984.
Catalog published, foreword by Julia Brown, essays by Pontus Hulten and Susan C. Larsen.

The Santa Barbara Museum of Art, California. *From Avery to Zurbarán: A New View of the Permanent Collection.* 3 December 1983–12 February 1984.
Catalog published.

Texas Gallery, Houston. *New Works by California Artists.* 6 December 1983–7 January 1984.

Modernism, San Francisco. *California Drawings.* 16 December 1983–28 January 1984.

1984 Baxter Art Gallery, California Institute of Technology, Pasadena. *Contemporary Ceramic Vessels: Two Los Angeles Collections.* 4–29 January 1984.
Catalog published, preface by Jay Belloli, interviews with Betty Asher and Howard and Gwen Laurie Smits.

Indianapolis Museum of Art, Indiana. *Painting and Sculpture Today 1984.* 1 May–10 June 1984.
Catalog published, foreword by James P. White, introduction by M. Bernadine Tabler, and essay by Helen Ferrulli.

Design Center of Los Angeles. *A Broad Spectrum: Contemporary Los Angeles Painters and Sculptors '84.* 7 June–15 August 1984.
Catalog published, essays by Fidel Danieli and Sandy Nelson.

The Santa Barbara Museum of Art, California. *Art of the States: Works from a Santa Barbara Collection.* 22 June–26 August 1984.
Catalog published, essay by Robert McDonald.

Hunsaker/Schlesinger Gallery, Los Angeles. *Major Work by California Artists.* 19 July–18 August 1984.

Los Angeles Municipal Art Gallery. *Art in Clay, 1950's to 1980's in Southern California: Evolution, Revolution, Continuation.* 24 July–26 August 1984.
Catalog published, foreword by Betty Warner Sheinbaum, essays by Susan Peterson, Gerald Nordland, and Eudorah M. Moore.

Arco Center for Visual Art, Los Angeles. *Los Angeles and the Palm Tree: Image of a City.* 31 July–22 September 1984.
Catalog published, foreword by Robert J. Fitzpatrick, essays by Emmet L. Wimple and Michael Kurcfeld.

University Art Gallery, San Diego State University, California. *Watercolors: A Contemporary Survey.* 13 October–10 November 1984.

Gallery at the Plaza, Security Pacific National Bank, Los Angeles. *Art and the Familiar Object.* 19 October 1984–6 January 1985.
Catalog published, statements by Vered Galor and Tressa R. Miller.

1985 The Santa Barbara Museum of Art, California.
Santa Barbara Collects. (Part One: European and American Art), 26 January–24 March 1985.
Catalog published, introduction by Robert Henning, Jr., and five other contributors.

University Art Museum, University of New Mexico, Albuquerque. *Tamarind: 25 Years.* 18 May–30 August 1985.
Catalog published, introduction by Marjorie Devon, forewords by Clinton Adams and June Wayne, and essay by Carter Ratcliff.
Traveled under the auspices of The Art Museum Association of America, October 1985–June 1987.

Gallery at the Plaza, Security Pacific National Bank, Los Angeles. *Contemporary Monotypes.* 29 July–8 September 1985.

Swen Parson Gallery, Northern Illinois University, DeKalb. *The Atelier in America: A Collaboration Between Printer and Artist.* 17 November–15 December 1985.
Catalog published, introduction by David F. Driesbach, essays by nine contributors.

Holly Solomon Gallery, New York. *Home Work, Paintings, Sculpture and Furnishings by Artists.* 5–31 December 1985.

1986 The Gallery of The University of Texas at San Antonio. *Collage.* 27 October–21 November 1986.

The Museum of Contemporary Art, Los Angeles.
Individuals: A Selected History of Contemporary Art, 1945-1986. 10 December 1986–19 January 1988.
Catalog published, essays by Keta Linker, Donald Kuspit, Hal Foster, Ronald J. Onorato, Germano Celant, Achille Bonito Oliva, John C. Welchman, and Thomas Lawson.

1987 University Art Museum, Berkeley, California. *Made in U.S.A.: An Americanization in Modern Art, the '50s and '60s.* 4 April–21 June 1987.
Catalog published, essays by Sidra Stich, Ben H. Bagdikina, James E. B. Breslin, and Thomas Schaub.
Traveled to: The Nelson-Atkins Museum of Art, Kansas City, Missouri, 25 July–6 September 1987; Virginia Museum of Fine Arts, Richmond, 7 October–7 December 1987.

Odakyu Grand Gallery, Tokyo. *Pop Art: USA-UK.* 24 July–18 August 1987.
Catalog published, essays by Lawrence Alloway, Marco Livingstone, and Masataka Ogawa.
Traveled to: Daimaru Museum, Osaka, 9–28 September 1987; the Funabashi Seibu Museum of Art, Funabashi, 30 October–17 November 1987; Sogo Museum of Art, Yokohama, 26 November–13 December 1987.

Selected Bibliography

Compiled by Barbara Bowman

INTERVIEWS AND STATEMENTS BY THE ARTIST

"The Artist and Politics: A Symposium." *Artforum*, September 1970, pp. 35-39, ill.

Bengston, Billy Al. "Late Fifties at the Ferus." *Artforum*, January 1969, pp. 33–35.

————. "Los Angeles Artists' Studios." *Art in America*, November–December 1970, pp. 100–109, ill.

Berges, Marshall. "Home Q & A: Billy Al Bengston." *Los Angeles Times*, 23 November 1975, *Home*, pp. 51, 53, 61, ill.

————. "Art on the Wild Side." *Design*, Spring 1977, pp. 6–9, ill.

Kalil, Susie. "Straight Talk from Pair of Hard-Working Artists." *Houston Post*, 12 December 1982, pp. 20-F–21-F.

Larsen, Susan. Tape recorded interview with Billy Al Bengston, 9 September 1980. California Oral History Project, Archives of American Art, Smithsonian Institution, Washington, D.C.

Meyer, Andrew. "Conversation with Billy Al Bengston." *Los Angeles Herald Examiner*, 27 September 1981, *California Living*, p. [6].

Peck, Stacey. "Home Q & A: Billy Al Bengston." *Los Angeles Times*, 10 August 1980, *Home*, pp. 24–25, 27, 31, ill.

Quinn, Joan. "Billy Al Bengston." *Interview*, October 1979, p. 62.

Robinson, William A., Perry Walker, and Henry Hopkins. "Bengston, Grieger, Goode: 3 Interviews." *Art in America*, March–April 1973, pp. 48–53, ill.

Rubenfien, Leo. "Through Western Eyes: Billy Al Bengston." *Art in America*, September-October 1978, pp. 75–83, ill.

Wasserman, Isabelle. "Inside the Arts: Still a Rebel, But Richer." *San Diego Union*, 24 April 1981, pp. E-1–E-2.

ONE-PERSON EXHIBITION CATALOGS

Billy Al Bengston: Paintings of the Seventies. Los Angeles: Security Pacific Bank, 1978. Essay by Fredericka Hunter.

Billy Al Bengston: Puerto Escondido, Watercolor Suite 1977. Los Angeles: James Corcoran Gallery, 1977.

Billy Al Bengston: Watercolors 1974-1980. Washington, D.C.: The Corcoran Gallery of Art, 1980. Essay by Jane Livingston.

A Decade of Billy Al Bengston: The Seventies. San Diego, California: San Diego State University, 1981. Essay by Jeff Perrone.

Monte, James. *Billy Al Bengston*. Los Angeles: Los Angeles County Museum of Art, 1968.

BOOKS

Alloway, Lawrence. *American Pop Art*. New York: Collier Books in association with Whitney Museum of American Art, 1974, pp. 32, 35, ill. pp. 30, 31.

Battcock, Gregory, ed. *Minimal Art: A Critical Anthology*. New York: E. P. Dutton & Co., Inc., 1968, p. 289.

Bengston, Billy Al, and Edward Ruscha. *Business Cards*. Los Angeles: Billy Al Bengston and Ed Ruscha, Inc., 1968.

Clark, Garth. *A Century of Ceramics in the United States 1878-1978*. New York: E. P. Dutton in association with the Everson Museum of Art, Syracuse, New York, 1979, pp. 134, 136, 199, 276, ill. pp. 150, 212. Preface by Margie Hughto.

Distel, Herbert. *The Museum of Drawers*. Zurich: Kunsthaus Zurich, 1978, ill. pp. 23, 35.

Domergue, Denise. *Artists Design Furniture*. New York: Harry N. Abrams, Inc., 1984, pp. 54–55, ill.

Kozloff, Max. *Renderings: Critical Essays on a Century of Modern Art*. New York: Simon and Schuster, 1968, pp. 276–77.

Lippard, Lucy R., ed. *Pop Art*. New York: Frederick A. Praeger, 1966, pp. 137, 140, 148, 160, ill.

Plagens, Peter. *Sunshine Muse: Contemporary Art on the West Coast*. New York: Praeger Publishers, 1974, pp. 25, 30, 95, 99, 115, 120, 122, 140, 142, 146, ill.

ARTICLES

An R following an entry indicates a review.

1958 Langsner, Jules. "This Summer in Los Angeles." *Artnews*, Summer 1958, pp. 58–59. R.

1959 Langsner, Jules. "Art News from Los Angeles." *Artnews*, April 1959, pp. 65–66. R.

Nordland, Gerald. "Art: At the County Museum." *Frontier*, September 1959, pp. 23–25. R.

S[eldis], H[enry] J. "In the Galleries: Two Artists at Ferus Try 'Beyond Painting' Media." *Los Angeles Times*, 1 March 1959, part V, p. 12. R.

1960 Langsner, Jules. "Art News from Los Angeles: Bengston, Grant." *Artnews*, March 1960, p. 51. R.

Nordland, Gerald. "Art: Valentines Etcetera." *Frontier*, February 1960, p. 18, ill. R.

————. "Art: The Expressionists." *Frontier*, May 1960, pp. 20-22. R.

1962 "Artists Take to the Place: Wide Open and Way Out." *Life*, 19 October 1962, pp. 83, 89, ill. p. 84.

"Brush-Strokes of a 4-Stroke." *Motorcyclist*, February 1962, p. 20, ill. R.

Langsner, Jules. "Los Angeles Letter." *Art International*, March 1962, p. 48, ill. p. 47. R.

R[aynor], V[ivien]. "New York Reports: In the Galleries: Fun Art." *Arts Magazine*, September 1962, p. 50. R.

S[andler], I[rving] H. "Reviews and Previews: New Names This Month: Billy Bengston." *Artnews*, May 1962, p. 18. R.

Seldis, Henry J. "In the Galleries: 'New' Drawings an Old Story." *Los Angeles Times*, 16 November 1962, part IV, p. 9.

1963   Coplans, John. "Pop Art, USA." *Artforum*, October 1963, pp. 27–30, ill. p. 27. Reprint of catalog essay for *Pop Art USA* exhibition at Oakland Art Museum.

———. "Notes from San Francisco." *Art International*, November 1963, pp. 91–94. R.

F[actor], D[on]. "Reviews: Six Painters and the Object and Six More, L. A. County Museum of Art." *Artforum*, September 1963, pp. 13–14, ill. p. 15. R.

Fried, Michael. "New York Letter." *Art International*, December 1963, p. 68. R.

Langsner, Jules. "Los Angeles Letter." *Art International*, January 1963, pp. 81–83, ill. R.

———. "America's Second Art City." *Art in America*, April 1963, pp. 127–31, ill.

Leider, Philip, and John Coplans. "West Coast Art: Three Images." *Artforum*, June 1963, pp. 21–25. R.

S[choneberg], S. C. "Reviews: Billy Al Bengston, Ferus Gallery." *Artforum*, February 1963, p. 41, ill. p. 43. R.

S[mith], V[ic]. "Reviews: The Pacific Coast Invitational, Fine Arts Gallery of San Diego." *Artforum*, February 1963, pp. 9–10. R.

1964   Coplans, John. "Circle of Styles on the West Coast." *Art in America*, June 1964, pp. 24–41, ill. cover.

———. "Formal Art." *Artforum*, Summer 1964, p. 42.

Geldzahler, Henry. "Los Angeles: The Second City of Art." *Vogue*, 15 September 1964, pp. 42, 56, 62, 64.

Kozloff, Max. "Art: West Coast Art: Vital Pathology." *The Nation*, 24 August 1964, pp. 76–79.

Leider, Philip. "The Cool School." *Artforum*, Summer 1964, p. 47, ill. p. 48.

1965   Coplans, John. "Los Angeles: The Scene." *Artnews*, March 1965, pp. 56–58, ill. p. 29.

———. "The New Abstraction on the West Coast U.S.A." *Studio International*, May 1965, pp. 192–99, ill.

———. "Billy Al Bengston." *Artforum*, June 1965, p. 37, ill. pp. 36, 38.

Hopps, Walter. "United States Exhibit, São Paulo Bienal." *Art in America*, October–November 1965, p. 82, ill.

"Neue Abstraktion: Billy Al Bengston." *Das Kunstwerk*, April–June 1965, p. 101, ill. p. 62.

Solomon, Alan. "Making Like Competition in L.A." *New York Times*, 11 July 1965, p. 10-N, ill.

1966   Coplans, John. "Abstract Expressionist Ceramics." *Artforum*, November 1966, pp. 34–41, ill. Adapted from catalog essay for *Abstract Expressionist Ceramics* exhibition at University of California, Irvine.

Getlein, Frank. "First U.S.-Backed Art Show for Overseas is Shown." *Washington Star*, 30 January 1966, pp. D-1, D-3, ill. R.

Giambruni, Helen. "Abstract Expressionist Ceramics." *Craft Horizons*, November–December 1966, pp. 17, 61, ill. p. 18.

Hopkins, Henry. "'West Coast Style': Something About Los Angeles." *Art Voices*, Fall 1966, pp. 60–61, ill. p. 66.

Hudson, Andrew. "Viewpoint on Art: Newman Brings Grandeur to Town." *Washington Post*, 30 January 1966, p. G-9. R.

———. "Letter from Washington." *Art International*, Summer 1966, pp. 130–31. R.

Kozloff, Max. "Art: São Paulo in Washington." *The Nation*, 28 February 1966, pp. 250–52. R.

Kramer, Hilton. "U.S. Art from São Paulo on View in Washington." *New York Times*, 29 January 1966, p. 22. R.

Plagens, Peter. "Present-Day Styles and Ready-Made Criticism." *Artforum*, December 1966, pp. 36–39.

Rose, Barbara. "Los Angeles: The Second City." *Art in America*, January–February 1966, pp. 110–15.

1967   Coplans, John. "Art Bloom." *Vogue*, 1 November 1967, pp. 184–87, 232–33.

Danieli, Fidel A. "Billy Al Bengston's 'Dentos.'" *Artforum*, May 1967, pp. 24–27, ill.

Ellis, Susan. "A Back-Seat Approach to 'New' Art." *Los Angeles Herald Examiner*, 8 January 1967, *California Living*, pp. 12–13, ill.

Livingston, Jane. "Los Angeles: Artists' Artists, Lytton Center." *Artforum*, October 1967, pp. 61–62, ill. R.

Seidenbaum, Art. "How Can You Call a Smooth Slab 'Love in Italian?'" *Los Angeles Times*, 28 May 1967, *West*, pp. 30–36.

1968   A[lbright], T[homas]. "'Motel Dracula' and Iris Blooms." *San Francisco Chronicle*, 9 September 1968, p. 38. R.

"Art: Artists." *Time*, 30 August 1968, pp. 38, 41, ill. p. 40.

Good, Jeanne. "Billy Al Bengston." *Art Calendar* (Los Angeles), December 1968–January 1969, pp. 21–24, ill.

Harrington, Stephanie, and Blair Sabol. "Outside Fashion." *Village Voice*, 6 June 1968, p. 26, ill.

Levinson, Robert S. "All Dirt Tracks Lead to the County Museum." *FM & Fine Arts*, December 1968, pp. 27–29, 42, 44, ill.

Livingston, Jane. "Los Angeles: Speed Sculpture, Pomona College." *Artforum*, May 1968, p. 66. R.

Meeker, James J. "Young Artists' Work Exhibited in Dallas." *Fort Worth Star-Telegram*, 20 October 1968, p. 5-G. R.

Monte, James. "Bengston in Los Angeles: The County Museum Presents the Artist's First Retrospective." *Artforum*, November 1968, pp. 36–40, ill. Reprint of catalog essay for *Billy Al Bengston* exhibition at Los Angeles County Museum of Art.

T[erbell], M[elinda]. "Arts Reviews: Bengston and Westermann." *Arts Magazine*, December 1968–January 1969, p. 56. R.

Wilson, William. "In the Galleries: 'Women' Exhibition Nicely Balances Art, Femininity." *Los Angeles Times*, 18 March 1968, part IV, p. 14. R.

———. "Aspects of Modernity in Orange County Shows." *Los Angeles Times*, 27 October 1968, *Calendar*, p. 52. R.

———. "Billy Bengston Earned His Stripes." *Los Angeles Times*, 8 December 1968, *Calendar*, p. 34, ill. R.

1969   Albright, Thomas. "Two L. A. Artists." *San Francisco Chronicle*, 27 March 1969, p. 49. R.

Getlein, Frank. "The Arts: Three Different Aspects of Contemporary Art on View." *Washington Star*, 9 March 1969, p. D-11, ill. R.

Gold, Barbara. "Art Notes: Motorcycles and Painting." *Baltimore Sun*, 9 March 1969, sec. D, p. 8, ill. R.

Lowndes, Joan. "Focus: The Artist Who Is Also A Man Of Speed." *Vancouver Province*, 23 May 1969, p. 3, ill.

———. "Art: The Living Room Shrine of Billy Al." *Vancouver Province*, 30 May 1969, p. 8, ill. R.

Richard, Paul. "Tough Yet Smooth." *Washington Post*, 23 March 1969, p. K-4, ill. R.

Townsend, Charlotte. "Bengston Creates Myth." *Vancouver Sun*, 26 May 1969, p. 28.

———. "Bengston Opens Superb Showing." *Vancouver Sun*, 28 May 1969, p. 37. R.

———. "Exhibition Reviews: Vancouver." *Artscanada*, August 1969, p. 37, ill. R.

1970   Blair, Kim. "Billy Al Bengston: Talent for Art and Life." *Los Angeles Times*, 4 September 1970, part IV, pp. l, 6.

Garver, Thomas H. "Los Angeles: Billy Al Bengston, Mizuno Gallery." *Artforum*, May 1970, p. 84. R.

Plagens, Peter. "Los Angeles: Billy Al Bengston, Mizuno Gallery." *Artforum*, June 1970, pp. 89–90, ill. R.

S[eldis], H[enry] J. "Art Walk: A Critical Guide to the Galleries." *Los Angeles Times*, 6 March 1970, part IV, p. 8. R.

W[ilson], W[illiam]. "Art Walk: A Critical Guide to the Galleries." *Los Angeles Times*, 27 November 1970, part IV, p. 16. R.

1971   Baker, Elizabeth C. "Los Angeles, 1971." *Artnews*, September 1971, pp. 27–39, ill.

Butterfield, Jan. "Approach of Artist Considered Unique." *Fort Worth Star-Telegram*, 31 October 1971, p. 4-G. R.

Freed, Eleanor. "Art: Happenings On and Off Main Street." *Houston Post*, 10 October 1971, Spotlight sec., p. 10. R.

Hobdy, D. J. "Artist Brings Work—But Not Motorcycle—to Town." *Houston Chronicle*, 6 October 1971, sec. 4, p. 12. R.

Plagens, Peter. "Los Angeles: Ed Moses and Billy Al Bengston, Mizuno Gallery." *Artforum*, February 1971, pp. 90–91, ill. p. 89. R.

Terbell, Melinda. "Los Angeles." *Arts Magazine*, February 1971, p. 45. R.

W[ilson], W[illiam]. "Art Walk: A Critical Guide to the Galleries." *Los Angeles Times*, 30 April 1971, part IV, p. 7. R.

Winer, Helene. "How Los Angeles Looks Today." *Studio International*, October 1971, pp. 127–31, ill.

1972   Burr, James. "London Galleries: Dustbin Art." *Apollo*, October 1972, p. 355, ill. R.

Butterfield, Jan. "Exhibition at Museum Reveals Ties Between Artist, Collector." *Fort Worth Star-Telegram*, 23 January 1972, p. 2-F. R.

———. "Link Between Artists, Collectors Explored." *Fort Worth Star-Telegram*, 30 January 1972, p. 4-F. R.

———. "Los Angeles Art in Texas Collections . . . An Interesting Phenomenon." *Southwest Art*, Summer 1972, pp. 44–47, ill.

Fuller, Peter. "In the Galleries: Billy Al Bengston." *The Connoisseur*, December 1972, p. 302, ill. R.

Kutner, Janet. "Scene in Art: Los Angeles School in Fort Worth Show." *Dallas Morning News*, 23 January 1972, p. 5-C. R.

Wolfram, Eddie. "Art." *Harper's & Queen*, October 1972, p. 86, ill. R.

1973   Fish, Mary. "Olitski and Bengston." *Artweek*, 21 July 1973, p. 5. R.

Freed, Eleanor. "Low Key Phenomena." *Houston Post*, 4 March 1973, Spotlight sec., p. 38. R.

Holmes, Ann. "Crisp New Art Snaps and Crackles—It's Pop." *Houston Chronicle*, 6 March 1973, sec. 1, p. 17, ill. R.

Kutner, Janet. "Scene in Art: Bengston Show Draws, Repels." *Dallas Morning News*, 16 February 1973, p. 30-A. R.

Montgomery, Cara. "Reviews: Los Angeles." *Arts Magazine*, March 1973, p. 67, ill. R.

Plagens, Peter. "From School-Painting to a School of Painting in Los Angeles." *Art in America*, March–April 1973, pp. 36–40.

———. "No/Yes on the West Coast." *Artforum*, May 1973, pp. 55–56, ill. R.

Richard, Paul. "A Luscious Color Feast." *Washington Post*, 24 February 1973, p. D-1. R.

S[eldis], H[enry] J. "Art Walk: A Critical Guide to the Galleries." *Los Angeles Times*, 26 January 1973, part IV, p. 8. R.

Smith, Griffin. "Billy Al's Humanization Makes a Successful Show." *Miami Herald*, 14 January 1973, p. 8-F, ill. R.

1974   Alf, Martha. "New Paintings by Billy Al Bengston." *Artweek*, 2 November 1974, p. 3, ill. R.

Frankenstein, Alfred. "Dull vs. Top-Notch Art." *San Francisco Chronicle*, 23 February 1974, p. 33, ill. R.

McConnell, Miriam Leila. "Straight Painting: Color, Form, Surface." *Artweek*, 12 October 1974, p. 3. R.

McDonald, Robert H. "Contemporary Abstraction—South." *Artweek*, 23 February 1974, pp. 1, 16. R.

———. "Bengston's Recent Works." *Artweek*, 16 March 1974, p. 3, ill. R.

Moser, Charlotte. "Bengston's Watercolors: Contained . . . . . . Freedom." *Houston Chronicle*, 25 August 1974, pp. 19–20, ill. R.

Plagens, Peter. "Abstract Painting in California." *Studio International*, July–August 1974, pp. 35–37, ill.

S[eldis], H[enry] J. "Art Walk: A Critical Guide to the Galleries." *Los Angeles Times*, 25 October 1974, part IV, p. 12, ill. R.

1975   Campbell, R. M. "L.A. 'Heavy' in One-Man Show." *Seattle Post-Intelligence*, 19 September 1975, p. 8, ill. R.

Forgey, Benjamin. "The Nation: Washington, D.C.: Cézanne to Dracula." *Artnews*, April 1975, p. 79. R.

Marmer, Nancy. "Los Angeles: Billy Al Bengston at Nicholas Wilder." *Art in America*, January–February 1975, pp. 87–88, ill. R.

Plagens, Peter. "Billy Al Bengston's New Paintings." *Artforum*, March 1975, pp. 34–35, ill.

Preisman, Fran. "Billy Al Bengston: New Paintings." *Artweek*, 8 March 1975, pp. 3–4, ill. R.

Rosenthal, Adrienne. "Bengstons of the Sixties." *Artweek*, 28 June 1975, p. 3, ill. R.

Seldis, Henry J. "Art: LAICA Exhibit Still in Mainstream." *Los Angeles Times*, 9 February 1975, *Calendar*, p. 70. R.

1976   Ballatore, Sandy. "Bengston: Painting as Environment." *Artweek*, 15 May 1976, p. 3, ill. R.

Campbell, Mary Schmidt. "Clay Show Features Unusual Format." *Syracuse New Times*, 29 February 1976, p. 11. R.

Crossley, Mimi. "Review: Billy Al Bengston at Texas Gallery." *Houston Post*, 8 February 1976, p. 31. R.

Moser, Charlotte. "New Work Shows Magnitude of Johns' Artistic Inquiry." *Houston Chronicle*, 8 February 1976, p. 9, ill. R.

———. "The Nation: Houston: Between Fantasy and Surrealism." *Artnews*, April 1976, pp. 65–66. R.

"Museum Clay at Everson." *Craft Horizons*, April 1976, pp. 26–29, ill. R.

Overend, William. "Behind Scenes at Bohemia-by-the-Beach." *Los Angeles Times*, 20 July 1976, part IV, pp. 1, 4, 7, 10.

Pieszak, Devonna. "Reviews: Billy Al Bengston." *The New Art Examiner* (Chicago), October 1976, p. 18. R.

Wilson, William. "Art Review: 'Unclassified' Reaction to Labels." *Los Angeles Times*, 16 February 1976, part IV, p. 5. R.

W[ilson], W[illiam]. "Art Walk: A Critical Guide to the Galleries." *Los Angeles Times*, 30 April 1976, part IV, p. 13. R.

1977 Crossley, Mimi. "Review: Art: Gallery Roundup." *Houston Post*, 24 June 1977, p. 12-F. R.

Moser, Charlotte. "Space, Age." *Houston Chronicle*, 26 June 1977, p. 11, ill. R.

Spelman, Martha. "Billy Al Bengston: Viva Decoration!" *Artweek*, 18 June 1977, p. 4, ill. R.

1978 Albright, Thomas. "Forgettable Works from Billy Bengston." *San Francisco Chronicle*, 10 March 1978, p. 60. R.

Crossley, Mimi. "Review: Billy Al Bengston." *Houston Post*, 23 June 1978, p. 18-E, ill. R.

Fischer, Hal. "Los Angeles: Billy Al Bengston, James Corcoran Gallery." *Artforum*, March 1978, p. 73, ill. p. 71. R.

Howell, Betje. "Downtown Exhibit: A Banner Show for Billy Al Bengston." *Los Angeles Herald Examiner*, 19 March 1978, p. E-12, ill. R.

Moser, Charlotte. "Artistic Cross-Currents." *Houston Chronicle*, 25 June 1978, p. 14, ill. R.

Muchnic, Suzanne. "Art Review: Bengston in a Mellow Mood." *Los Angeles Times*, 28 March 1978, part IV, p. 6. R.

1979 Bass, Ruth. "New York Reviews: Billy Al Bengston." *Artnews*, November 1979, p. 196, ill. R.

Colby, Joy Hakanson. "Billy Al Bengston: Goading the Viewer—Naturally." *Detroit News*, 21 October 1979, p. 6-E, ill. R.

Crossley, Mimi. "Reviews: Art: In the Galleries." *Houston Post*, 2 December 1979, p. 20-AA. R.

Kalil, Susie. "Billy Al Bengston: Sensuality and Structure." *Artweek*, 22 December 1979, p. 3, ill. R.

Kramer, Hilton. "Art: Drawings by a 'Disciple' of Gorky." *New York Times*, 21 September 1979, p. C-18. R.

Perrone, Jeff. "Reviews: New York: Billy Al Bengston, Acquavella Gallery." *Artforum*, November 1979, pp. 79–80. R.

———. "Reviews: Philadelphia: 'The Decorative Impulse,' Institute of Contemporary Art, University of Pennsylvania." *Artforum*, November 1979, pp. 80–81, ill. R.

"Prints & Photographs Published." *The Print Collector's Newsletter*, May–June 1979, p. 55, ill.

Rickey, Carrie. "Los Angeles: Billy Al Bengston, James Corcoran Gallery." *Artforum*, March 1979, p. 72, ill. p. 71. R.

Tatransky, Valentin. "Arts Reviews: Billy Al Bengston." *Arts Magazine*, December 1979, p. 25. R.

1980 Christensen, John. "Bengston: An Artist in Perpetual Motion." *Honolulu Star-Bulletin*, 14 July 1980, p. E-1, ill.

Hazlitt, Gordon J. "Venice, California: Unique among the World's Bohemias." *Artnews*, January 1980, pp. 94–98.

Lewis, Louise. "Ukiyo-e Chic." *Artweek*, 24 May 1980, p. 2, ill. R.

Newman, Patricia. "New Processes Add Tangible Shape to Venerable Art Form." *Smithsonian*, August 1980, pp. 60–64.

Stewart, Frank. "Traces of Paradise." *Honolulu Star-Bulletin*, 27 July 1980, p. C-18, ill. R.

1981 Baro, Gene. "New York Letter." *Art International*, August–September 1981, p. 120. R.

Forgey, Benjamin. "An Artist with a Place in the Sun." *Washington Star*, 31 January 1981, pp. C-1–C-2, ill.

Johnson, Patricia C. "Art: Bengston's 'Honolulu' Challenging Colors." *Houston Chronicle*, 23 November 1981, sec. 5, p. 8, ill. R.

Miller, Elise. "The L.A. Look: Billy Al Bengston at S.D.S.U. and the Babcor Gallery." *San Diego Magazine*, May 1981, pp. 138–40, 262, 264–65, ill. R.

Muchnic, Suzanne. "Art Review: Bengston—More Than a Decorator." *Los Angeles Times*, 11 May 1981, part VI, pp. 1, 4, ill. R.

Plagens, Peter. "Art in Los Angeles: Seventeen Artists in the Sixties." *Art Journal*, Winter 1981, pp. 375, 377, 379, ill. R.

Richard, Paul. "Shades of California: The Sunlight Expressions of Painter Billy Al Bengston." *Washington Post*, 31 January 1981, pp. G-1, G-9. R.

Wortz, Melinda. "Art in Los Angeles: 17 Artists, 16 Projects." *Artnews*, November 1981, pp. 161–65, ill. R.

1982 Rickey, Carrie. "Studs and Polish: L.A. in the Sixties." *Art in America*, January 1982, pp. 80–89, ill.

Wilson, William. "Galleries: La Cienega Area." *Los Angeles Times*, 7 May 1982, part VI, p. 8. R.

1983 Brenson, Michael. "Art: The Tightrope Helen Frankenthaler Walks." *New York Times*, 9 December 1983, p. C-30. R.

Curtis, Cathy. "Images from the Islands." *Artweek*, 30 July 1983, p. 6, ill. R.

M[uchnic], S[uzanne]. "The Galleries: La Cienega Area." *Los Angeles Times*, 6 May 1983, part VI, pp. 13–14. R.

Nelson, Sandy. "Beginning in the Middle: Billy Al Bengston's Pictures for the Eighties." *Images & Issues*, May–June 1983, pp. 30–33, ill.

Wortz, Melinda. "New Editions: Billy Al Bengston's." *Artnews*, October 1983, p. 92, ill. p. 91.

1984 Geldzahler, Henry. "California As World Art Capital." *California Magazine*, April 1984, pp. 78–85, ill.

Hunter, Fredericka. "Artist's Dialogue: A Conversation with Billy Al Bengston." *Architectural Digest*, January 1984, pp. 146, 150, 152–53, ill.

Ianco-Starrels, Josine. "Art News: Aussie Artists on View." *Los Angeles Times*, 22 September 1984, *Calendar*, p. 87. R.

Klein, Ellen Lee. "Arts Reviews: Billy Al Bengston." *Arts Magazine*, February 1984, p. 35, ill. R.

Muchnic, Suzanne. "The Beach House that Art Built." *Los Angeles Times*, 29 July 1984, *Calendar*, p. 88.

———. "When Artists Turn Architects, You Can Expect the Unexpected." *Houston Chronicle*, 20 August 1984, sec. 5, p. 2.

1985 McDonald, Robert. "Art Review: Bengston Exhibit Puts Sizzle in a Cool Night." *Los Angeles Times*, 21 September 1985, part V, p. 1, ill. R.

Wilson, William. "The Art Galleries: La Cienega Area." *Los Angeles Times*, 10 May 1985, part VI, p. 10. R.

1987 Conrad III, Barnaby. "Los Angeles: The New Mecca." *Horizon*, January–February 1987, pp. 17, 30, ill.

Photography Credits

Photographs reproduced in this book have been supplied,
in many cases, by the owners or custodians of the works as
cited in the captions. The following list applies to photographs for which additional acknowledgment is due.

Gray Crawford: Pl. 51

M. Lee Fatherree: Pl. 48

Brian Forrest: Pls. 3, 7, 8, 12, 13, 14, 16, 18, 20, 21,
23, 29, 30, 31, 32, 33, 38, 39, 40, 43, 53, 55, 56,
58, 59, 60

Rick Gardner: Pls. 17, 19, 22, 25, 28, 35, 37, 41, 49,
50

Gene Ogami: Pls. 2, 5

Philipp Scholz Rittermann: Pl. 44

William Thornton: Pl. 15

p. 1: Billy Al Bengston at his 50th birthday party, 1984.
Photo: Ann Kresl.

pp. 4, 5: Billy Al Bengston at his Venice studio,
California, 1986. Photos: Winston Conrad.

Billy Al Bengston:
Paintings of Three Decades
was produced for the
Contemporary Arts Museum, Houston, The Oakland
Museum, and Chronicle Books, San Francisco
by Perpetua Press, Los Angeles.
Edited by Letitia Burns O'Connor
Designed by Dana Levy
Typeset in Ehrhardt and Gill Sans by
Wilsted & Taylor, Oakland
Printed in Japan by Dai Nippon Printing Co., Ltd., Tokyo
in an edition of 7,500 copies

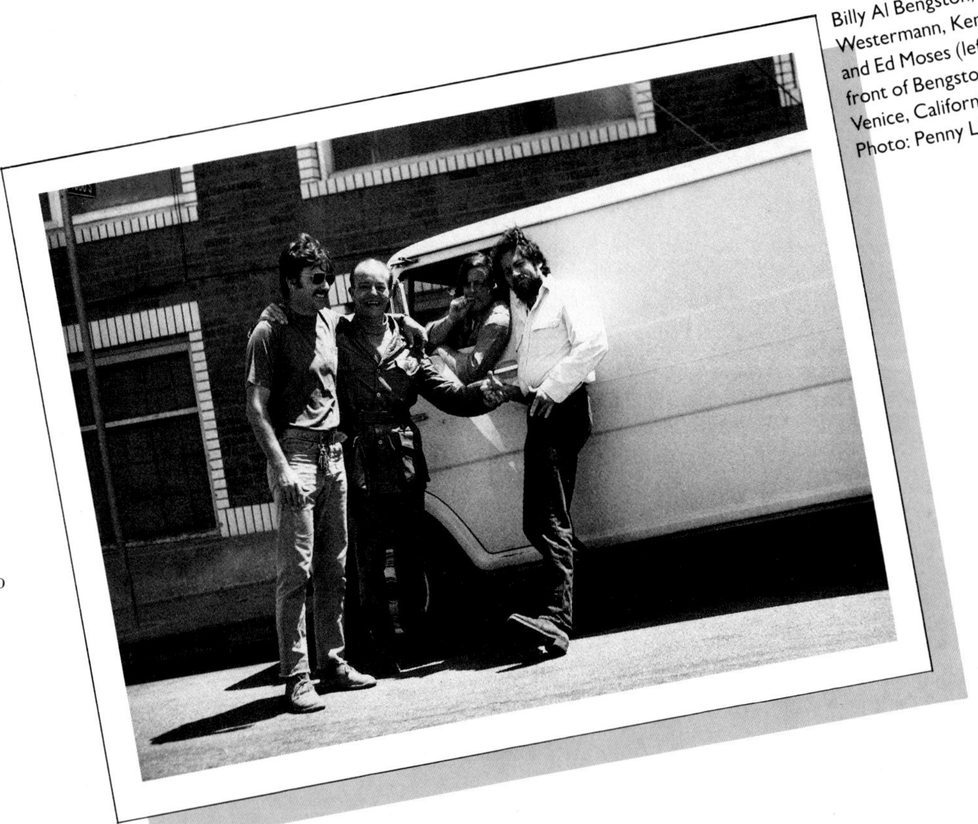

Billy Al Bengston, H. C.
Westermann, Kenneth Price,
and Ed Moses (left to right) in
front of Bengston's studio,
Venice, California, ca. 1972.
Photo: Penny Little.